A Boy of the Dominion

F. S. Brereton

[ZHINGOORA BOOKS]

This edition is published by
Zhingoora Books.

Contents

CHAPTER I

Finding a Profession

It was just past ten o'clock on a chilly morning in the early spring when Joe Bradley emerged from the shop door of the little house which had been his father's, and stepped, as it were, abruptly into life. The banging of the door and the turning of the key were a species of signal to him, as if to warn him that the past, however fair or foul it may have been, was done with, and that the future alone stared him in the face.

"There it is," he said, somewhat sadly, handing the key to a man who accompanied him. "You've paid me the money, and have arranged about your lease. The business is yours."

"And you can wish me success," came the answer. "Hope I'll do better than your father."

"I hope it, with all my heart," said Joe, his lip a little tremulous. "Goodbye! Good luck!"

He could hardly trust himself to say even that; for Joe was but seventeen years of age, and changes are apt to prove trying to one so youthful. Moreover, there are few, fortunately, who at the age of seventeen find themselves face to face with the future all alone.

Joe pulled the collar of his overcoat up over his ears, for the wind was keen and cutting, and thrust his hands deep into his trouser pockets. For a little while he watched the retreating figure of the man to whom he had sold his father's business, and then glanced aimlessly up and down the single street of which this little northern town boasted. Let us declare at once that hesitation was not a feature of Joe's character; but there was an excuse for such a display on this cold morning. For, as we have just said, when he stepped out of his shop he, as it were, stepped into this big world; he cut himself adrift from the past and all its pleasant memories, and faced the wide future.

"What to do, that's the knotty question? Can't stay here, that's quite certain. Then where do I go? It's a corker!"

If one puts oneself in the place of Joe Bradley for a few moments, thoroughly understanding his position, it will be admitted that there was good cause for hesitation, and that a dilemma such as he found himself in would puzzle anyone, and even one gifted with greater age and discretion. For beyond the

4

fair education which he had contrived to pick up, and some knowledge of mechanics and cycle fitting, Joe could boast of no special training; in any case, he knew of nothing in this little northern town which could give him employment.

"I've simply got to move away—only where, that's the question," he repeated to himself for perhaps the fiftieth time that day. "I've sixty pounds in my pocket. That's my capital. If I do nothing I live on that money, and the day draws nearer and nearer when I must work or starve; so work is the thing I want. Exactly so—work. What work? Where?"

He pursed his lips up and whistled—a little habit of his—then he looked up and down the street again, his brows furrowed, evidently thinking deeply. And while he stands there before the cycle shop which had been in his father's possession, we may as well take advantage of his indecision to take a careful look at Joe.

Seventeen he called himself, and the face was that of a lad of about that age, though perhaps, if anything, just a trifle too serious for one so young. But it was unlined, save for the wrinkles which were now upon his brow while he was thinking. It was a frank, open face, and when one caught him smiling, which in other days was often enough, there was something particularly taking about Joe Bradley. Indeed, he was a gay, light-hearted fellow, just the one, in fact, who, finding his fortunes suddenly darkened, might very likely mope and pine and suffer from a severe attack of the blues. But Joe had too much character for that. The shrill whistle he had given broke into a jaunty tune, while he plunged his hands even deeper into his pockets. No, there was no sign of the blues about him, but merely a show of anxiety clearly reflected on a face which bade fair, one of these days, to be handsome. There was grit, too, about Joe's features; there was budding firmness about the jaw and lips, while the eyes belonged to one who could look friend or foe in the face without flinching. Otherwise he was rather tall for his age, squarely built, and decidedly active.

"Hallo!" called someone to him, and swinging round Joe found himself facing the doctor's assistant.

"Hallo!" he responded, smiling.

"Where away?" came the question, while the doctor arrested his bicycle and balanced it with one foot on either side.

"That's just it," said Joe, looking serious. "I was just asking myself the same thing. It's a conundrum."

"A conundrum, eh? Don't understand, Joe."

"Then it's like this," explained our young friend, while the doctor regarded him closely. "I've just handed over the key of the shop to Mr. Perkins. He's paid me sixty pounds for the business as a going concern. So I'm out of work and homeless. I'm just wondering what to do and where to go. I've sent my box to the station, but exactly in which direction I shall travel is a toss up."

"In fact, you've the world before you, and find it hard to say which part shall be honoured with your presence," smiled the doctor. "Well, Joe, one thing's certain—this place is no good to you. You'd collect dust here, and that's no good to anyone. Make for London, or—George!—why shouldn't you—why not emigrate?"

"Emigrate?"

"Yes; go to Canada or Australia. Strike out a line for yourself. There are thousands who are doing it—thousands who haven't got so much as sixty shillings in their pockets. Think it over."

"I will," declared Joe, his eyes shining.

"Then come and see me to-night and we'll have a talk. Must move along now; I've a patient to visit."

The doctor was off within a few seconds, leaving Joe still standing outside the shop so recently vacated, still with his ears well within his collar and his hands deep in his pockets. But there was a new expression on his face, while the eyes were distinctly brighter. For here was a suggestion; here was a way out of the dilemma which for the past three weeks had faced him. Till then he had hardly known the meaning of the word trouble. He had been content to work in the cycle shop with his father. But the latter's sudden death, the necessity to sell the business and move away had thrown our young friend into a whirl that was bewildering. And this suggestion that he should emigrate was the first solid one that had been made to him.

"Why not?" he asked himself. "Others have done so. Of course I could, if I liked, take the other course Father points out to me. Supposing I were to open the letter?"

He withdrew one hand from his trouser pocket and plunged it into an inner one. When he brought it into the light again there was a long sealed envelope between his fingers. Joe turned it round and read some writing on it carefully.

"To my son, Joe Bradley," he read. "The contents of this letter will explain to you many things which I have never cared to refer to. But I beg of you never to open it till you are in direst need, or have earned the right to do so. Make your way in the world; gather riches. Then you can open and read."

"Make your way in the world and then open. I will," declared Joe aloud, forgetful of his surroundings.

"Will what? Eh? You ain't ill, Joe?" asked a man who had approached from between the houses. In fact, he had suddenly emerged from an alleyway that cut in between the shop which Joe had so recently vacated and the next one, belonging to the nearest grocer. Swinging round, our young friend found himself face to face with the local constable. A huge, hairy face was grinning at him from beneath an absurdly small helmet.

"Will what?" demanded the constable, his smile broadening till he showed an uneven array of teeth, from the centre of the upper row of which one was missing. Joe's eyes were attracted by the gap, and in a flash he remembered that Constable Near had come by the injury during a contest with some poachers. "Will what?" demanded the hairy fellow again. "It's a queer thing to hear a young fellow saying as you spring out upon him. There was you, Mister Joe, standing all alone, wool-gathering I should reckon, and holding out a paper before you. 'I will!' you cries, as if you was gettin' married. What's it all about?" Joe told him crisply. "I'm wondering what on earth to do with myself," he said. "Doctor Tanner suggests emigrating."

"And why not?" exclaimed the constable. "Why not, me lad? If I was young again, same as you, I'd go. Don't you make no error, I'd hook it termorrer. And I'll tell yer fer why—this country's too full of people. Out there, in Canidy, there's room for me and you, and thousands like us. There's free grants of land to be had; there's labour fer all, and good wages."

"And no failures?" asked Joe shrewdly.

"In course there's failures. In course there's people too tired to work when they do get out, and there's others taken in and robbed by those who should know better; but there's success fer most, Mister Joe. There's better than that; there's indipendence—indipendence, me lad! For two twos I'd sell up and be going. Now look you here, come along to the station, where I'll show you a few figures."

Here was a treasure; Joe snatched at the opportunity, and accompanied his old friend the constable to his own cosy little cottage. Nor was he there for long before he learned that it was possible to obtain an assisted passage to Canada, with the definite promise of work on landing. Moreover, with the money he had he could easily pay his way and still have enough to make him independent when he arrived.

"You jest think it all over," said Constable Near, when he had shown Joe various papers. "You're young enough, and supposing you don't like Canada, why, you could go along on to Australia. But like it you will; I've heard tell of it often."

"Then I'll go into the matter," Joe answered. "If I want more particulars I'll call in again. Thanks, constable; I already feel that I have fewer difficulties."

It was with a lighter and a brisker step that he emerged into the street again. Cramming his hat down on his head, Joe tucked his collar about his ears again—for it was very cold outside—and went striding off towards the country. "Can't think in this town," he told himself. "I always get back to the shop, as it were, thinking of Father and of his letter. That letter's a temptation to me. I won't open it; I swear I'll make my way before I venture to break the seals. Now about Canada—or shall it be Australia?"

It was a sensible idea of Joe's to clear out of the town and all its old associations. For, recollect, he was young, and almost up till that moment had had a father to refer to in all his youthful difficulties. But Mr. Bradley, never a very robust man, had died somewhat suddenly some three weeks earlier, and Joe was now an orphan. As to his parentage, he was even then somewhat vague. His mother he had never known. She was not even a memory to him, having died shortly after his birth. Of his father he knew little more. Obviously he was one who had been born to better things than a cycle shop. There were many in this northern town who wagged their heads when speaking of Mr. Bradley, and the doctor, a shrewd judge of character and of men, had long ago decided the point; only, being a discreet fellow, had mentioned it to none other than his wife.

"There's something about that Mr. Bradley that bothers me, my dear," he had said. "He's a gentleman through and through, while his personal appearance, his reserve, and his manners generally proclaim that he has seen better days. He never grumbles; but I know there is a history behind his reserve. The boy takes after him, too; he keeps much to himself, and is obviously superior to boys of a similar station."

That was the general opinion of the keeper of the cycle shop, and seeing that Mr. Bradley gave himself no airs, and was always pleasant to all and sundry, he was, in his quiet, retiring way, a popular character in the town. His death had been followed by the usual gossip. Then a buyer for the business had speedily turned up, and with his help and that of a local solicitor Joe had had no difficulty in settling all his affairs and in paying all debts. As we have said, here he was with sixty pounds in his pocket, good health, good temper, and good appearance, and the world before him. But he had no fixed purpose in life. He was like the man who enters upon business without a plan of action; like the general without a settled scheme of campaign, and likely enough to expend his whole strength in useless and profitless skirmishes. Joe, without a plan to work with, was certain to see his little fortune slip from between his fingers before he found remunerative work.

"Must get out of the place and think," he told himself. "Here's for a sharp walk."

Head buried in his collar still, and hands deep in his pockets, he went striding away into the country, nodding to those acquaintances who gave him good day. It was a little later when he heard in the far distance the echo of a motor horn.

"Big car," he told himself, for his father had dabbled in motor-car repairs, and Joe had learned more than a smattering of those useful and wonderful machines. "Coming along fast, too. Fellow's in a hurry. They'd better pull up soon, for the corner yonder is a sharp one, and there are cattle on the road."

His eyes followed the long greasy ribbon ahead, winding in between the hedges till it was cut off at an abrupt angle where the road doubled almost upon itself. The corner was, in fact, one similar to those to be found so often in England, perhaps a relic of the early days when roads were first constructed, and some selfish owner declined to allow their passage, save and except they passed round the confines of his property. Whatever the reason, here was a greasy strip of macadam doubling upon itself, with a herd of cattle ambling aimlessly along it. Boom! The horn sounded again, while the whirr of machinery died down a trifle.

"Driver has seen the triangle marking a dangerous corner and is slowing," Joe told himself. "He'll have a surprise when he gets round; it'll be a case of brakes hard on."

Boom! Boom! The car was up to the corner. It came shooting round, not necessarily at too fast a pace; for your modern, low-hung car can legitimately attack curves at a speed of twenty or more miles an hour. But the careful driver allows for the unexpected. Wagons are to be discovered often enough at a corner, and invariably on the wrong side of the road. Pedestrians, gifted with wonderfully thick heads and, one suspects, with a degree often enough of stupid obstinacy, insist on adhering to the centre of the road. Yes, there are often unexpected obstacles, and here there were cattle. Round the car came—a big red one—its glass wind shield flashing in the light. Burr! Screech! The brakes went on instantly, and the scream of metal came to Joe's ear.

"Old car," he told himself again, with the air of one who has had experience. "New cars don't make a sound with their brakes. My! He's put 'em on hard; he'll skid if he isn't careful."

He just had time to observe the fact that there was a single individual in the car, seated in the driving seat, and then what any experienced motorist might anticipate happened. The car skidded; its nose shot to one side, and Joe got a glimpse of it broadside. Then it swung round again, slued across to the side of the road, turned completely till its back passed before his eyes and was again

9

replaced by the front. Whereupon, with irresistible impulse behind it, it charged the bank, ran up it and turned over with a thud, coming to a stop within ten feet of the nearest beast, with its four wheels still spinning. Joe jammed his hat firmly on to his head and raced towards the scene of the accident.

"Chap killed, I expect," he said. "Anyway, he's under the car. I saw it come down over him; beastly place that corner! Besides, the fellow was going too fast. His own fault; inexperienced, perhaps."

It took him a matter of three minutes to reach the scene of the upset, when he found the drover gazing at the upturned car as if spellbound, his mouth wide open, his small store of intelligence utterly gone.

"Drive the cattle into that field and then give me a hand," cried Joe, seeing that he must give a lead. "Quick with it! The driver is under the car, and we must get him out. Don't stand gaping, man! Bustle! Bustle!"

He pointed to a gate near at hand giving entrance to a grass field, and ran on to the car. The wheels were still spinning, at least those in front were, while the back ones had come to a rest. A man's cloth cap was lying just outside the car, while the lifting trap, which often enough is fitted to the floor of the back part of cars, had swung downward. Joe leaned over, thrust his head through the opening, and peered beneath the car. There was a man's arm just beneath him, and farther along he could see the rest of the unfortunate fellow's body.

"Hallo!" he called. "Hurt?"

A groan answered him. He heard the late driver of the car gasping, then he was answered in a weak voice, the words interrupted by gasps.

"Wind knocked clean out of me," he heard. "Can't move; I'm pinned down by the top of the front seat. Get the car off me."

Joe moved rapidly; slowness was not one of his failings. He vaulted to the other side of the car and peered beneath it; then he lifted his head and gazed around.

"Hallo!" he called again, going to the opening he had used before. "Where's the jack? Can I get at it?"

"Back of the car," came the gasping answer. "Don't be long. I can scarcely breathe; the whole weight of the thing seems to be on my chest."

Joe raced to the back of the upturned car, wrenched at the brass handle which operated the lock of the cupboard usually to be found there, and, tearing the door open, discovered a jumbled mass of rags, spare motor parts, an inflator pump, and a lifting jack. He whipped the latter out in the space of a few seconds, and darting round to the side of the car, looked shrewdly at it. Then, careless of the damage he might do to the coachwork, he placed the jack beneath the lowest edge, pushed it into position and rapidly worked the lever which operated it. Slowly he managed to raise the side of the car a matter of some three inches.

"How's that?" he called.

"Better," came the answer, in what seemed to be a tone of relief. "There's not so much pressure on me now. But I'm pinned fast; I think my trousers are under the other side. What'll you do?"

"Leave it to me," called Joe. "I'll not go away till you are released. Still the car is a heavy one, and there are only two of us here. I've told the drover to put his cattle into the field near by and then come and help. Stay still, or you may jerk that jack out of place. I'll get hold of the drover, and we'll see what can be done."

"Be he killed, maister?" he heard, as he lifted his head. "He were coming that tremendous fast, that I knew he'd smash. I hollered; but it warn't no sort o' good. He just come round like a rocket."

"He's alive, but pinned down by the car," Joe explained. "We must have something to use as a lever. Look for a strong rail."

They went together along the hedge seeking for something to suit their purpose, and presently came upon two lengths of timber beside a stack of hay. Joe led the way back to the car, running as fast as he could.

"Now, we want something to use as a point for our levers," he said. "A pile of bricks would be best, but there are none hereabouts."

"How'll stones do?" asked the countryman, his mouth still agape. "There be plenty jest here."

Close to the gate there were quite a number of squared blocks which had probably at one time been built as a support for the gate post. Joe seized upon one, while the lusty drover brought a couple.

"Now, let's consider the matter," said Joe. "With these long poles we shall be able to lever the car up; but that isn't enough. We want to turn her clean over. We want a rope."

The driver had that, for a wonder. "I be one of those careful sort," he explained, with a giggle. "Most times there ain't no need fer a rope. But still I carries one, 'cos you never do know, now do yer? I carries one in case there's a fretful beast. And here it is."

Joe already had his plans made. There was a tree on the opposite side of the road, within five yards of the upturned car. He took the rope and made it fast to the far edge of the car. Then he carried the other end to the tree, passed a loop round it, and beckoned to the countryman.

"Hold on," he said. "As I lever the car up, take in the slack and hold fast. Mind you don't bungle, or that poor chap may be killed."

11

A minute later he had his long lever in position, with the end well beneath the edge of the car, and a pile of stones some fifteen inches from the point of leverage. With such a pole as he had—for it was fourteen feet long, perhaps—he had now tremendous power, and firm pressure at the end first caused the pole to bend, and then lifted the car with ease.

"Hold on!" he shouted, and, obedient to the word, the drover hauled in the slack of his rope. "Again! Once more! Now stand fast; that's enough for the moment."

By dint of careful effort Joe had now raised the edge of the car a matter of two feet, and having built his stone fulcrum still higher, he soon had the space beneath even greater. Waiting to see that the drover had firm hold of his rope, he then dropped his lever, and, stepping under the car, dragged the imprisoned driver out.

"Much damage?" he asked.

"Shaken, that's all. Nothing broken, I believe. I've been feeling myself all over. Arms all right, you see; legs ditto. Chest, er—yes. No ribs broken, I imagine, though I feel as if I had been under a steam roller. You're a fine fellow; I owe you a heap."

"Then you rest there for a little," said Joe, dragging him to the hedge, and well out of harm's way. "We'll turn the car right side up if we're able."

It was fortunate that at that moment two men came along the road in a trap. Dismounting, they assisted in the work, and very soon the car was righted, coming down on to her four wheels with a bump which might have been expected to shake the engine out of her. But no harm was done; beyond badly-bent mud guards, there seemed to be no damage. Even the steering gear was unharmed. Joe busied himself with the engine, threw the gear lever into neutral, and soon had the motor running.

"I'll take you along to the doctor," he said, going to the damaged stranger. "Like to come?"

"You can drive? Got a licence?" came the questions—and then, as Joe nodded—"Right! Here's something for the men who helped; please thank them for me."

Two minutes later Joe was driving the car back into the town he had so recently left. His first day's battle with the world had resulted in an adventure.

CHAPTER II

An Ocean Voyage

"Not a single bone broken, I assure you," declared Dr. Tanner, when he had thoroughly examined the stranger, to whose help Joe had so opportunely come. "Bruises, of course; plenty of them. There's a swelling here on the back of your head almost as big as a turnip. You'd better rest quietly for the night."

"But—but I have business to attend to," declared the stranger, who we will at once introduce by his correct name of Hubbard. "I'm due in Manchester to-morrow, then in Birmingham, and later in Coventry. I can't sit down and rest."

"You must, or take the consequences," answered Dr. Tanner, smiling. "Come and have some tea. Joe, you join us; I've that yarn to have with you about Canada. Now, Mr. Hubbard, what do you advise a young fellow like this to do? He's not on his beam ends; far from it. He has a little capital; but he's adrift as it were. Has no occupation, and no means at present of earning a living."

"Then I'll offer him work at once, work to last a week," declared Mr. Hubbard. "Only a week, though, mind that, my young friend and rescuer. I'm no great hand at driving a car, and after this accident I feel that my nerve is shaken. Come along and drive the car. You managed beautifully this afternoon. Come as a friend; I'll pay all expenses, and give you three pounds into the bargain."

"Done, sir!" It was characteristic of Joe that he accepted the post at once. In fact, he leaped at it; for it was exactly to his liking.

"But don't forget it's not a permanency, Joe," sang out the doctor, lifting a warning finger and shaking it at him. "Permanent jobs are the only posts for young fellows. They learn then to be useful, to manage things. Temporary jobs lead to unsettlement. Besides, you know the old adage, "a rolling stone gathers no moss". Moss is wealth and position, all that makes for happiness, and you want to gather it with both hands. Eh, Mr. Hubbard?"

"Spoken like a wise counsellor," came the laughing rejoinder. "But you began to speak of our young friend."

"Well, there he is," said the doctor, pausing in the act of pouring out a cup of tea, and pointing to Joe with the spout of the teapot, "there he is, employed at this moment as chauffeur to yourself, but likely to be without a job in the course of a week. What are his prospects in this country? Fair, we will say; for he is one of the steady lads. What are his prospects in Canada or Australia?"

"Depends; he's a worker, you say?"

Joe flushed as he listened to this conversation that reflected on himself, then he laughed good-humouredly.

"A worker, yes; steady, certainly," replied the doctor.

"Then Canada will brighten his prospects. I know the country; I'm doing business for a firm out there, and so can speak with some knowledge. Certainly Canada will improve his prospects. He's got capital?"

"Sixty pounds," said Joe, who was listening eagerly.

"Then forget it. Buy your ticket for the crossing, and then earn your way. Forget the dollars till you've learned experience, then invest them as you'll soon ascertain how to do. Bless us, but I wish I was in his shoes! Think of the interest of such a life; think of the enjoyment of working one's way up, of climbing higher! This humdrum existence we most of us lead is tame beside such an opportunity for flattering one's ambition."

"In fact," asked the doctor, "you advise emigration?"

"Indeed I do," came the prompt answer, while Mr. Hubbard stirred his tea. "Mind you, I don't say that there is no opportunity in this country for youth and ambition. What I do say is this. Where a man has no ties, where a young fellow has lost his parents, and has little or no influence to start his career, then Canada calls loudly to him. There he will make new ties, new friends, new hopes. There he can have land for the asking, if farming is what he wants; and success is assured, one way or the other, if only he will put his back into the work. Of course, I know what you're going to say, Doctor," he went on, arresting the latter's interruption with uplifted teaspoon. "Men come back again; men fail. Of course they do; the lonesomeness of the long winter gives the half-hearted the blues. Others attempt to follow a vocation for which they were never suited. Weak men break down under the strain. Slackers get deported; but young active fellows, with pluck behind them, and with grit and strength and health, they make good every time, sir. They help to form the backbone of Canada."

Joe's eyes glowed as he listened. His cheeks took on a colour to which they had been a stranger of late, since trouble had come upon him. He began to wonder what life in Canada would be like. He leaned forward, one hand at his cup, his eyes shifting from the doctor to this voluble stranger. Moreover, Mr. Hubbard was no ill-looking man to watch; there was eagerness and keenness written on every feature of his face. Perhaps he was thirty-five years of age, perhaps even younger. But he was shrewd and level-headed without a doubt, also he gave one the impression that he was a man who had travelled far and seen much, and who ventured his opinions only when he knew his subject. It was plain that Canada was an open book to him.

"The long and the short of the matter then is this," smiled the doctor, vastly interested in his visitor, "you advise Joe to go."

"I advise him to go, and I'll put him up to the ropes. There!"

Mr. Hubbard helped himself to cake, fixing his eyes sharply on our hero; and Joe returned the glance unflinchingly. "You'll make good, or I'm right out of my calculations," declared Mr. Hubbard, after quite a long scrutiny of his features. "Then's the time when a man finds life enjoyable, for he knows he's done well; he ain't got much to regret."

That evening Joe heard more of Canada from his friend the constable. He supped at the local hotel with his employer, and turned in early. The following morning, after bidding farewell to the doctor and a few others, he brought the car out of the yard, ran to the station, there to pick up his box, and then came to a halt opposite the hotel door.

"Been at work, I see," said Mr. Hubbard, surveying the car. "You've straightened those mud guards and cleaned her. That's push; some fellows wouldn't have thought of it. Others would have been too proud to do the cleaning. Now let her hum."

It does not require that we should follow the two on their trip about the country. Suffice it to say that, thanks to previous experience, Joe drove the car with ease and dexterity, a fact which his employer had already noted.

"And mighty lucky I am to have hit upon you," he laughed, as they buzzed on their way to Manchester. "First, for the fact that you dragged me out of my prison after that upset, and now because you were free to come with me. I'm so stiff to-day that I couldn't have driven had I wished, and I rather expect it will be a few days before I am quite fit again. So it's a huge convenience, for my business wouldn't wait."

A week later the two ended their trip at Liverpool.

"Where we see to this passage of yours to Canada," said Mr. Hubbard. "Now, if you'll be advised, you'll go steerage. As you're emigrating, best start in right at the beginning with the people who'll be alongside you. I shall pay for your passage."

In spite of Joe's protests, Mr. Hubbard insisted on doing this, and did not finally say goodbye to our hero till he had seen him aboard the Canadian Pacific liner which was to bear him to his destination. Moreover, his gratitude to Joe took the form of an outfit as well as a passage.

"Clothes of every description are very dear out there," he said, "so you'll want a kit with you. Everything warm, mind. That's the way. In the hot weather you can leave off what you don't need; but in the winter warm things are wanted."

In the end Joe found himself with a strong box containing several flannel shirts and underwear, a pair of high boots and two pairs of strong nailed ones, socks in abundance, a suit of corduroy and one of strong tweed, two neck handkerchiefs, a slouch hat, and various other articles, not to mention a kettle, a teapot, a tin mug, basin, and plate, with the necessary portable knives, forks, and spoons, and a canteen containing tea and sugar and a tin of condensed milk. "Looks stupid to be taking all that rig, don't it?" asked Mr. Hubbard, with a quizzical smile. "But then, you see, I've been through the mill. You'll get to Quebec and then go aboard the train. Well, food doesn't grow by the wayside nor on the cars. You've got to take it along with you and cook whatever you want; so don't forget to buy up a tin or so of sausages and such things. With those and the kit you've got here you'll be in clover. Now, lad, there's the bell for landlubbers to get ashore. Don't forget to give me a call one of these days when you're round by Ottawa; and always remember to make good. Goodbye!"

Their hands met, they looked keenly into one another's eyes, and then he was gone. Joe was alone again, alone upon the deck of a ship swarming with people, but alone for all that; for everyone about him seemed to have friends. He plunged his hands deep into his pockets and whistled a merry tune; for if he were alone, Joe felt happy. The fingers of his right hand nursed the banker's draft for those sixty pounds he had banked; the fingers of his left handled the cash which his liberal employer had paid him. His coat bulged to the right where his father's letter was secreted, and somewhere on the ship was the steel trunk which contained his kit. Alone! Joe scoffed at the thought, and went on whistling merrily.

"All ashore!" someone bellowed, while sailors ran past him on some errand. The steam siren of the ship sent a wide spray of water over the passengers, and then, as if thereby it had cleared its throat, it set up a deep, reverberating roar that deafened all other sounds. The deck thrilled and throbbed; the water right astern was churned into milk-white foam, while the shore seemed to be moving. Joe leaned over the side and waved frantically to Mr. Hubbard. Down below, he could see a thousand faces. A thousand handkerchiefs waved frantically up at him. Alone! Why, they all seemed to be friends; they all seemed to be wishing him good fortune. Even the tall, stern waterside policemen seemed to unbend and smile.

"Hooray! Hooray!" shouted Joe, unable longer to restrain his enthusiasm. "We're off."

"Hooray!" came back from the throng on the landing stage. Then, as the ship's head paid off to the pull of a tug, and another thrill went through her as her turbines turned, the blaring notes of a trombone came to the passengers. It was "Auld Lang Syne", and the tune sent people sobbing. Joe watched a big fellow close beside him, and saw the tears stream down his face. But the scene changed with the tune, and that in an instant. It was "Rule Britannia" now, and the man was standing erect and as stiff as a poker.

"Old soldier," thought Joe. "Going out?" he asked.

"To Canidy, yessir," came the answer. "Going out along with the missus and the youngsters. Couldn't get work here in the old country. I don't grumble, mind you. I'm not the one to shout out about aliens crowding the likes of me out. It's the training that's wrong. I've none; I'm good only for casual work and unskilled jobs, and there's thousands more for 'em. But Jim—he's my brother— he went out this five years ago, and he's made a pile already—a pile, sir, enough to pay a passage for me and the missus and the children."

There was hope in the honest fellow's face; he was looking with a glad heart to the future, and no doubt at that moment was bidding farewell to a past which, if not too pleasant and uncrowded with thoughts of plenty and of enjoyment, at least had its touches of colour, its memories, and its faces.

By now the steamer was well in midstream, and the throb of the engines was better felt. Not that your turbine leads to much vibration; but still, with the horse-power possessed by these leviathans, it is only reasonable that there should be some commotion. Joe walked to and fro along the deck, and then began to feel hungry. He went to the companion, a wide gap leading to the lower deck, and descended. There was a woman halfway down vainly attempting to escort four children, all of small stature.

"Allow me," said Joe, and promptly picked up two of them. "Going out to Canada?" he asked, though the question was hardly necessary, seeing that that was the ship's only destination.

"Winnipeg, sir," came the answer. "Husband went out a year ago; I'm going to join him. Thank ye, sir!"

Joe dived still lower into the depths of this monster ship, and found himself in a huge hall with long tables set along the length of it. Cloths were already laid, and there were mugs and plates in unending rows, while dishes containing sliced cold meat were placed at intervals. Already a number of people were seated, and Joe at once took a place close to a respectable-looking couple.

"Pardon," he asked, bumping the man as he sat down.

"Eh?"

"I apologized for knocking your arm," said Joe, flushing at the bluntness of this individual.

"Ah, me lad, thank ye," came the hearty answer. "Only it sort of took me by surprise. I ain't used to overmuch politeness; we don't seem to get much time where I come from. Been out before?"

Joe shook his head, and asked for the plate of meat and bread and butter.

"Then you're green?"

Joe smiled. "As grass," he said briskly.

"Going to work or to play?" asked this stranger, as he stuffed a huge piece of cake into his mouth.

"Work—got to; I'd rather, any day."

"Farming?"

"That's my intention," declared Joe, helping himself liberally.

"Then you'll like it. I'll be able to put you up to the ropes. You're going out just at the right time, too, for it'll be fine weather. Tea, me lad?"

Joe accepted with pleasure, and began to look about him. People were beginning to swarm down into this species of dining-hall, and they presented all sorts and descriptions. There was a party of men shepherded by an official of the Salvation Army, a dozen or more young married couples, and as many women going out to join their husbands. A small regiment of Scandinavians passed by, and were followed by a crew of Russians.

"Don't look as if they'd had so much as a bath between 'em, do they?" grinned his neighbour. "But they've been travelling these many days, and most like have crossed over from the continent during the night. They're the boys fer work. Give me a Russian or a Scandinavian on the farm. They earn their dollars and don't grumble. Now, lad, if you've not been aboard one of these ships afore, you'd do well to settle your bunk and take possession of it. There's a couple of likely youngsters along here that we know of. They've come from our part of the world in England, and they're decent fellows. Maybe you could pitch upon a cabin fer three. If not, you'll have to sleep in the bunks out in the open. Jim and Claude," he called, "here's a mate fer ye; get right along and fix your bunks."

Joe liked the look of the two young fellows instantly. They were about his own age, and better dressed than many. He exchanged a smile with them, then, having finished a meal which was excellent, to say the least of it, and undoubtedly plentiful, he accompanied his two new friends to the sleeping deck. Here were rows of canvas bunks suspended on steel uprights and cross pieces, the whole looking clean and compact and comfortable. At the vessel's sides were cabins of considerable size, and, since they were amongst the first on the scene, they had no difficulty in securing one to accommodate the three.

"We'll be fine and comfortable in there," said one of the young fellows named Claude. "We'll bring our things along just to prove possession. Shouldn't leave anything about if I were you; for there might be a thief aboard."

Joe took the warning to heart, and so that there could be no danger of a robbery where he was concerned, went to the purser promptly and there deposited his banker's draft, his father's precious letter, and the majority of the loose cash he possessed.

"Now let's have a look round, and see if we can do anything to help," said Jim, leading the way to the upper deck. Here they found a seething crowd, for the ship was packed with emigrants, to say nothing of her complement of first- and second-class passengers. She presented, in fact, a good-sized township, with facilities for dealing with every class of business, of which catering was not the least important. In the centre of the crowds of emigrants our hero was soon attracted to a railed-in space wherein was a mass of sand, and in this a number of children were digging. Elsewhere men lounged and smoked, while women sat on their worldly possessions, many of them looking forlorn and lost.

"Give them two days to settle down, and all will be happy and contented," said one of the stewards who happened to be passing. "We're going to have a smooth crossing, so that will help."

He pushed his way through the throng and dived down below. A stewardess followed him, and others came bustling after her. Officials now were engaged in inspecting the tickets of the passengers, while a summons brought the emigrants in a long waiting queue to a table set in the dining-hall, where one of the doctors with an assistant took careful stock of them, particularly to observe whether or no each person had been recently vaccinated.

Joe was glad to creep into his comfortable bunk that night, as it had been a day of movement; but a good sleep did wonders for him, and when he rose on the following morning he was as fresh as paint.

"How do yer like it?" asked the pleasant fellow, close to whom he had sat on the previous day when he descended for a meal; for, following a habit on emigrant steamers, he took the same place at table.

"There's something interesting all the time," said Joe. "This sea air gives one an appetite."

"Then peg in, lad," came the hearty advice. "Here's tea; help yerself. Here's eggs and bacon, or will you have sausages?"

The meal was an eye opener. No doubt there were many poor fellows aboard who had not sat down to such a breakfast for many a long day, for we must recollect that emigrants are not always prosperous when they set out from the shores of Old England. It made Joe wonder of what size was the storeroom on this ship, and how it was that the purser or his assistants managed to gauge what would be required *en route*.

"Now you jest come along on deck with me and the missus and have a yarn while I smoke. Do yer smoke?" asked the man who had been so friendly.

"Not yet," was Joe's blushing answer.

"And a good thing too. Not that I'm against it, seeing that I smoke hard, and most of the day. What's yer name?"

"Joe Bradley."

"Mine's Sam Fennick. Sam's enough, and Joe'll do fer you. You ain't been out before, you say. Who's sent you?"

Joe was a confiding fellow, and told him his story; for Sam seemed an excellent friend and listened with interest.

"What'll you do?" he asked. "You'll land up in seven days, or perhaps eight, at Quebec. There you'll go before the emigration authorities, and will be examined again by the doctor. If all's well, you can start right off on your own, providing you've sufficient dollars in your pocket to make 'em sure you won't be a pauper. Paupers ain't what Canada wants. She wants men with a little cash, not much—just enough to keep the wolf away for a few days. But above everything, they must be workers. And the Government over there won't have slackers. She deports 'em double quick. Well, what'll you do?"

"Look out for a farm," said Joe; "but where, beats me."

"Then jest you think of New Ontario. It's the coming country. Now, see here, mate; I'll give yer a piece of advice. You get along down from Montreal. Accept a job on a farm, and stay there till the winter. Then have a turn with the forest rangers. They don't do much in the winter, it's true; but a few are kept going. Or you might go along with a gang to a lumber camp. It'll keep you from rusting. Next spring you could work again on a farm, and come the following cold weather you ought to be able to look to yourself. We're off to seek a location in this here New Ontario."

"Then why couldn't I come with you?" asked Joe, for he liked the look of this Sam Fennick.

"And so you shall, but not at first. It'll take us best part of two months to find a likely location. Then we've to make a heap of arrangements, so I doubt our getting to at the job till late in the year. So you'd better fix elsewhere; you can come along when we're ready."

It may be imagined that Joe spent many an hour discussing matters with Sam, and soon began to long for Canada to heave in sight. However, there were many miles of sea stretching between the ship and the Gulf of St. Laurence, and they were not passed before he was involved in another adventure.

CHAPTER III

Volunteers called for

It was rather late on the third morning of the voyage when Joe had his attention attracted to one particular portion of the huge ship in which he had taken passage to Canada. Not that this one particular portion had escaped his notice; for, like the majority of young fellows nowadays, our hero was certainly quick at observation.

"Them things hum and squeak and flicker most of the day," said Sam Fennick, withdrawing a somewhat dilapidated brier pipe from his mouth and pointing the bowl at a deck house situated on the upper deck. "What's it all about, youngster?"

"Marconigrams coming and going," answered Joe; for the little house alluded to was given up to that recent wonderful invention which allows of messages being sent across space, without the aid and intervention of the customary wires. "The young officer there used to live in our neighbourhood. I once thought of becoming an operator myself, and, in fact, had many lessons from him."

"You had?" asked Sam, staring at Joe; for every hour that the two conversed revealed to Sam that Joe was a little better than the ordinary. Indeed, it is only reasonable that we should be fair, and admit that in coming to such a conclusion Sam was strictly right. After all, emigrants are not made up of the most intelligent or of the highest educated of our population. Too often they are men and women seeking a new life because of the failure of that which they had previously followed; or they are young people with a fair education, and with little else. In Joe's case, thanks to his own restless ambition, and to the fact that his father had devoted many an hour to him, the lad was acquainted with much unknown to the average emigrant. And here was something. To Sam a marconigram was neither fish, flesh, nor fowl; he didn't precisely know what it was, whether it had actual shape, nor what was its colour.

"Eh?" he asked. "You know the chap as works up there? And you've had lessons? What's a marconigram, anyhow?"

Joe explained with enthusiastic lucidity.

"I've sent 'em, too," he said. "There was a station not so far from us, and that's where I met Franc. It's nice having him aboard the same ship. But he is busy, isn't he? There must be something happening out of the ordinary. Wish I could go up there and join him; but it's forbidden. He told me that particularly."

It was only natural that our young hero should wish to see something of a chum associated with former days. But Franc, the young Marconi operator, was never get-at-able when on duty. It was only between the spells of work in his office that he met Joe down on the emigrant deck for'ard. Now, at the time when Sam and Joe were together, Franc was undoubtedly busily engaged. Moreover, there was a subdued air of mystery, if not of anxiety, about the officers who occasionally passed amongst the emigrants.

"What's up?" demanded Sam bluntly of one as he passed. "That thing yonder"—and he again withdrew his pipe and pointed the bowl at the Marconi office—"that thing's busy, I guess. Sending messages as fast as the air'll take 'em. What's up, mister? Revolution back in the Old Country, eh? What?"

He received merely a curt answer; the officer hurried on, leaving Sam none the wiser.

"All the same, there's a ruction stirring somewhere," he said; "I can see it with half an eye. The captain's walking up and down his bridge as if there was lions after him. What's it all mean?"

It became clearer, as the hours passed, that there was something seriously wrong in some direction, though where or what the trouble might be none could guess. Joe descended with his friend to dinner, and it was not till he mounted to the deck again that he gained tidings of what was happening. A huge column of pungent smoke was rising from the fore hold of the ship as he gained the deck, while sailors were moving about with wet cloths tied round their mouths.

"A fire down below," said Sam, with a catch in his voice. "Lor'!"

"Fire!" shrieked one of the passengers, a woman, as her eyes lit on the smoke. Then the alarm was echoed from a hundred quarters. Men came rushing up into the open. Women screamed, and one huge fellow, a Russian by his appearance, came rushing across the deck and cast himself into one of the boats.

"Silence!" commanded the captain through his megaphone, coming to the front of the bridge. "Quartermaster, turn that man out of that boat."

"Aye, aye, sir!" came from a burly individual, already advancing on the spot in question. "Now then," he said, when he had reached the boat, "you hop out, quick."

But the Russian was not inclined to do so. Terror had taken firm hold on him, and he sat clutching the thwarts, heedless of the quartermaster and of the fact that the boat sat firmly upon its guides on the deck, and offered as yet no sort of protection. But he remained there for only a minute, for the quartermaster hopped over the thwarts, seized the Russian by his coat and by the seat of his trousers, and threw him out without ceremony.

"Passengers," called the captain, in a voice so steady that he might have been inviting them to dinner, "there is nothing as yet to be alarmed at. Please go on with your work or your pleasures as if nothing were happening. I call upon every man and woman to set a good example, remembering that there are children amongst us."

That was enough. Men who had run forward with alarm written on their faces went back to their wives and children at once. Others gathered into anxious knots and went on with their pipes, while the children, unconscious of their danger, romped about the decks.

"All the same, it's a ticklish business," said Sam, after a while. "They've got the hatches off, and I expect they're trying to clear out the stuff that's afire. That looks bad, for as a rule they'd leave the hatches on and turn steam sprays on to the burning cargo. Perhaps the sprays can't get at the stuff that's afire."

"In any case, the crew won't be able to continue for long at the work unaided," added Joe. "Look! There's one overcome by the smoke; they've carried him off along the deck to the doctor."

In the course of the next hour four men were rendered incapable by the pungent smoke issuing from the hold, while the smoke itself had become even denser. Huge clouds arose through the hatchway and, caught by the breeze—for all this while the ship was forging ahead at her fastest pace—went billowing out behind her. So dense, in fact, was it, that the passengers for'ard could not see the bridge nor any other part of the giant vessel.

"Want volunteers?" asked Joe of an officer hurrying along the deck.

"Eh?" came the curt and hurried answer.

"Do you want any help?" repeated Joe. "There are plenty of us who would be eager and willing. That would free the men who are needed for the usual work of the vessel."

"Well now, that's a fine idea. See here," said the officer hurriedly, "I'll get along to the skipper and ask him what his wishes are. Of course he may say he's right as things are, but then the 'Old Man' may think differently. Meanwhile, you get a few likely chaps together. If they're wanted, everything'll be ready."

He went off at a quick pace, striding over the deck, and Joe saw him clambering to the bridge, where he sought the anxious captain.

"Well?" demanded Sam, for the idea of volunteers being called for had never occurred to him. "What'll you do?"

"Get a few men together at once," said Joe. "You stop here, and I'll send 'em over to you. That'll allow them to gather without creating a fuss. Anything is likely to increase the uneasiness of the passengers, and we don't want to add to the alarm they already feel."

He left Sam smoking heavily by the rail and went off amongst the passengers, who, in spite of their efforts to remain calm, were obviously filled with alarm. For if huge clouds of smoke had been coming from the open hatch before, it was billowing out now in vast volumes, smoke, too, which set everyone on the bridge choking, for there was a slight headwind, and the breeze the ship herself made in her rapid passage through the air helped to carry the smoke backward. As to the first- and second-class passengers, they had been driven to take shelter on the lower deck right aft, and were therefore entirely invisible. Joe accosted Jim and Claude, the two young fellows who were his cabin companions, and, whispering to them, sent them over to Sam. In the course of some ten minutes he had selected a couple of dozen young fellows, all of whom he had chatted with at various times during the past two days. That, indeed, is one of the curious results of travel aboard a ship. One becomes acquainted with one's fellow passengers during the first day; their inner history is often known by the evening of the second; while, long before the trip is ended, often enough their innermost thoughts, their ambitions, and their hopes are the property of one or other of the many friends they have made on board. In any case, Joe was the sort of lad who makes friends quickly. Free from that stupid side which sometimes afflicts the youth of this and other countries, he had a welcoming smile for everyone, and was ready to exchange his views with Dick, Tom, or Harry. It was not remarkable, therefore, that he had already become acquainted with a number of young fellows, bachelors like himself.

"I'll choose them in preference to the married men," he told himself. "The latter have pluck and dash enough, I know; but they have wives and children, and their services will be required by the families. Hi, Bill!" he called to another of his chums, beckoning him, "volunteers are likely to be wanted to help the sailors. Are you——"

"Right!" declared the man abruptly.

"Then get across to Sam Fennick; he's away over there at the rail. Just go on smoking as if nothing out of the way were happening. Got a good-sized handkerchief in your pocket?"

"No, no; I ain't got that," admitted Bill, after hunting about his person.

"Then get off to the cabin steward, or to the purser, if you can find him, and ask for three dozen towels. We can easily get a bucket of water up on deck, and that will give us the right thing to put round our mouths."

It was perhaps five minutes later when Joe went sauntering back to Sam. Quite a couple of dozen men had already congregated about him, and stood for the most part lolling against the rail and smoking contentedly; but there was not one who was not watching the smoke issuing from the hatchway critically.

"Seems to me as there's more of it, and it's kinder hotter," said Sam, almost in a whisper, as Joe came to his side. "Well, you've got the boys together, and the right sort too. Now, if I'd been asked, I'd have been flummoxed from the very beginning, and as like as not I'd have chosen the wrong sort."

"They're all single men," answered Joe. "Married men will be wanted to set an example of coolness to the passengers and allay their fears. Has that officer come along again? Ah, here's Bill! Well?" he demanded, as the latter came over to him with a bundle beneath his arm.

"Got 'em easy," panted the latter. "A steward gave 'em to me right off. Now?" He asked the question in excited tones and in a loud voice.

"Keep cool, and don't speak too loud," Joe cautioned him. "We want a bucket of fresh water. Who'll get it?"

Jim went off promptly, and when he returned some three minutes later it was to meet the officer coming towards the group.

"Ah," said the latter, singling Joe out, "you're the young fellow that spoke about volunteers. Well, now, the skipper says that he'd be glad of 'em, but they must be carefully selected—single men only, you know."

"How'll these do then, mate?" asked Sam, swinging his open palm round so as to embrace the little band of men Joe had selected. "This here young chap"— and he pointed to our hero—"seems to have the right ideas always tucked away at the back of that head of his. You'd no sooner gone than he was away selecting his men. Every one of 'em single, too, 'cos he says as the married 'uns must be calm, and set all the rest an example. And he's got towels for every man, and a bucket o' water here to soak 'em in. Spry, ain't it?"

For perhaps a whole minute the officer looked Joe coolly up and down. Indeed, at any other time his open inspection might have been interpreted as a rudeness. But there was something more than mere curiosity in his eye. He stretched out a hand sailor fashion and gripped our hero's.

"You're young," he said bluntly, "but you've the right sort of pluck, and a headpiece with which to back it. Bring your men along; I like the look of 'em. But first to explain. This fire's been going ever since two in the morning. It's somewhere in a lot of cotton goods right under a heap of other cargo, and try as we have we can't stifle it. Nor can we get at it with our sprays. So we're attempting to move the other stuff, and then we'll pitch what's alight overboard or swamp it with water from the hoses. It's the smoke that's the trouble. You come right along."

He led the way to the hatchway, Joe and his men following, while almost at once a crowd of steerage passengers massed themselves along the rail which cut them off from that part of the deck, and detecting the object of the little band, and realizing that they were volunteers, sent up a hoarse cheer of encouragement.

"Just you skipper the lot, youngster," said the officer, turning when close to the hatchway. "Keep those not at work below well to windward, then they'll be able to breathe easily. You can see that the skipper's put his helm over, so as to blow the smoke more abeam, for the people aft could hardly breathe. Now, you come down with me and I'll show you what's wanted; then you can set your men to at it."

Joe damped a towel in the bucket of water and tied it round his mouth and nose. Then he followed the officer over the edge of the hatchway, and gripping the iron ladder which descended vertically, soon found himself standing some thirty feet below on a pile of huge boxes.

"Machinery, and heavy stuff too," said the officer, taking him across to a part where there was little smoke. "Now, you can see for yourself whereabouts the fire is. The smoke tells you. Ah! there's another man done for!"

Joe's surroundings were indeed sufficient to cause more than the usual interest, for the scene was filled with movement. Overhead the square of the open hatchway framed a beautiful if confined area of blue sky, across which a few white clouds were scudding. But it was not always that one could see this view, for huge columns of smoke issued from the hold in front of him and went swirling up, to cease entirely at moments and then to gush forth again, for all the world as if someone were stationed in the depths amongst the cargo and were using a gigantic bellows. For the rest, a couple of huge reflectors threw the light from a number of electric bulbs into the hold, though without any seeming effect, for the dense smoke made the darkness almost impenetrable. Here and there a man rested well to one side, his mouth bound up with a handkerchief, while deeper in, entirely invisible, were other men. One heard a shout now and again and the clatter of moving boxes. Overhead, too, dangled a rope swinging from a derrick. It was at the precise moment when Joe's quick eye had gathered these details, that a couple of men came into sight staggering across the boxes and bearing a man between them.

"Dropped like a rabbit, he did," gasped one of them, as they placed the man on his back on one of the boxes. "Went down jest as if he'd been shot. Above there! Lower away."

A head appeared in the opening of the hatchway, while a second later a cloud of smoke shot upward, hiding the head and setting the owner coughing. But the derrick above swung over promptly, and the rope descended.

"You two men get to one side and rest," said the officer. "I and this friend here will see to the man. Now," he went on swiftly, "lend a hand while I pass the rope round this poor chap. That's the way. Now steady him while I go aloft. You'll get your men down as you want 'em."

He had already spoken to an officer on duty down below, and now went clambering upward. A moment later Joe was guiding the unconscious body of the sailor as he was hoisted upward. Then, cramming the towel close round his nose and mouth, he dived into the clouds of smoke till, aided by the electric light, he saw an officer.

"Shall I bring some of the men down now, sir?" he asked. "I've two dozen up above, all ready to lend a hand. I thought it would be best to employ them in two batches."

The officer, a young man of some twenty-five years of age, rose from the box he was helping to lift, coughed violently, and then accompanied Joe back to the part directly under the hatchway.

"My word," he gasped, when at length a violent attack of coughing had subsided and allowed him to speak, "we'll be glad to have you. That's hot work in there. You've two dozen, you say? Then bring along half of them; they'll be mighty useful."

Joe went swarming upward at once and, arriving on the deck, promptly told off twelve of the men. He was down again with them within a few seconds, at once leading them forward to where the work was in progress.

"That you?" asked the officer, peering at him through the smoke and coughing. "Then get to at these boxes. We're pulling them aside, and till we've got a heap more away we shan't be able to reach the spot where there's fire. When we do, things won't be so easy. There'll be a burst of smoke and flames, I should imagine."

"Then we'd better have the other half of this gang ready with sacks and blankets damped with water," cried Joe. "A hose wouldn't stop the fire, and the water would do a heap of damage. Eh?"

"You're the boy!" gasped the officer. "That's an idea; will you see to it?"

Joe nodded promptly, and then set his gang to work to help the sailors already employed in moving the cargo. Dashing away as soon as he saw that they understood what was required of them, he swarmed up to the top of the hatchway and called loudly to one of the gang above.

"Find one of the officers if you can, or, better still," he said, "go along to the purser. Ask for twenty or thirty old blankets. Take a mate or two with you and bring the lot along here; then swamp them with water. When you've got them ready have them slung down into the hold. You've followed?"

The young fellow nodded eagerly. "Got it pat," he declared, swinging round. "I'll be back inside ten minutes."

Joe slid down below without further waiting, and, joining his men, attacked the cargo with energy. Half an hour later, perhaps, after a bulky parcel wrapped in matting had been dragged from its place, a sudden burst of smoke drove the workers backward. It was followed by a hot blast of air and then by tongues of flame.

"Looks bad," declared the officer, rising to his feet from the box on which he had been seated; for he was taking a well-earned rest. "There's stuff below there that's well alight. Look at that! There's smoke and flames for you."

"And we'll need to drown the fire at once," cried Joe. "I'll bring the other gang down and set them to fight it."

Once more he clambered over the boxes from the dark depths of the hold, and, gaining the open space beneath the hatchway, shouted loudly. At once a head appeared, and another call brought the second half of his gang tumbling downward.

"Each of you take one of the damped blankets," said Joe, standing beside them. "See that the towels are well over your mouths and noses, and then follow me. We've got to the seat of the fire, and have to do our best to damp it out. Now, follow one after the other."

Seizing a blanket himself, he led the way till within twenty feet of the spot where the last bale had been torn out of its position. The workers whom he had left had been driven backward to that point, and were crouching down with their heads as low as possible, coughing and choking as dense masses of smoke swept about them. Joe saw red tongues of flame, and at once, without hesitation, advanced on the spot, holding the blanket before him. But if he imagined he had an easy task, he was quickly to learn that he was mistaken. The choking clouds of pungent smoke which swelled past him and hid him from the men was the least part of the difficulty. It was the heat which threatened to defeat his efforts. For a hot blast surrounded him. He felt of a sudden as if he had plunged into a furnace, while his nostrils burned as if he were inhaling flames. Then the blanket, in spite of its soaking, steamed heavily and began to shrivel.

"Forward!" Joe commanded himself. "This is not the time to give back. Push on and get your blanket down right on the spot where the cargo is alight."

Pulling himself together, as it were, and summoning all his energies, Joe dashed forward over the uneven flooring, the heat wave about him increasing in intensity. A gust of hot air, an intensely burning breath gripped him, while lurid flames swept past him on either hand. Even the wetted blanket showed signs of giving way before such an ordeal, for one corner curled upward and then burst into flame. But Joe was a stubborn fellow. He was not the one to be beaten when so near the goal, and half stifled and roasted he pushed on, cast his blanket over a spot which appeared to be white with heat, and trod it down manfully. He retreated then as fast as he could, followed by a dense smoke which made breathing impossible.

"Next!" he shouted, when he could speak. "Don't stop. We must pile the blankets on as thick as possible."

It says much for the courage of those steerage passengers that not one of the volunteers hesitated. Helped by the members of the crew, to whose aid they had come, they rushed forward pell-mell, casting the wetted blankets over Joe's; then, having trodden them down, they retreated before the dense smoke which drove them out. They sat in groups and anyhow, gasping beneath the open hatchway, some of them even having to beat the fire from their clothes.

"We've fixed that fire, I think," gasped the officer at last, for the smoke seemed to be less intense. "If so, it's the luckiest thing I've ever encountered."

"Wait," cautioned Joe. "That smoke's more pungent. That looks as if the fire were still burning."

Five minutes later it was clear that he was right; for flames suddenly shot out at the gang of workers, scorching their hair and driving them backward. Nor was it possible to advance again with wetted blankets. For an hour the gallant workers struggled to subdue the blaze by throwing water from a couple of hoses into the hold. But that effort too proved useless. It was clear that the fire had got beyond control, and that the safety of the passengers depended on the ship reaching a port very soon, or coming in with another vessel. Then, and then only, did the news circulate that Franc, the young Marconi operator and Joe's friend, had been placed out of action.

"It's just broken up our chances," groaned the officer who had been working beside our hero. "That fellow has been calling for four or five hours so as to get in touch with another vessel. But there was none within reach fitted with the Marconi apparatus. Now he's fallen down the gangway, and lies in the doctor's quarters with one leg broken and himself unconscious. It's a regular bad business."

CHAPTER IV

Joe Gathers Credi

"All passengers come aft," shouted the captain as Joe and his gang, together with the sailors, clambered out of the reek of heat and smoke and ascended from the hold. "All passengers must collect their belongings at once and come aft of the bridge. Be quick, please; we can allow only ten minutes."

Blackened and singed by the heat, with their clothing scorched and actually burned in some places, Joe and his helpers came up through the hatchway and almost fell upon the deck, for they were exhausted after their long fight in a stifling atmosphere. Then the hatches were thrown on and wedged down.

"We've got to leave things like that," said the officer to whom Joe had first of all suggested that volunteers should be called for. "We shall turn on the steam sprayers and hope that they, together with the want of air, will kill the fire. You've done well, young fellow. The captain's been asking for your name. But just you hop along right away and gather your traps, else you'll lose everything."

In a little while it began to look as if our hero might lose even more than his belongings, or rather that the loss of his kit would be of little moment to him; for the fire in the hold, which perhaps had been little more than smouldering before, now blazed out with redoubled fury. Indeed, it was not long after the steerage passengers had gone scampering aft, dragging their children and their belongings with them, that the deck right for'ard became almost too hot to walk on, while the sides of the ship were red-hot.

"The deck'll fall in soon if this goes on," said the same officer, accosting Joe as he came aft. "I've known a steamer afire keep moving till she reached port, and then she was red-hot from end to end. But we've a steel bulkhead just on a level with the bridge, and I guess that's keeping the blaze forward. So it'll be the fo'c'sle that'll be burned out, and that deck'll fall in before long. Then the blaze'll become worse. You fellows were grand; you did your best for us. Now you come along to the captain."

They found that anxious officer striding up and down the bridge, as if there were nothing to disturb him. But there were perhaps a thousand eyes upon this chief officer of the vessel, and, knowing that, he set an example of wonderful sangfroid.

31

"I thank you greatly," he said, as the officer brought Joe on to the bridge. "Mr. Henry has told me how you raised volunteers, and likely volunteers too, and Mr. Balance has reported how well all behaved. I thank you, sir, in the name of the ship's owners and her crew and passengers. It's a nasty business."

"Thank you, sir," answered Joe, blushing at the receipt of such praise. "I was wondering whether I could be of further service."

"Eh? Why, yes; but how?" asked the captain.

"I was thinking of your Marconi operator, sir."

"Eh? Ah, poor chap! That's the most unfortunate thing that could have happened. But—I don't quite follow," said the captain, looking closely at Joe.

"Only I knew him well, sir, and often worked with him. I've frequently sent a Marconi message. There's no great difficulty if you are fond of mechanical things and have learned the code. I worked hard at it, as I thought once of going into the Marconi service."

"The deuce you did!" came the sharp answer, while the skipper of this huge ship, with so much responsibility on his shoulders, turned a deep red colour beneath his tan and whistled shrilly. "You can—but you don't mean to tell me that you could handle his apparatus, that you could call up and talk with a ship if she happened to be within reach of us?"

"Let me see the things and I'll soon tell you," said Joe quietly, feeling nevertheless somewhat nervous lest his recent lack of experience should have resulted in forgetfulness. For it must be remembered that although a code such as is used by Marconi and other telegraphic operators becomes second nature, and is as easy to them as is writing to the average individual, yet such codes with want of practice soon become forgotten. Joe might have forgotten; want of practice might have stiffened his wrist. His "transmitting" powers might be now so cramped and slow, that an operator "receiving" aboard some other ship would not pick up his message; also, the converse might well be the case. His ear, unaccustomed now for some little while to the familiar sounds so particular to a telegraph instrument, might fail to pick out the meaning of dot and dash coming across the waves of ether so rapidly.

"Let me have a look into the office and also a talk with Franc. He'll tell me what is the company's usual call. I'm not so cocksure of being able to send and receive for you, sir; but I can try, and I think I'll succeed."

"That's fifty times better than being dead sure and failing miserably," cried the captain. "I'd sooner by a lot have a fellow tell me he'd try, than go off full of assurance and conceit. Of course you can see the operator. But he's hurt badly; they tell me he was stunned. Take him along, Mr. Henry."

It was a fortunate thing for the passengers aboard the vessel that Joe found his friend able to speak and understand. Indeed, the unfortunate Franc was fuming and fretting on account of the injury that had come to him; not because of the damage he had suffered, or of the pain, which was considerable, but because of his helplessness and the ship's dire need help. He raised his head as Joe entered, then called out gladly.

"Why, I'd forgotten you entirely, Joe!" he almost shouted. "I might have remembered that you knew the code and had worked the 'transmitter'. Get right along to the office and call up help. We want a ship to come over and take off the passengers, and then stand by while we run on into port. Here, I'll give you the company's call."

A few minutes with his friend told Joe sufficient to send him along to the Marconi office full of assurance, and within a quarter of an hour the apparatus, silent since Franc came by his damage, was flicking and clicking again, causing a thousand and more anxious pairs of eyes to be cast upward at the raking masts and at the web of wires suspended between them.

"There's an answer," he told Mr. Henry, when he had sent the call across the water on a dozen and more occasions. "Wait till I can say who it is. What am I to tell them about our position?"

The officer at once wrote down the ship's approximate position on a piece of paper, while Joe tapped on the key and listened to the receiver.

"Tell 'em we've fire in number one hold, and are almost roasted," he said. "Ask 'em to come along and take off our passengers, unless she happens to be steering the same course, when, if she'll run on beside us, there may not be need to transfer the passengers. Ah, she's calling you."

Rapidly did Joe get accustomed to the apparatus. No doubt he could neither send nor receive a message at the same rate as his injured friend; but if the messages were slow and laboured, and not always too correct, they were accurate enough for his purpose. Indeed, it was not long before he was able to send a long dispatch to the captain.

"S.S. *Kansas City* answered us," he wrote. "She's steering west-north-west, and on a line to intercept us. Doing fifteen knots and a little better. She's a hundred miles away, and will look out for us. She sends that she's bound for Halifax."

"That'll suit well," said Mr. Henry, coming back from the bridge and the captain. "She ought to fall into company with us about midnight or early in the morning, and, of course, if there's need, we can slow down or stop altogether, while she turns north and runs direct up to us. But we can see this thing through till morning. By then the fo'c'sle'll be little better than an ash heap. It'll be a case of clearing the passengers and then fighting the flames, or the ship'll go to the bottom. See over here; it's worth looking at, if only to remember."

He took Joe out of the office to the rail of the vessel and then drew his attention to the steel plates for'ard. If they had been of a dull red heat before, they were now of a bright redness, while flames were actually issuing from some of the lower portholes. As for the deck, it was a smouldering mass of blackness, to which a thin cloud of smoke clung tenaciously.

"You'd want thick boots on to walk across it," said Mr. Henry, "and then you'd never know when it might fall in and take you into a furnace. I tell you, a fire aboard ship is almost as bad as one in the forests of Canada. Ever heard tell of them?"

"Never," replied Joe, shaking his head.

"Then they're bad, real bad, and you've to move quick if you want to live through one. Now aboard a ship you can batten things down, just as we've done; or you can rouse up some of the cargo, get a hold of the stuff that's alight, and heave it into the water. That's what we tried and failed to do. Now there's nothing more but to wait till we join company with the *Kansas City*. Reckon there's a crowd of people will be glad to say goodbye to this vessel."

A saunter between decks proved that rapidly to our hero. Not that there was any great alarm or any marked sign of uneasiness. People congregated in little bunches; men stood lounging and smoking together, talking in eager, low voices. Here and there a woman was weeping; but there were few who showed less courage than the men, and, indeed, not a few displayed noble devotion.

"How's things going?" asked Sam, accosting our hero and whispering his question. "They tell me you've been up with the captain and have been working the Marconi office. You'll come in for something, me lad. Guess the skipper of this ship did a lucky thing when he booked you as a passenger. But what's happening?"

Joe told him in a few words. "We've got into contact with another ship," he said.

"Which means that you have," answered Sam, catching him up abruptly. "Give things their right names, lad. But there, I've seen it with you afore. It's jest like Joe Bradley to leave himself out of the question. So you've got talking with another vessel?"

"The *Kansas City*," Joe explained. "She's steering a course south of us and almost parallel. She's coming north a little of her course, and should reach us early in the morning. If need be, and we cut off steam, she could come due north and get alongside before midnight even."

"Then that's a bit of news that'll help people," said Sam, satisfaction in his voice. "I'll go and tell folks about here. Truth is, there's a few got the jumps bad, but we've give 'em a lesson. Jim and Claude and me, when we all came aft, saw that one or more of them foreigners was likely to prove troublesome. We found some of 'em packing their kit in the boats and pushing agin the women; but I fetched one of 'em a smack that'll make him sit up fer a fortnight, while when a bunch of 'em—low-down rascals, as I should name 'em—got out o' hand and went howling along towards the officers' quarters with the idea, it seems, of putting their dirty hands on the skipper and forcing him to quit the ship and put 'em aboard the boats, why, me and some of the boys you got together went for the beggars. There was a proper turn-up between us, and there's a few nursing their heads at this moment; but it jest settled matters. You see, the best of the foreigners came in and joined with our party, and what with that and the hiding we gave these fellows, why, things has quieted down wonderful. Only, of course, there's anxiety; a chap can't be altogether easy when he's sailing on a red-hot furnace, with miles of sea about him."

There was, in fact, wonderful order and coolness displayed on the ship, and nowhere more than amongst the emigrant passengers. Indeed, all vied in endeavouring to keep up the courage of the women and to leave the officers and crew of the vessel to carry out their work unimpeded. As for Joe, he spent the next few hours in the Marconi office, keeping in constant touch with the *Kansas City*, and every hour he was able to report that she was nearer.

"You'd better send along and ask her to make slick up here," said Mr. Henry, as darkness closed about them. "Some of the plates for'ard have burned through, and the air rushing in is making the fire blaze up terribly. The skipper is going to shut off and lie to. It's the only way of saving the vessel."

He handed Joe a written message, which the latter transmitted through his instrument, reporting in turn that the other ship had now changed her course and was coming direct toward them. Meanwhile the burning vessel was brought to a standstill, the throb of her engines ceasing save for an occasional thrill, as one or other of the screws was rotated so as to keep the stern always before the wind. The bugles rang out for tea almost at the accustomed hour, and, to the amazement of many, the emigrants found food and drink ready for them, but not in the same quarters. They were now huddled together, without cabins and without bunks to lie in, except in the case of the women and children, who, thanks to the unselfishness of the first- and second-class passengers, were accommodated in the cabins previously occupied by single gentlemen.

It was near midnight when at length a loud booming in the distance, and the turning of a brilliant light upon them, intimated to the people aboard the burning ship that the *Kansas City* was within reach of them. A deep cheer broke from a thousand lips, while many people burst into tears. Then Joe and his little band were again requisitioned.

"The captain's compliments," said Mr. Henry, "and he wishes that you will organize the men again, so that there may be no confusion when embarking the women. Get double the number this time if you can, and place them in batches near every boat. The stewards will help, and between you it ought to follow that there will be no confusion. But there's never any saying when you have to deal with foreigners."

"Then Sam's my man this time," thought Joe, going in search of that worthy. "If between us, as Mr. Henry says, we can't keep order, why, what's the use of us at all? Ah, there he is! Sam!" he called loudly.

"Going to tranship us?" asked the latter.

"Yes; women and children first. They've asked me to organize double the number of helpers. Let's call out the old lot. We can select the others very quickly; a few Russians and Scandinavians amongst them would help greatly. Ah! There's Jim, and Claude with him. Boys!" he called, waving to them.

It may be imagined that the work of selection was not accomplished in a minute; for with the coming of the relief ship there was huge confusion amongst the emigrants, as also amongst the first- and second-class passengers. The courage of many, bravely shown through a number of trying hours, broke down suddenly. Men, and women too, who had set a fine example to their fellows, were seen to lose their heads and their coolness. Passengers dashed to and fro, bumping into any who crossed their path, while one or two became absolutely violent in their efforts to push nearer to the spot where the gangway would be lowered. However, Joe and his friends were soon collected together, and then, with Sam's help, a body of forty or more was rapidly selected.

"You tell 'em off; you've the orders and hang of what's wanted," said Sam, lighting his pipe for perhaps the twentieth time.

"Then break up into parties of five," said Joe. "Now get along to the boats, five to each. Don't let a soul enter unless you have the captain's orders. Sam, you and I will help the stewards; I see that they are already ranging the women and children into lines. Some of the poor things look half-distracted."

The ordeal was indeed a severe one for many on board, and rendered not a few of the women completely helpless. However, what with the help that the stewards gave, aided by the stewardesses and Sam and Joe, the long lines were soon quieted. Then, beneath the flare of huge electric lamps, the work of transferring women and children to the *Kansas City* was conducted, the latter ship lowering her boats for that purpose, while those aboard the burning vessel were reserved for a future occasion.

"Men now," shouted the officer standing at the top of the gangway; and at the order the men aboard filed slowly downward and were taken off, till none but the crew, the stewards, and Joe and his gang remained.

"Now," called Mr. Henry, seeing our hero and his party, "your turn."

Joe walked directly up to him, with Sam at his side, while the captain descended from the bridge at that moment and joined them.

"We volunteer to stay," he said. "We've talked it over. It seems that now that the passengers are gone, particularly the women and children, you will tackle the fire again. You will want help for that. We're game to stay. We'd like to stand by till this job is finished."

"And, by George, so you shall!" cried the captain, bringing a hand down on our hero's shoulder and almost flooring him. "By James, sir, so you shall stand by us! A pluckier lot I never hope to run across, and I've never seen men better handled. You, sir, Mr. Joe Bradley, I understand is your name, and this other gentleman whom you call Sam, have behaved with conspicuous gallantry. I can tell you, gentlemen, it means much to the officers and crew of a vessel such as this is if, when a pinch comes, when danger faces them, there are men at hand to quieten the foolish, to reduce the would-be rioters to subjection, and to fight the danger side by side with the crew. It means a very great deal. Often it means the difference between security and disaster. Stay, gentlemen—we are about to fight those flames again, and you can help us wonderfully."

By now the *Kansas City* had sheered off a little, lying to some three or four hundred yards from the blazing vessel, which presented a truly awful appearance, for in the darkness her red-hot plates shone conspicuously. Lurid flames belched from her lowest ports forward, while at one part, where the plates had burned through, there was a wide ragged gap through which a veritable furnace was visible.

"We've got to flood the fo'c'sle," said Mr. Henry, as he stood beside Sam and our hero. "The carpenter, 'Chips', as we call him, is hammering up a staging at this moment, and when that's popped into a boat a man will be able to reach that opening where the plates have gone. We couldn't do it by lowering a seaman over the side, for the simple reason that the deck away for'ard is far too hot to allow anyone to walk on it. So we shall try from the sea. At the same time, we shall pull off the hatches and pour water in amongst the stores till they're flooded. You come along to the hatchway. It's not likely that we'll be able to go down. But later on, if we're fortunate, we might be able to do so, and so get closer to the fire."

Working without confusion, and indeed in no apparent haste, the crew soon pulled the hatches off the hatchway. Meanwhile a pinnace had been lowered, and into her the carpenter had built a species of platform raised some ten feet above the thwarts. Peeping over the side, Joe saw that there was a crew already aboard her, while men were paying out a ship's hose over the rail, where there was no heat and therefore no danger of the hose burning. In a little while two lusty fellows were perched on the top of the staging, and, operating the nozzle of the hose together, were directing a stream of water in through the ragged gap which existed for'ard, and which we have already mentioned. By then, too, Joe and his friends had contrived to get three hoses going through the hatchway, though their efforts seemed to be little rewarded.

"We're not reaching the actual seat of the fire, and the place is so huge that even a flood of water fails to swamp the flames," said Joe, as Mr. Henry came along to see how they were progressing. "There's one thing helping us, and that is the absence of smoke. I suppose the stuff which sent out that pungent smoke has got burned, and there is no more of it."

"Shouldn't wonder," came the answer. "As to reaching the fire, you must just keep at it. This hatchway is too hot yet to allow a man to clamber down the ladder."

It was decidedly hot, for when Joe put his hand on the iron ridge which surrounded the open hatch he withdrew it with a sharp cry. Indeed, the metal was almost red-hot, while a fiery heat as from a furnace ascended, cooled a little perhaps by the sprays of water sousing in from the hoses.

"I believe a fellow could reach the fire if only he could get below there and bear the heat," said Joe, perhaps half an hour later. "Look here, Sam, I'm going to make an effort. I'll tie a noose in the rope from the derrick, sit in it, and then get lowered. The men can play a hose on me while I'm descending, and even when I'm down below. Let's see if I can bear it."

A shout from Sam brought Mr. Henry, and an order from the latter soon secured a long length of steel cable with strong electric lamps at the end of it. At his suggestion this was made fast to the wire rope, in which a wooden seat was fastened. Then Joe stepped into the noose, gripped the rope and the hose, and called on the engineman to lower slowly.

"You don't need to trouble about the electric lights," called out Mr. Henry. "They're well insulated and perfectly watertight. The only thing that will damage the cable is the heat. Raise your arm if it's too great for you. We'll haul you up in a jiffy."

Out swung the rope, and Joe with it. For a while he was dangled well above the open hatchway, with a sheer fall of forty feet beneath him, and a glowing furnace somewhere in the hold for'ard. Whisps of smoke curled up about him, while the heat was almost stifling, but not so severe as it had been when he and his helpers had attacked the flames at closer quarters.

JOE ATTACKS THE FIRE AT CLOSE QUARTERS

Page 72

JOE ATTACKS THE FIRE AT CLOSE QUARTERS

"Lower away," he shouted, and then nodded to Sam to turn his hose on him. "Keep the water going, and start my hose," he called to those at the edge of the hatchway. "Now, slowly does it."

Very gently the engineman slacked out the rope running over the top of the derrick, causing Joe to slowly disappear within the open mouth of the hatchway. Meanwhile those in charge of the hoses paid the one out which Joe carried, and Sam, as if he were bent on doing his young friend an injury, sent a stream of water squirting against our hero till the latter was drenched, and till the force of the impact of the stream caused him to sway and twist at the end of the sling.

"Steady!" he shouted. "Less water; you'll drown me!" and, obedient to the order, Sam shouted to the men and saw that the stream was reduced. He sent a cascade downward now, for Joe had descended still lower, causing the water to fall on his shoulders and then go tumbling and hissing to the floor beneath. And, thanks to this deluge, and to the water spouting from the hose he carried, Joe was able to prepare the way before him. He could hear the fluid actually hissing, and see it rising in thick clouds of steam as it fell on iron and woodwork. It bubbled as it tumbled in a heavy cascade on huge masses of tightly-packed machinery directly beneath him, and then it began to settle into quiet pools.

"Steady!" he shouted again. "Hold on till things get a little cooler."

But ten minutes later he called to them to lower away, and in a little while had stepped from the sling and was actually advancing into the hold. A sailor joined him, and then Sam, both filled with enthusiasm. There were five hoses going within the hour, while another was all the while directing a powerful stream through the gap forward. Smoke gave way in time to steam, while the clouds of the latter, which had risen from every heated surface, and particularly from the vessel's plates, became far less in quantity. When three hours had passed, the atmosphere in the hold was almost pleasant, and certainly not too hot for safe working, while the fire appeared to have been conquered entirely. Then the ship's head was turned towards the west, and once again her turbines sent the decks throbbing. They came to Sam and Joe in the bunks which they occupied and told them of it; for the intense heat which they had faced, the stifling smoke, and the strenuous fight they had made had had their natural effect. Both had been hoisted from the hold in an insensible condition.

"Eh?" asked Sam. "She's right? Fire under? Then call me late in the morning. I've never yet travelled first class aboard a ship, and this bunk's just lovely. Hallo! That Joe? Eh? He's unconscious? Well, I am sorry; guess there's many a one will say he helped a heap to save this vessel."

41

They slept profoundly side by side, and the sun was high in the heavens before either opened his eyes. When Joe looked round, it was with a groan of recognition and remembrance. His hands were blistered all over and in bandages. His face was smeared with some greasy preparation, while there no longer trace of eyelashes, eyebrows, or hair. He was bald—a terrible object—with lips and tongue hugely swollen.

"My word," exclaimed Sam, staring at him, "what a sight!"

Joe giggled. After all, however tired, however sore with a struggle, he could look on the queer side of things. "My eye!" he gurgled, for speech was almost impossible. "Just you take a look at yourself; it'll make you feel downright faint, I do assure you." Then he went off into a laugh, which ended in a cry of pain and tribulation, for cracked and swollen lips make laughing painful. As for Sam, he rose in his bunk, leaned outwards, and stared into the mirror. It was with a groan of resignation that he threw himself backward, for, like Joe, he was wonderfully disfigured.

"The wife wouldn't know me," he said. "What a sight! No wonder you giggled."

But time does wonders for sore hearts and sore heads. Five days later, when the ship put into Quebec, both were moderately presentable, though Joe still had his hands in bandages. But think of the reward! A thousand and more disembarked passengers from the steamship *Kansas City* awaited their arrival and cheered them to the very echo as they landed. It was Joe's welcome to Canada, the land wherein he trusted to make his fortune.

CHAPTER V

One of the Settlers

"Now we get right in to business," said Sam, two days after the ship had brought them to Quebec, and he and Joe had gradually recovered their usual appearance. For, till then, they were hardly presentable, both having had every hair singed from their heads, while Sam, who wore a moustache, as a rule, merely retained a few straggling ends of that appendage. As for Joe, his hands were so blistered, that even now he was able to do little for himself.

"But you've got something inside there in your pocket that'll make amends," grinned Sam, as they sat in the parlour of the little hotel to which Sam had taken his wife, and whither Joe, Jim, and Claude had accompanied them. "You've got notes in that 'ere pocket that'll make you ready and eager to get burned again. There! Ain't I speaking the truth? I'm fair jubilant."

A cockney from his birth upward, Sam had not, even now, lost touch with the Old Country and its manner of speech, though into his conversation there was now habitually pressed many a Canadian slang expression, many an Americanism which to people of the Old World is so peculiarly fascinating. He pulled a huge leather wallet from his own hip pocket, a capacious affair that accommodated quite a mass of material, and was fellow to one on the far side harbouring a revolver. Not that Sam was of a pugnacious frame of mind; on the contrary, he was just one of the numerous citizens of Canada whose daily thoughts were centred in "making good". Indeed, as is the case with all in the Dominion, with few exceptions, Sam was out, as he frankly admitted, to make a pile, to build up a fortune.

"And I'll tell you for why," he had once said to our hero. "It ain't only because dollars look nice and can buy nice things. It ain't only because I'd like to be rich, to put by a heap and feel and know that me and the missus needn't want when the rainy day comes along, and we're took by illness or old age. Don't you go and believe it. There's people will tell you that Canadians think and dream of nothing but dollars, and jest only for the sake of the dollars. Don't you go and believe it. They're jest like me; they've been, many a one of 'em, down on their beam ends in the Old Country—couldn't get work, for one cause or another. Then they've emigrated, fought their way through, nearly gone to the wall maybe, and then made good. It's making good that fascinates us, young feller. Making good! Jest that and mostly only that. I'd be a proud man if I could put by a pile; for, don't yer see, it shows as I've succeeded. That's what I and many another are after. We've been failures, perhaps. We want to show the world that we're good for something. Dollars spells success—that's why we're after them all the time."

But Sam was not pugnacious, as we have observed. He dragged his huge leather case from one hip pocket and his revolver from the other, laying both on the table.

"I always carry a shooter," he said to Joe, "and so'll you after a bit. The usual run of fellow you come across is a decent, hard-working man. But this here country's full of 'bad men', as we call 'em. Ne'er-do-weels, remittance men, as some are known, loafers, and thieves. A chap as shows he's got sommat to defend himself with has a good chance of sendin' 'em off; so I carry a shooter. But we was talking of the stuff you'd got in your pocket, same as me. That makes up for burned hands."

Very deliberately he began to count out the values of the flimsy, blue-backed money notes rolled in his wallet, while Joe dived into an inner pocket and did likewise. He drew out quite a respectable bundle and counted the amounts also.

"Two hundred and fifty dollars," said Sam solemnly. "Reward for work done aboard the burning ship."

"Seven hundred and fifty dollars," murmured Joe, blushing when he thought of the amount.

"Jest so—reward for pluck and fer gumption," declared Sam. "My, wasn't you bashful up in the office when we was called in! You was for refusing almost. Said as you'd done nothing. That ain't the way of Canadians, lad. You did do good work; it was you who organized the volunteers and led 'em. That's a deal. It ain't nothing! It helped a whole heap, and therefore a reward was earned. That's the way in Canada—but let's get to business. What'll you do?"

"Act on advice you've already given," said Joe, pocketing his money. "My idea is to learn farming out here, and some day to take up a quarter section of land. But I'm going to learn the work first. I couldn't so much as milk a cow at this moment."

"Jest so," observed Sam dryly. "That's sense, that is. There's prosperity in this country, as I've told you often enough, but only for the workers. There's millions of acres, too, and no fear that if you wait you'll find none left for you. But where men fail is if they come out ignorant like you and pitch upon a quarter section when they ain't got the knowledge to choose their country. Their difficulties would often enough kill a man with farming knowledge; but, bless you! without even that knowledge, often enough with precious little money, they goes under almost afore they've had time to look round. So I say it's sound advice to you to say, 'Learn the farming work first'. Then take up your quarter section; for you'll be eighteen by then. Now, New Ontario's booming. Me and the missus will make there and prospect for a little. A single man can take a hundred acres in New Ontario for nothing. So can a married man; while, ef he's got a child under sixteen years of age, he can have two hundred fer the asking. Any more that's wanted costs two shillings and a halfpenny an acre. Cheap, ain't it? Wall, now, we comes again to you. You learn farming this summer. In the winter, get along into the towns and take most any job; next summer come right along to us. We'll have fixed a location by then, and you can take up a holding close handy. We'll get Claude and Jim in too, with one or two others, and we'll run co-operative farms. That is, instead of each man having a bunch of hosses, we'll keep enough for all, and help plough each other's holdings. We'll buy seed in bulk and get it cheaper fer that reason. And we'll sell our stuff in the same market, making one doing of the transport—so you come along next summer."

"I will," agreed Joe. "I've thought it over a lot, and will do as you advise; meanwhile, I shall bank most of the money."

"And mighty wise of you; only, see here," said Sam, his face wrinkling. "There's money to be made often enough by a wise fellow if only he has a little capital. With the sixty pounds you brought along, and the hundred and fifty you've been given, you've a tidy nest egg. Now you bank most of it, keeping twenty pounds for emergencies. One of these days, along where you're working, you'll drop on a site where the railway's approaching, and where there's likely to be a town. Towns spring up in new countries like mushrooms. Acres bare now, and worth perhaps two shillings, are worth twenty and thirty and more pounds in English money within a few years if they gets covered by a town. So, likely enough, you may drop on sich a place. Then draw the money you've banked, buy your land, and sit down to wait. Only, don't put all the money into one holding. Spread it about, young fellow. Don't put all the eggs into one basket."

There was little doubt that Sam was perfectly right, indeed, the experience of huge numbers in the Dominion goes to prove that. Towns do spring into being almost with the rapidity of mushrooms. A tiny settlement composed of wooden huts, called "shacks", and perhaps a log church, may, in the matter of three or four years, develop into a town, and, later on, even into a city. Those with knowledge and experience, and possessed of far-seeing eyes, may, by a fortunate purchase in the early days reap a big reward, and many a one has done so.

"So that's fixed," said Sam. "And now fer orders. We leaves here to-morrow fer Sudbury—that's beyond Ottawa. There me and the missus gets off the train. We'll buy a "rig", as a cart and horse are known, and we'll make off to the north-west looking fer a holding. You'd better come along with us to Montreal, where you can switch off fer Toronto, and look out in that direction fer a farm job, or you can come right along to or beyond Sudbury. Round Toronto you get Old Ontario, the country that's been known and settled this many a year. They're mostly fruit and dairy farmers about Toronto. North-west Ontario, New Ontario as it's called, is a different country. People kinder missed it till lately. It wasn't known that it was jest as good as many another, and no colder. But it's booming now, and there's where you'll find heaps of men jest wheat-growing. You could, of course, go right along to Manitoba, getting off at Winnipeg or somewheres close. But it's wheat-growing land there also; so ef you're going to join up with us later on you might jest as well stay somewheres near in Ontario."

Joe put on his cap and went out for a sharp walk. He clambered up the steep, old-fashioned streets of Quebec, still preserving their old French houses, to the Plains of Abraham, once the scene of a fierce engagement between English and French, when the gallant Wolfe won Canada for our Empire from the equally gallant Montcalm. He looked out from the heights across the flowing St. Lawrence River to the Isle d'Orleans, where Wolfe's batteries once thundered against the forts of Quebec, and past which the fierce Irroquois Indians, in days long since gone by, paddled their war canoes and kept the French colonists from crossing. And all the while he debated his future movements, for with the practical mind that his father had helped to train in him, Joe wanted to see his way clear. He had his future to make; a false step now might delay that success at which he aimed, at which, according to the worthy Sam, all newcomers and old colonists of the Dominion aim. Let those who would sneer at the seemingly grasping methods of many in Canada not forget what Sam had to say. Dollars do not spell happiness; they spell success. The immigrant who has few, if any to speak of, on arrival, and who fails to make wealth, is a failure, and failure causes a man to become despondent and to lose self-esteem. But gain, riches to one who was poor, who broke from old paths, left home and friends and all to start a new life, dollars in his case spell success, success that raises his head and his own self-esteem.

"I'll go along to Sudbury," Joe told himself. "Then I'll look out for a farm, and I'll bank all the money save fifty dollars. That's it; pay for my transport, and then bank all but fifty dollars, keeping father's letter with me."

The following morning found our hero aboard the train bound for Sudbury. They occupied places in a long car with two rows of seats, one on either side. At the far end of the car there was a miniature kitchen, where a fire was burning in a stove. Others who had crossed from England were with them, and the party soon settled down to their journey. Mrs. Fennick, with experience gained by earlier travel, had provisioned a basket, and with the help of Joe's kit, containing kettle and teapot, the little party were never at a want for good things to eat and drink. At night the seats, which were arranged in pairs facing one another were pulled out, making a respectable couch for one person, while the negro attendant lowered other bunks hinged to the side walls of the enormous car high overhead.

Late the following day the train pulled up at Sudbury, and they got down. Then Joe, Claude, and Jim waited till the Fennicks had bought a rig and had set out on their journey, when they, too, shouldered their bundles and strode off along the track, out of the town and into the open country. An hour or more later his two companions had accepted an engagement with a farmer whom they met driving along the track. Joe bade farewell to his two chums and strode onward.

"I'll make away more into the open," he told himself. "I'll get away from the settlements, so as to see what the life is really like, and whether the loneliness is so irksome as some make out."

Trudging along contentedly, he had covered some miles by noon, and then sat down to devour his luncheon. All that day he tramped, and the following one also, spending the night in the open; for it was beautiful weather, and frosts had long since departed from the land. Here and there he came upon settlements, and many a time was employment offered him, for the busy season with farmers was at hand, and labour always scarce. Sometimes he passed isolated farms, and on the third night put up in the shack of a settler who had little cause to complain of his progress.

"Came out as a youngster," he told Joe. "Took jobs here and there for four years, and then applied for a quarter section. It happened to be free from trees, though there was many an old rotting stump in the ground. I ploughed a quarter of the acreage the first year and secured a fine crop. Next year I did better, and broke up still more ground. If things go along nicely I shall do well, while already the section is worth some hundreds of dollars. Am I lonely? Don't you think it! I've too much doing in summertime and sufficient in winter. The chaps as is lonely are those who've lived in towns all their lives, and are used to people buzzing about them, and to trains and trams. They want to go to a theatre or a picture entertainment most every night, and having none about find things lonesome. I don't. If I want company I get the rig and drive off to a neighbour, or use the sleigh if the snow's too deep. Then there's a moose hunt at times, while always there's work to be done—tending the cattle, feeding the pigs and poultry, sawing logs, and suchlike. In summer there's picnics with the neighbours—shooting and fishing too at times. No, I ain't lonely."

Joe left his hospitable roof and pressed on towards the north-west, with his back to the railway. And a little later he came upon a small settlement, with farms immediately adjacent. Here he had no difficulty in obtaining work as a farm hand, the payment to be ten dollars a month and his board and keep.

"Know anything?" asked his employer, a man of some forty years of age, a colonial born, to whom Joe soon took a liking.

"Know anything about farming?" repeated Peter Strike, the man in question.

"Nothing," was Joe's answer, with an accompanying shake of the head.

"Never farmed, eh?"

"Never; couldn't milk a cow."

"Yer don't say so," grinned the farmer. "Now you'll do, you will, fine."

Joe was at a loss to understand. It seemed somewhat curious to him to hear that a hand engaged on a farm would do well when it was known that he was utterly ignorant. He explained the difficulty.

"Of course you don't understand," said Peter, guffawing loudly; for Joe's open speaking delighted him. "Of course you don't, 'cos back in England a man would be expected to know everything. But I'll tell you how it is with us. You're English; wall, now, in past years Englishmen got such a name with us colonials that we wouldn't employ him if we could help it. Eh? You'd like to know why? That's easy. Your Englishman would reach here dressed in knickers, perhaps—a regular swell. Us colonials with our old clothing would be fair game for him. Then he'd know everything. He'd be wanting to do things as he'd done 'em back in his own country, and not as we've learned they has to be done here. He'd want to teach his master, and grumble—my word, nothing pleased him! Now that's all getting altered. We find immigrants readier to learn, and you're one of 'em. Mind you, there's faults with others besides the Englishman who knows everything. There's faults with us. There's a sight of colonials who think they know more than they do, and when they get having advice from a man fresh out to the country—why, they get testy. It makes 'em angry. They ain't too fair to the newcomer. But guess that's getting altered, as I've said. Anyway, you don't know anything, ain't that it?"

"Nothing," laughed Joe; for the open-hearted Peter amused him.

"Then you come along in and see the missus and the children. Afterwards there's a job for you."

Joe was introduced to Peter's family circle, consisting of his wife and four small children. He found the shack to contain three rooms, a somewhat liberal allowance.

"Most of 'em has but one or two," explained Peter. "A man who has to be his own house builder can't afford too much time for fixing rooms. However, I made two, the kitchen here and the bedroom. Later on I built a lean-to, making an extra room. That'll be for you. Now we'll feed. Like beans and bacon?"

"Anything," said Joe heartily. "I've had a long tramp and am hungry. This fine air gives one an appetite."

"It's jest the healthiest place you could strike anywhere," cried Peter, his face glowing. "We've been here this four years. I bought the section from a man who had broken most of it and then got tired. You see, we've prairie all round, save for the settlement close handy. They say that the railway'll soon be along here. Anyway, there's no muskegs (swamps) hereabouts, and therefore no mosquitoes to speak of."

"He don't know what's a muskeg," laughed Mrs. Strike. "Tell him."

"It's a swamp, that's all," came the answer, "and there's miles of them in Canada. Often enough they're covered with low bush and with forests of rotting trees that ain't worth nothing as timber. But here we've open prairie, with plenty of wood, and huge forests at a little distance; so it's healthy. Now, you come along out and fix this job," he said, when Joe had finished the meal and had swallowed a cup of tea. "I'm so busy I haven't had time to see to a number of things, specially since my man was taken ill and left. There's the pigsty, for instance; it wants cleaning out. You jest get in at it."

Joe had long since donned his colonial outfit. He wore a slouch hat, with which no one could find a fault save for its obvious newness. An old pair of trousers covered his legs, and thick, nailed boots were on his feet. His jacket he had carried over his arm, and it was now reposing with his baggage, while a thick brown shirt and a somewhat discoloured red handkerchief completed his apparel. He followed Peter to an outhouse, and found at the back a range of wooden pigsties which might, with truth, be said to be in an extremely unsavoury condition. There was a fork and a spade near at hand, together with an old tin bucket.

"Right," he said briskly, turning up the ends of his trousers; "I'll make a job of it. I should say that a chap who had no knowledge of farming could do this as well as any other. I'll come along when I've finished."

Peter stood watching his new hand for some few moments, and then strode off out of sight. Joe turned his sleeves up, climbed into the sty, and set to work with a will.

"Not an overnice job," he told himself, "but then it's part of farming work. If I turn up my nose at this sort of thing and think myself too good for it—why, that would be a nice sort of beginning! Someone has to clean the sties on a farm. I'm the labourer, and so it's my job."

His jovial whistle could be heard in the shack as he worked, and brought Mrs. Strike to the door with an infant in her arms.

"Why, it's the new hand," she told her husband. "He's whistling, as if he liked the job you'd given him. Now I think that was a little hard. You can see as Joe's a better sort of lad. He's had an education, and I wouldn't wonder if he was something in the Old Country. And you put him right off to clean out the sty."

She regarded her lord and master with some severity; but the latter only grinned. Peter had a most taking face; in fact, his features were seldom severe, and more often than not wore a smile. He was a tall, burly man, with broad shoulders and long limbs. Possessed of fair hair and of a peaked beard, he was quite a handsome fellow, though wonderfully neglected as to his raiment. Indeed, contrasting Joe and Peter, one would have said offhand that the latter was the labourer and Joe the owner of the property.

But that is just the curious part of things outside the settlements in Canada. The more patched a man's garments, the more probable it is that he is successful. A colonist is not there judged by his fellows because of his clothing. He is judged by results—results of his labours on the soil or his astuteness in business. Compare this with England, where fine clothes make fine birds, where appearance is of so much importance, and do not let us sneer at either people. Custom has brought either condition about, and no doubt with good reason.

As for Peter, he was grinning widely as his wife turned somewhat sharply upon him.

"You've given him right off the nastiest job, and he quite green," she said.

"And I've done so with a reason," laughed Peter. "There's men I have hired before who had obviously seen something better back where they came from. They would have kicked at doing that sty. They would have forgotten that their old life was nothing to me, and that they were seeking their living in this country. Their old pride would be too much for 'em, and I would have to suffer. Now a chap who comes out here has to drop pride. If he's ignorant, he oughtn't to be above starting right at the bottom. I like hearing that lad whistling; he ain't too proud to earn an honest living, even if the job is what it is."

"Hallo!" he called, coming over to Joe some half-hour later and looking into the sty. "How're you doing?"

"Fine," said our hero, borrowing an expression somewhat common in the Dominion. "Almost finished."

"Then you've been mighty slippy," admitted Peter, his eyes opening when he saw that our hero had indeed almost finished the task. "This lad'll do for me," Peter said to himself. "He works, he does. He's the kind of fellow who likes to get ahead, whether he's working for another or for himself. My, if he ain't washing the place down now!"

Evidently his new hand was cleanly also, and that was pleasing. Peter began to think that in gaining Joe's services he had made quite a bargain.

"That'll fix it right, lad," he sang out. "You've made a fine job of it. Jest you hop out now, and put the fork and spade back where you found 'em. It's yer first lesson in farming and in other things."

Joe looked up smiling. "Eh?" he said.

"Yes," went on Peter, "Mrs. Strike's been pitching into me for giving you such a job first off; but I wanted to see for meself whether you'd kick, or whether you meant to get on whatever came along. Reckon you'll do—now come along in and feed the hosses."

When a month had passed, Joe found another ten dollars added to the fifty he had kept by him; also he had settled down wonderfully with the Strikes, and was already getting along with his farm work.

"He's a treasure is that lad," admitted Mrs. Strike warmly, when she and her husband were alone one evening. "It don't matter what it is that's wanted, he'll do it. If it's one of the children to mind, he'll smile and wink at the bairn. If it's water for the shack, he's willing. And if it's a log for the stove, he jest takes the saw and goes off whistling. That lad'll get along in the world."

"He's fine," agreed Peter. "He's the sort we want out from the Old Country."

Whether he was or not, Joe had taken kindly to the new life, without a shadow of doubt. His attentive mind was constantly absorbing details from the garrulous Peter or from his neighbours, and the end of that month's service on the farm had taught him quite a smattering of the profession he was to follow. As for being lonely, that he certainly was not; he was almost too busy even to have time for thinking of such a matter. Then, too, there were neighbours, while each shack actually possessed a telephone. However, if there were monotony in the life he was living, it was not long before an exciting incident occurred that would have aroused anyone even more lethargic than our hero.

CHAPTER VI

A Canadian Bad Man

"You jest put the hosses into the rig and make along to Hurley's," said Peter, Joe's employer, one early morning when the land was already ploughed, harrowed, and sown, and there was little to do but tend the animals and await the growth of the wheat crop, upon which Peter anticipated so much. "And don't stop longer than you need, lad. He's a bad man is Hurley, one of England's ne'er-do-weels, who came out years ago, and has now taken to farming. I've lent him a seeder this two seasons, and he hasn't returned it. Jest hitch it on to the back of the rig and bring it along."

"And you can take something from me along to Mrs. Hurley," said Peter's wife, who was one of those kind-hearted colonists one so often meets. "She's a poor, down-trodden thing, and most like she doesn't have too many of the good things. Here's butter for her, and eggs, and a leg of pork."

Joe was by now quite an adept at the management of the rig, and soon had his horses harnessed in, an operation of which he had been supremely ignorant before his arrival. He mounted into the cart, having placed Mrs. Strike's basket there already, cracked the whip, and went off across the prairie track between the ploughed acres already sprouting into greenness.

Hurley's quarter section was a matter of four miles away, and Joe had met the man only once before. But already something of his reputation had reached his ears, and Joe had gathered that amongst a farming class of industrious fellows this Hurley was looked at askance.

"He's a bully, and a sullen bully with it all," Peter had said once before. "He don't keep a hand more'n a month, as a general rule, while I reckon the boy as he has apprenticed to him has none too good a time. Hurley's a man I don't take to."

Bearing all this in mind, Joe whipped up his horses and took them at a smart pace across the fields. On every hand lay wooded country, with clearings to right and left, where the industry of the settlers had felled the trees, paying toll to the Government of Canada for them, and had then rooted the land, broken it, and placed therein the seed which was to spring into such bounteous growth. In every case a log hut was erected somewhere on the quarter section, consisting of one hundred and sixty acres; and these log huts often enough disclosed from their outward lines something of the character of the inmates, for in one case the shack was barely twelve feet by twelve.

"Jim Canning's," Joe told himself, for he had met Jim and liked him. "A confirmed old bachelor; been in Canada for ten years and more, and seems to like living by himself. He's a jovial fellow. Hallo, Jim!" he shouted, seeing that worthy crossing his section towards him. "How'dy."

Observe the expression, and gather the fact that even his own short residence in the Dominion had already caused Joe to copy those who lived about him. He was becoming quite a Canadian in his speech. Already one could detect something of that pleasant drawl that marks the sturdy colonial.

"Hallo, Joe!" shouted the stranger, beaming at our hero and disclosing handsome features, sunburned to a degree, while even his chest was of a deep brown; for Jim wore no collar, and had discarded the customary neckcloth. He was, in fact, a tattered-looking object—a huge patch in the seat of his trousers, a shirt which might have been blue or green or red in its palmy days, but which was now of a curious brown, evidently from much exposure to the sun. "How'dy," he cried. "Where away?"

"Hurley's, fetching a seeder."

"Huh! Then you look lively back agin," came the answer. "There's ructions down there. Hurley's been fighting with his hands, and though I believe they've settled the quarrel for the time bein', you never know when it won't break out again; he ain't no use ain't Hurley."

They waved to one another and then parted, Joe jogging along the rough track, now with the wheels on one side deep in an old rut, which threatened to upset the rig, and then bumping over boulders and tree stumps, which made riding anything but comfortable. But what cared Joe? He whistled shrilly; his face was rosy and tanned, his eyes clear, his broad-brimmed hat thrust back on his head, till a lock of hair showed to the front. Nor could his own clothing be very favourably contrasted with Jim's; for Joe's shirt had a large rent in it, made that very morning. A portion of the brim of his hat was missing, while the ends of his trousers were threadbare, to say the least of them.

"Clothing don't make the man, anyhow," Peter had said many a time. "You ain't any the wuss fer a rent in yer breeks."

"Hallo, Joe!" came a hail across from another quarter section. "How's the Strikes?"

Joe shouted back a greeting, and was soon exchanging others with farmers farther on. Indeed, he called at one of the shacks, a magnificent affair, showing the pluck and ability of its owner. It belonged to a city clerk from the city of

London, one who had been ignorant of farming conditions, and when Joe was last in this direction it was not entirely finished.

"I thought I'd just drop in and see the house," he said, as he pulled up at the door. "It wouldn't have been neighbourly to have passed without a call."

"That it wouldn't," laughed a small but active lady, who emerged and shook hands with him. "Hi, Jack, here's Mr. Joe come to see us! Isn't the shack a beauty, just?"

She stood away from the shack, regarding it with a proud eye. And Joe eagerly extolled its magnificence; for this city clerk had built a house which none need be ashamed of.

"Not bad by half, eh?" he grinned, as he came up to Joe. "My cousin, who's farming with me, gave a hand. There's four rooms inside, and a covered way to the stables and the piggeries. It's cost us a heap of labour, but it's done now, and mighty pleased we are. How's the Strikes? Crops showing well, eh? We're doing fine; and the wife is making money with her fowls and eggs and such things. My boy, I wouldn't be back on an office stool for double the pay. I'm free here—free, my boy! I can breathe out in this country. And look at the kids—they're as healthy as we could wish."

Joe took in his surroundings with an observant eye, and heartily congratulated his friends. Here he saw before him an example of what a man from a city can do in the Dominion, if only he have the pluck and the tenacity to face the difficulties and disappointments which are sure to come along at first, and have the perseverance to work.

"How did you manage?" he asked Jack, the owner of the place.

"Manage! Well, now, like this. I was ill back in the Old Country, and I'll say this for the people who employed me—they treated me handsomely. They paid my salary for a whole year; then the doctor recommended Canada, and out we came, drawing all our savings. Tom, my cousin, had been here four years working on the farms, and we went into partnership right away. Of course I knew nothing. I trusted to him, and I've learned steadily. It's been uphill work, my boy. But there you are."

He held out an open palm towards the house, eyeing it with supreme satisfaction. And no wonder. Here was a man who through ill-health had failed, more or less, in England. Canada had given him a new lease of life and new opportunities. But let us remember that the Dominion gives nothing without effort on the side of immigrants. Jack had worked—his elaborate shack showed that distinctly—while he had been aided and abetted by a clever wife who fell in at once with the ways of the country, who did not grumble because she was far outside a town, but set to work to master the intricacies of chicken rearing, or butter making, and a thousand and one things, hidden arts to her till that moment. And the result was success—success and happiness.

Joe shouted a farewell, promised to call in for a meal on his way back, and again whipped up his horses. In half an hour the rough track and his rig brought him to the door of the Hurleys, a tumble-down shack, showing obvious slackness on the part of the owner; and as he climbed out of the rig he heard cries and shouts coming from the interior of the shack.

"A ruction," he told himself. "Perhaps I'd better wait; other people's quarrels have nothing to do with me."

He paused half in and half out of the rig for a little while, till, of a sudden, the door of the shack flew open, and a lad some fifteen years of age dashed out. After him came a burly, bearded fellow, whose knitted brows and scowling face showed that he was in a temper. There was a whip in his hand, and no sooner was he out of the door than he sent the lash curling about the flanks of the lad who had preceded him, causing the latter to give vent to a cry of pain and to take cover by the rig. Then Hurley—for he it was—swung round on our hero.

"Huh!" he growled, drawing in the slack of his lash. "What do you want? You ain't been asked here. Clear off!"

Joe dropped from the rig and stepped a pace nearer. "I've come for Peter Strike's seeder," he said.

"Strike! Eh? You get off!" came the furious answer, for it seemed as if Joe's arrival had increased the anger of the individual. "You get right off, or I'll give yer strike jest as I'm a-going to do with this little rascal. Come you here, Tom; I'll learn you to leave the door of the stable open of a night and have all the cattle treading over the corn. You ain't coming? Then I'll have to fetch you."

The huge bully bore down upon the trembling lad he had addressed, and who seemed too scared to move. He cowered by the side of the rig till Hurley was upon him, and was then dragged towards the door of the shack.

"What! You ain't gone?" growled Hurley, seeing that Joe had made no movement, but stood beside the rig regarding him, and gripping the butt of his whip. "Ef you ain't away in a jiffy, I'll give you summat of the same too."

"You'll give me the seeder first," said Joe, keeping his temper, and showing an unflinching front, "and then you'll take your hands off Tom. Even if he did leave the stable door open, he's sorry, no doubt, and there's no excuse for treating him so badly. I'd be ashamed if I was a big fellow the same as you."

Hurley let his lower jaw drop with amazement, showing a set of irregular teeth which were all discoloured. He almost foamed at the mouth, while his eyes narrowed with anger and seemed to disappear within their sockets. Joe could see the fingers of his one free hand crushed into the palm, while the man's muscles hardened and stood out prominently under the skin of his arm. He bellowed when he answered.

"So you'd like to concern yourself with things that ain't got nothing to do with you," he shouted. "You're one of the green chaps from over the water that thinks things out here should be run as if the boys was dressed in silk, and every one of them mammy's darlings. I'm going to lick this kid, and when I'm done, if you ain't gone, I'll give you a hiding jest the same."

Joe began to gather the fact that he was in for trouble, and debated what he ought to do. There may be some who, under similar circumstances, would have clambered into the rig and driven off; but few, very few we imagine. Joe, at any rate, was not to be numbered with them; he clenched the hand not gripping his whip and watched to see what happened. And Hurley did not keep him long waiting. He took the boy Tom by the scruff of his neck, forced him against the doorpost of the shack, and proceeded to bind him to it with a length of cord.

"That'll do," said Joe curtly, walking towards him. "Let that lad go!"

"Eh? Why, ef I don't think you're mad!" declared the bully, opening his mouth in amazement. Indeed, he never once thought seriously that our hero would interpose between him and his victim. For Hurley stood six feet in his socks, and was burly and heavy. Joe perhaps topped the measure at five feet nine, and wanted to fill out a great deal yet before he could compare with this fellow. If he had any advantage over such a man, and that was an extremely doubtful point, it lay in his activity. Joe was light and "nippy" on his feet. In the boxing ring he could dodge round his opponent till the latter was exhausted almost in his efforts to force the battle. Hurley, however, was heavy and fat and unwieldy; besides, the bully's face bore abundant evidence of indulgence. There were heavy lines beneath the eyes; the healthy tan and colour of the average colonist who works in the open was conspicuous by its absence, and instead his face was deadly pale. His deep and rapid breathing, too, told of his soft condition.

"He'd smash me like an egg," Joe told himself. "This is going to be a nasty business. But I can't, I really can't back out of it. Look here, Hurley," he said, attempting to reason with the angry man, "leave Tom alone. You know better than I do that your neighbours would never stand seeing you knocking him about. Bullying don't go down out in these parts."

There came a roar from Hurley. Reason was thrown away on the maddened ruffian, and if only the truth had been known, he had imbibed a sufficiency of liquor that morning to account for a great deal of violence. Indeed, this was a habit which had grown with him, and which spelled ruin to his farming and to the happiness of his home. The veins in his bull-like neck swelled out prominently, then he launched himself at Joe, and, swinging the whip overhead, sent the lash coiling about his face. Our hero answered with a rapidity that must have been startling. He dashed in with the quickness of lightning and brought the butt end of his whip handle down with a crash on the middle of Hurley's head. A minute later they were locked in one another's arms and engaged in a desperate struggle. Hurley gripped Joe round the shoulders, compressing his chest and arms. Then Joe managed to wrench his right fist free, and without a particle of hesitation sent it again and again into the bully's face, till blood streamed down upon him, while Hurley shouted and foamed with rage, and strained as if he would crush the life out of his youthful antagonist. His breath came in gasps, so great were his exertions. His eyes were bloodshot, and altogether he wore anything but a taking appearance.

"Now, let me go, and end the matter," said Joe, keeping his wits, and pressing the man away from him as far as possible.

"Not till I've half-killed you," came the grunting answer. "I'll learn you to interfere; I'll break yer back, young feller."

And thereupon he proceeded to attempt to put that plan into execution. He lifted Joe as if he were a feather, swung him round and hurled him against the shack, jarring the breath out of his body. It was only with a great effort that our hero kept his senses and struggled to hold an upright position, then, just as he had got his breath again, the man was on him. Joe let out with his right and left fists in quick succession, getting home on the bully's face on each occasion. Then, stooping quickly, he picked up his whip, and, gripping the handle again, brought the butt heavily across Hurley's head, sending the man staggering backward. Indeed, the fellow seemed to be incapable of further exertion, for he rested his back against the shack and stood there panting.

Joe went to the boy at once, cut the rope which bound him, and pointed to the shack.

"Get your traps at once," he said, "then climb into the rig. I'll take you along with me."

He turned once more to see what was happening to Hurley, and was only just in time to spring aside, and thereby escape a sweeping blow from a heavy fork handle with which the ruffian had armed himself.

"I'll show you who's master," shouted the fellow, his beard bristling with rage, his hat fallen from his head, and his clothing all awry. "I'll show you who's winner here, I will. I'll brain you before I've done with you."

Up went his formidable stick again, to be swung over his head; then with a rush he advanced on Joe. But the latter dodged behind the rig, and for a while attacker and attacked were separated. Joe, in fact, could have retired. But there was the lad Tom to be considered, for at this moment he emerged from the shack, a huge bundle under his arm.

"Go back, right in," bellowed Hurley. "I'll finish you too if you're not careful. Go right in; I'll give you what you've earned when I've done with this cub. Eh? You ain't going to?"

The smallest hesitation on the part of Tom was sufficient to send the blood again rushing to the face of the bully. He looked a terrible object as he sprang at the boy, and there is little doubt that he would have done him a serious injury, had not Joe again pluckily come to the rescue. Darting out from behind the rig, he was just in time to catch the end of the stout handle which Hurley wielded as it swung back over his shoulder. Then, with a howl of rage, the brute turned on him.

"You again!" he shouted. "Then that for you! That, and that, and that!"

He rained blows on our hero, one catching him across the shoulder and almost felling him. The remaining two he was lucky enough to escape by leaping aside. But he realized that such an attack could not last for ever, nor was he likely to escape another time. It was with a quick movement, therefore, that he closed with Hurley. His fists went crash into the man's face, and then they were once more locked together. But here the bully had all the advantage, and his strength was increased by the rage he felt. It mattered little to him that Tom, with a pluck that did him credit, seized Joe's whip and struck his tormentor over the head time and again. Hurley did not seem to feel the blows; all his frantic rage was concentrated on Joe.

"I'm a-going to kill you right out," he grunted. "I'll larn you to come interfering with me and mine."

He swung Joe upward clear of the ground and then hurled him downward, once again driving the breath out of Joe's body. But he was not defeated. The lad had more pluck than strength, to give him his due, as, gasping for breath, he rose swiftly and once more tackled his opponent. Reaching forward, he planted a heavy blow in Hurley's face, and contrived to spring away before the man could seize him.

"Go in again! Punch him for all you can!" shouted Tom, taking an active interest now in the proceedings, and dodging round the combatants, as if he were seeking another opportunity to strike his tormentor. "Watch him, though; he's got that stick again. If I'd a gun I'd shoot him."

"You would, would you?" growled Hurley, his head down, his neck sunk into his shoulders, and a demoniacal expression on his face. "You'd shoot me, young feller? But I'll deal with you in a while. Maybe I'll kill you. This fool here I will, sure as eggs."

He spat into his hands and gripped his stake again. As for Joe, had he been armed with a revolver, there is little doubt but that he would have made good use of the weapon; for if ever a man looked murderous it was Hurley. More than that, had Joe but known what the interior of the shack disclosed, and been armed, he would have fired at this ruffian without a second's hesitation; for Hurley's attack on Tom was not his only act of brutality on this eventful morning. He had begun to bully the boy an hour ago, in spite of his unhappy wife's appeal, and when she had at length endeavoured to intervene, he had struck her insensible. That was the class of ruffian our hero had to deal with. A glance at his face, at his gaping lips, his firm-clenched teeth, and his bristling beard showed that his mental condition approached madness. And now, having regained his breath in some measure, he fixed his eye on Joe and rushed at him as a bull would at one who had roused his anger.

"Watch him!" shouted Tom again, as if the warning were actually needed. "Here, let's run for it."

But it was too late to think of that. Besides, Joe had his master's property to consider. He stood his ground, therefore, and held up a warning hand.

"I warn you to desist," he shouted. "I have done you no wrong, but have prevented you from ill-treating this boy. You are much older than I am, and should know what the end of this will be. Then, stand off."

"Stand off, and know that you've interfered? Not me!" came the growling answer. "Besides, I know how the thing's going to end. I'm going to kill you sure for being fool enough to interfere with other people."

Hurley waited for no more. He had paused as Joe held up a hand and spoke; but now he hurled himself forward, and struck out blindly with his stake. As for Joe, he stepped aside and dealt the man a swinging blow behind the ear as he passed him; but it was his last effort. The fight was too unequal, for here was a man armed with a long stake and able to reach him with it. Up went the formidable weapon again, and when it fell Joe's head was beneath it. He fell with a crash and lay quite motionless. As for Tom, he dropped his bundle and went off at a run towards the nearest quarter section, shouting for help at the top of his voice.

"That's what I call justice," growled Hurley, looking at the result of his violence. "I promised I'd knock him out, and I've done it. Now for the next business. This row'll put the North-west Police on me, and the neighbours'll be only too ready to join in. I'll hook it."

He went to Joe and bent deliberately over his unconscious figure, and then, with the hand of one who had obviously had experience, he ran through his pockets. When he rose again he was tucking away within his coat the roll of bills which represented all our hero's savings, added to the small fund he had kept out of the bank, and in addition the precious envelope which Joe's father had left to him.

"Sixty-five dollars free," growled Hurley. "That's a windfall, seeing that there's scarce a cent in the shack. It'll do for the time being. Here's an envelope—valuables, perhaps. I'll look into it later. Now, I'll cut this farming and be off."

Hurley was a cool ruffian, even if at times he was violent. He entered the shack, and emerged after some five minutes carrying a bundle of clothes and a rifle. Then he mounted the rig, having previously picked up the whip which Joe had used, cracked it, and set off down the track in the direction of the railway. He left the figure of Joe Bradley lying motionless and forlorn on the very ground, where he had made such a brave fight to protect a lad little younger than himself against the attack of a hulking bully.

CHAPTER VII

Into the Backwoods

"Jest you sit right up and take a sip at this. Now then, head back; make a try, lad. It'll pull you round; time's pressing."

PETER AND JACK BAILEY FIND JOE UNCONSCIOUS

Page 109

PETER AND JACK BAILEY FIND JOE UNCONSCIOUS

Joe heard the voice afar off and stirred. There was a familiar note about it, a kindly bluntness to which he was accustomed. So being the sort of lad whose nature it was to make an effort always, if only for the reason that he was of a decidedly active temperament, and perhaps also because he hated, like many another person, to be beaten, he lifted his head, feeling at once a hand placed beneath it. Then he opened his eyes and stared upward, blinking all the while, at a huge expanse of blue sky such as dwellers by the edge of the Mediterranean rave about.

"Eh?" he gasped, attempting to moisten his lips. "Time to get up, eh?"

"Jest take a sip, and then you'll be feeling lively," he heard again in the well-known voice. "You ain't knocked out altogether. That thar Hurley ain't quite beaten you, I guess."

The mention of the bully's name brought Joe to an upright position. He sat up abruptly, and then, seeing a tin mug just before his face, and being consumed by a terrible thirst, seized the said tin mug and drained it.

"Ah!" he gasped. "I wanted that. Where's Hurley?"

"That's jest the very question we're axin' ourselves. Sit up agin, lad," he heard, undoubtedly in Peter Strike's voice. He turned at once and gazed into the rough, unshaved face of his master.

"You?" he asked in bewilderment. "Why, I left you way back at the shack!"

"So you did, lad, so you did; but that's two hours ago, and perhaps more. I was out lookin' at the pigs, and thinkin' as the time was coming close when I'd drive some of 'em over to Sudbury, where I'd be sure to make dollars on 'em, when the missus comes rushin' out. 'Peter,' she shouts, 'where have you got to? Drat the man!' she says aloud to herself, 'drat the man! Where's he got to? Never here when I want him, but—ah, there you be!' she hollers out, suddenly catching a view of me over by the pigs. 'There you be, Peter.'"

Joe sat up with a vengeance now. His stay with the excellent Peter and Mrs. Strike had taught him to like them very much, and Peter's description of what had happened was so faithful to what must have actually occurred. Joe himself had heard the bustling spouse of his master calling her lord in peremptory tones, and he grinned now at the recollection.

"Yes," he smiled, "you were there."

"I was that," laughed Peter. "And then I heard that there had been a ruction, and that you was in it. Of course I slipped into the shack fer my gun at once, hopped on to a hoss, and was away fer Jim Canning's in a jiffy. He'd got his hosses harnessed into the rig already, and we went on in company till we struck along by Jack Bailey's. Wall, now, he's a bright lad is Jack, though he ain't so very long from an office stool in London. There he was with his cousin George, with the rig loaded up with provisions.

"'Most like we'll be away from home a bit,' sang out Jack as we come up. 'So we've put together a little grub and drink, besides a kettle and sichlike. What'll you do?'

"'Get right along to Hurley's and see what's happened,' I answered. 'This Tom's come in in a hurry, and maybe things ain't as bad as they seem. Anyway, we'll make along there. I'll gallop ahead. I've rung up the central station Sudbury, and told the missus to call for the North-west Police, because this job's bound to be a police job anyway.' Wall, here we are. How's yerself?"

Peter had filled his tin mug again, and when he offered it to Joe the lad took it with pleasure. He could sit up alone now, and presently could actually stand, though he felt giddy. However, they brought a chair from Hurley's shack and placed him in it. Then Jack Bailey, the immigrant who not so long ago had been a clerk in the city of London, and who was now on the high road to becoming a successful farmer in the Dominion, stood over him and gently dressed the wound Hurley had given.

"Not so bad, after all," he said cheerily, as he carefully washed the part where the bully's stick had fallen. "Little more than an inch long, and not deep. It won't even send you to bed. Just stay still while I clip the hair away and tidy things up a little."

For ten minutes he busied himself with Joe's head, snipping the hair away all round the ugly wound which Hurley had given our hero; for your city clerk is no fool, and Jack knew that no scalp wound can be safely left unless the hair be removed and thorough cleanliness thus ensured. He produced a little roll of strapping which his thoughtful wife had provided, and, having placed a small dressing over the wound, applied the strips of strapping, getting them to adhere by the simple expedient of lighting a match and heating the adhesive material.

"Now you'll do," he said, surveying his work with some pride. "How do you feel? Giddy, eh?"

Joe felt distinctly giddy and positively sick; for a concussion is often followed by sickness. But he was game, and fought down the feeling heroically; in fact, he struggled to his feet, plunged his hands into his pockets, and actually whistled.

"Showing as you ain't beaten by a long way," said Peter, emerging from the shack and looking with approval at our hero. But there were grave lines about his face, and for a little while he was in close and earnest conversation with his friends. Perhaps an hour later a horseman came galloping towards them, and was hailed with pleasure.

"That you, Mike?" sang out Peter. "I sent along over the 'phone for you, and guessed it wouldn't take you long to reach."

"Horse was already saddled, and me almost mounted when the message came," replied the newcomer, dropping out of his saddle. "I was jest off in the opposite direction, so it war lucky you 'phoned jest then. I rode down to the station, and put horse and self aboard a freighter about to steam out. They dropped me down about opposite here, and I've legged it for all I could. What's the tale?"

A magnificent specimen of humanity he was, this newcomer. Even Joe was not so sick that he could not admire him. For Mike Garner stood six feet in his stockinged feet, nothing less, and was burly in proportion; also he seemed to be as agile as a cat, while none could accuse him of fatness.

His muscular calves filled the soiled and stained butcher boots he wore. A pair of massive thighs swelled his khaki breeches, while the dun-coloured shirt was stretched tight over a brawny chest, open at the neck, and with sleeves rolled to the elbows, exposing a pair of arms tanned to the colour of nut-brown, and swelling with muscle and sinew. In fact, Mike was just a specimen of that fine body of men, the North-west Police of Canada, who, in spite of paucity of numbers, keep law and order in the land. But it is only fair to mention that out in the settlements their task is simple, as a general rule; for your newcomer to Canada, as well as the old settlers, are law-abiding people, given to toil and thrift and not to broiling. However, here and there there is trouble, and Mike had galloped over to investigate the case of Hurley.

"What's the tale?" he asked abruptly, dropping his reins over the big horse's neck and leaving it there unattended, while he came towards the shack rolling a cigarette. "Hurley's broken out, you say. Guessed he might. I've had an eye on him this two years back. There's been complaints of ructions at the shack. We had a man in a month back who said he'd been knocked about."

"It's wuss this time," answered Peter gravely. "I'll give yer the yarn in a few words. I sent this here chap Joe over to fetch a seeder Hurley had borrowed two years ago and hadn't returned. Wall, he heard shouts as he come up to the shack, and saw Hurley whacking Tom here, the lad he'd got apprenticed to him. Joe wasn't having that, nohow. Eh?"

He looked over at our hero as if for corroboration. Then Tom chimed in.

"Hurley's a bully," he cried. "He was tying me to the post when Joe asked him to leave off. He was polite, was Joe. But Hurley swore and threatened him too. Then he struck at him, and there was a shindy. My, but Joe stuck to his man and hammered him in fine style! If it hadn't been for the rake handle, Joe would have beat him, big though Hurley is. But he struck Joe over the head, and then I ran for help."

"Seems to me as this here Joe did well," declared Mike curtly. "Wall, now?"

"There ain't much to tell. Tom reached Jim Canning's, and he rang me up. We was all of us along here as quick as possible. Hurley took the rig and drove off, and there ain't a doubt that he's taken a gun with him. He cleared Joe's pockets of every cent—about sixty dollars, he reckons—as well as a letter of some value. But that ain't all. There's been trouble in the shack. That ere brute set upon his wife and made an end of her."

When the whole tale came to be understood, there was little doubt that the brute Hurley had flown into a furious temper, and had become almost mad with passion. His unfortunate wife he had killed with a knock-down blow, while the reader has learned of his subsequent movements.

"Wall?" asked Peter, looking expectantly at Mike.

"You wait a bit, mate," said the other. He dropped his cigarette, lifted his hat solemnly, and entered the shack. There was a severe air on his handsome, sunburned face as he emerged.

"Of course," he said, "we've got to follow; that is, I have. If you gentlemen——"

"You don't need to ax," exclaimed Peter, with added bluntness. "We're here. Ef you want us, we're right alongside you all the time. Murders ain't often done in the settlements, but when they are, then it's every man's job to find the brute as did it. You lift yer little finger, and you've every man Jack willing and ready."

"Thanks," said Mike swiftly, looking about him and proceeding to roll another cigarette. "We'll move slippy; we'll get right back along the tracks this fellow made, and make use of the first telephone. This Hurley didn't have one, so we can't send news from here. If he's taken to the railway, we'll send along either way, and they'll have him quick. But most like he's turned north, in which case we've a pretty business before us. Ready now?"

"You kin guess so," said Peter, clambering on to his horse. "Tom, you ain't afraid to follow?"

That young fellow shook his head vigorously; his eyes were sparkling. At that moment he looked more of a boy, more resolute than he had done ever since he came to the Hurleys'. "I'm game," he said. "If Joe was game to tackle him alone, I'm right with the lot of you."

"Then you climb right into Jack's rig and take Joe with you. He'll want a bit o' nussing for a while. Reckon, Mike, if this here business is going to take us away north, we'd do well to lay in a stock of ammunition. What say?"

The policeman was in his saddle already and turned his head.

"We'll get all we want from the station," he said. "Let's move."

Waiting to allow Mike to gain some yards start, so that he might follow Hurley's track without difficulty, the others followed in single file, first Peter, and then Jack and his cousin in their rig, with Tom and Joe beside them, while Jim brought up the rear. Half an hour later they struck the railway, running clear and unfenced across the land. Here Mike turned east, still following the wheel marks left by the rig which Hurley had stolen. About four miles farther along the marks left the railway and ran towards a stretch of wooded country. Perhaps a quarter of a mile within this they came upon the rig itself, deserted, while the horses and Hurley himself were nowhere to be seen. Mike dropped out of his saddle, where Peter joined him. As for Joe, the jolting and the excitement of the chase seemed to have done him a vast amount of good, for his head had ceased to ache, and he was hardly giddy. But for the pain in his scalp and a certain stiffness about his limbs, he might never have come by an injury.

"Unhitched his cattle here and made off with 'em," declared Mike, standing well clear of the rig, and walking slowly round it. "Struck due north, as I guessed he might. He'll be hiding up amongst the woods, and it'll take a tracker to find him. Tell you, Peter, it ain't no manner of use for us to follow right off. We might lose his tracks any moment, then there'd be difficulties. Guess the best thing to do is to camp right here and wait. I'll make back to the railway and 'phone along. Late to-night, perhaps, or to-morrow morning I'll be back agin with you, and then I'll have someone along with me as can follow any track, as can scent out a white man almost. You sit tight right here. Got it?"

"You've hit it true," agreed Peter. "There ain't no manner of sense in plunging on. This country right north is jest a huge forest for miles. There's swamps, too; then stretches of rock over which a man might ride and never leave a sign that a white man could follow. So we'll camp right here, and you kin get back and fix things. Don't forget that we'll want shooters. I've a revolver and a gun; Jack there and George ain't got a gun between 'em, nor Joe nor Tom. It ain't sense to go after a chap same as Hurley without having the things to meet him with. He'll shoot, he will."

"Sure," declared Mike, with the directness of one who knew; "he'll shoot on sight. There's a rope waiting fer his neck, and he knows it. You boys had best understand that right away."

He glanced round at the party, his eyebrows elevated, a question on his lips. But they sent him off promptly, laughing at his caution, eager as ever, whatever the dangers, to follow the miscreant who had killed his wife and wellnigh done the same for our hero.

"Best get the hosses out o' the rigs and let 'em feed," said Peter, who took the lead now that Mike had gone. "Jack, you and George has the cooking things and the grub, so reckon it's up to you to cook us a meal. Jim and me'll scout round a while. We ain't likely to cover the tracks left by Hurley, and it'll be well to follow a goodish bit, so as to make sure he ain't too handy. It wouldn't be kinder nice to get eating and then have a bullet plumping amongst us."

There was bustle about the little clearing for some few minutes. Joe lent a hand to the Baileys, and soon had the horses out of the rig and tied by a long rein to trees, allowing them freedom to graze. By then Tom had gathered sufficient sticks to form a fire, and had helped to take the horses from Jim's rig; for the latter had already departed with Peter. In a little while there was a blaze in the centre of the camp, and Jack had a kettle of water suspended over it with the help of a couple of forked sticks. George produced from a mysterious parcel a lump of meat, and having cut it into dainty slices, skewered them in a long row on a maple stick he had cut and cleaned, and at once began to toast them over the flames.

"Makes you get hold of an appetite, young fellow," he said, winking at Joe. "Now don't it? There's a flavour about open-air cookery that just sets a man's mouth watering. Ever been out camping?"

"Never," admitted Joe. "Ripping, I should say."

"Then you're about right," cried George, his face ruddy beside the flames. "I mind the time when I first came out to Canada. Didn't I just pity Jack back in the Old Country! For I went off with a prospecting party north to see what sort of a line there was for a new railway. It wasn't half as bad as people had painted, for there were few muskegs, as the swamps are called, and fewer mosquitoes. As for food, there wasn't a day passed but the Indians along with us brought in beasts of every sort; so we dined handsomely. And camping was a fair treat. Talk about a difference between it and the old life—living in a tiny villa south of London, mugging in a London office, and being half-stifled with winter fogs! There we were in the open day and night, such nights too! Fresh air, fresh food, and heaps of exercise all the time. I just revelled. This steak frizzling here, and the scent it throws out, reminds me of that time."

Joe sniffed eagerly. His headache and even his pains were gone now, while the trouble his wound gave him was infinitesimal. In fact, it was the weight of the blow which Hurley had delivered which brought unconsciousness. The wound was trifling. A thick skull had resisted damage, and now that his brain tissues were recovering from the jar they had received, Joe was almost himself again. He sniffed with eager anticipation, and agreed that open-air cooking had its attractions. He went to the far end of the maple switch and, holding out a hand, took it from George.

"You'll make a cook all right," laughed the latter. "Now see that none of the steaks get burned. I'll pop tea into the kettle and get other things ready. Those two will be back before very long; it stands to reason that they won't go very far. Take my advice, Joe; get inside a blanket just as soon as you have had a meal, and sleep. You'll be as fit as a daisy come morning."

About an hour later, when the first brew of tea had been finished, Jim and Peter put in an appearance.

"We kin camp without a thought of danger so far as I kin see," said the latter, throwing himself down by the fire. "That thar Hurley's made tracks slick north, and he ain't going to wait for no one. We followed the trace of his hosses' hoofs fer three mile and more. By the way, they ain't his hosses; they're mine. Jingo! That makes another count up agin him. But I was saying as he's gone north slick as anything. He'll want no end of catching. Seems to me this chase'll last a week on end, and ef that's to be, I'll make across to the railway after I've had a bite, and get on to the nearest telephone. Then I kin ring up Jack's wife and my own and tell 'em. How's that?"

"Just what was bothering me," cried Jack, who was at that moment burying his teeth in a juicy steak. "I was saying to myself a little while ago that it seemed as if this wouldn't be a one-day affair, and I was bothering to let the wife know. Not that I'm going back till the matter's finished. Not much—this is a duty."

"You've put it fair and square," agreed Peter, with flushing face. "This here are a duty, sure. Out in the settlements there ain't so many cases of murder and theft. A man soon gets known, seeing as there's so few of us, and mostly in settlements close together; and ef he's a bad man—why, out he goes sooner or later. But bad men mostly gets into the towns. There's a sight of 'em always hanging about the saloons, and so on. Some of 'em make a regular business of watching out fer green 'uns, fellers just out from home; and mostly the rogues strip the poor chaps of every dollar. They're up to all sorts of tricks. Most like they'll pretend to have land to sell, ready-made farms, you might say. The bad man is Canada's curse, jest that and nothing less; and reckon not a few of 'em is the relics of the wasters and the wont-works who was sent out here long ago from the Old Country, to get 'em out of the way or to give 'em a new chance."

"In fact, just the class that modern-day Canada is determined not to have," chimed in George. "And one can't blame the Government. In future, jailbirds won't be sent direct to the Dominion instead of to prison, simply because they'll be turned back at the ports; just the same as folks with obvious disease of the lungs will be turned back. But you can pass me along another of those steaks,

Tom; and don't go on looking at 'em like that. Pitch in at them, my boy. There's enough there and to spare fer everybody."

Tom had indeed been eyeing the frizzling steaks somewhat hungrily, and, if the truth had but been known, it was only from force of habit. Hurley had been very much the master. His apprentice had put up with short fare and many blows.

"How was it you was put with him, lad?" asked Peter, when he had finished his meal and had lit up a pipe preparatory to his setting out for the railway. "Surely the folks who put you there hadn't met Hurley?"

Tom shook his head emphatically. "They'd never seen him," he said. "My uncle wished me to come out from England, and saw an advertisement offering to take a lad for a premium. He paid the money and I came, only to find that I was a sort of slave."

"Huh!" growled Peter. "Jest what I thought. That's another turn the bad man gets up to. But boys ain't always treated same as that. I've had 'em meself, and know others who've taken lads. The Barnardo Boys' Home sends a goodish lot out to Canada and places them out on the farms. But, bless you! they ain't finished with 'em by a long bit, and rightly so. There's inspectors who go round and make surprise visits, and if they find that a boy isn't getting fair and square and liberal treatment, why, away he's taken, and put somewhere else. And the result is that we're bringing up in Canada a heap of young chaps who come out jest at the very right age, when they ain't yet learned any farming and when their minds is—wall, now, what are the term?"

"Receptive," cried Jack, who was quite a scholar. "The young, untutored mind is readily receptive."

"Put it like that," agreed Peter, who was a wonderfully talkative and jolly fellow. "The kids learn, and ain't got no bad tricks to unlearn. Folks has got to set great store by 'em, for they're likely obedient lads, and there's more demands for 'em than there's boys. They get looked after. There ain't no bullyin' and half-starving same as in Tom's case. What's more, farmers is willing and eager to pay 'em wages and keep 'em, and not jest have their work for nothing, and a handsome premium into the bargain. That 'ere Hurley's a bad hat."

He knocked the ashes out of his pipe, leaped to his feet, and swung his leg over his horse. Without troubling to put a saddle on the beast, he hitched the rein free from the tree and went off whistling.

"A good chap," said Jim. "Known Peter this many a year. Good master, eh, Joe?"

"None better," came the prompt answer. "They treat me as if I were a son. He's used to this tracking?"

"He's a good man, you may say," agreed Jim. "But he don't often track men—moose perhaps, and a bear sometimes. This Hurley'll be a different matter."

"Now, Joe, jest you get right off to bed," commanded George, who seemed to take almost a paternal interest in our hero. "By sunrise to-morrow you'll be feeling fine, and you'll thank me."

That the advice was good there was little doubt, and since Jack supported it with vehemence, Joe obeyed, though he felt far from sleepy. Indeed, he was almost too excited to be that; for, recollect, the events of the day had been sufficiently rousing for a youth of his age and experience. He had been engaged in a desperate struggle with a bully, with a man who would have killed him with pleasure, and who, in fact, did his best to bring about that ending. And now he and his friends were in chase of the murderer. He, Joe, was away in the wilds of Canada, in the backwoods, with the open sky above him, about to Sleep beneath it for the first time in his life. He drew a blanket which Jack had brought round his body, and lay down on a bed of spruce that Jim had cut. And there for a while he lay without movement, his eyes blinking at the glowing embers of the fire. A little later his head dropped lower, while the men chatting in low voices round the fire heard his sonorous breathing.

"Good plucked 'un, him," remarked Jim, pulling his pipe from his mouth and pointing the stem at the recumbent figure. "There's many as would have backed out of that 'ere ruction and left Tom to fend for hisself. He's the sort we want in this country. A chap as can put up a fight with a murderer double his size can face the troubles that come to all colonists. Pass the 'bacca, Jack. I came away in such a hurry that I've none."

"Do you know his history?" asked Jack Bailey after a while, when they had smoked silently for some few minutes, the smoke from their pipes ascending into the cool evening air and mingling with that from the fire where it met the leaves overhead. "He's a better sort—one of the better class in England."

"As you can see," agreed George. "Heard anything of him, Jim?"

"Jest this," came the answer. "There's a man named Fennick as was close handy to me this five years back. Well, seems he came out with Joe, and they write to one another every now and again. In fact, this Joe's going along to join him one of these days as soon as he's learned farming. Fennick just swears by the lad; says as he organized a band of volunteers on the way out when the ship got afire, and helped to fight the flames. So Joe ain't fought a murderer only; that's why I agreed as he was a good plucked 'un. Now I'm fer bed; most like we shall have a hard day of it ter-morrer. I know Mike; he's a boy fer pushing ahead. There's nothing tires him. Gee! I wouldn't wonder if we was in fer a hairy sort of time on this business. Joe are likely to come up agin trouble beside which his fight with Hurley warn't nothing."

Peace reigned over the slumbering camp within half an hour. The watchful stars glowed down upon the little band and seemed to guard them. Slowly the hours drew along towards morning, when the pursuit of the murderer would be taken up in earnest. And which one of the band could say what sort of experience awaited them? Perhaps Jim would be right. It was more than likely that Joe might find himself plunged into a conflict beside which his fight this day was a mere scrimmage. But whatever the prospect might be, it did not disturb his slumbers. Joe hardly so much as turned till the first rays of a brilliant sun streamed into his eyes on the following morning.

CHAPTER VIII

Hank makes his Appearance

The sound of hoofs trampling through the wood was the first thing that came to Joe's ears as he sprang from his spruce bed and looked about him. Someone was coming towards the camp through the forest, while about the still-smouldering fire lay the figures of his sleeping comrades.

"Peter and Mike coming back, I expect," he told himself. "But supposing it were Hurley?"

There was just a bare possibility that the sounds were produced by that individual, and, lest it should be the case, Joe gripped a thick stake and awaited events. Then a shout escaped him, while an answering welcome hail sounded through the camp and set every one of the sleepers stirring.

"I see you right enough!" shouted Peter, laughing as he dropped from his horse. "I seed Joe grip a hold of a stake when he heard us, thinking maybe we was Hurley. He was game, he was, to put up another fight with the bully. But we ain't, you see, lad, and so let's get to breakfast."

It appeared that Peter had met with Mike late the previous night, and the two had rested beside the railway; and now they came into the camp, bringing with them a couple of followers. These proved to be Indians—not the Red Indian one sees often pictured, but lean men with bent figures, and dressed in shabby buckskins. Their black hair was trained back from their faces and tied at their necks. Their thin faces were seamed and lined as if with many troubles, while their bent figures, their wrinkles, and their general appearance gave one the impression that Mike had brought old men with him.

"But don't you think it," said the policeman, when he dropped from his horse and was seated near the fire awaiting a meal. "They're men I've employed this many a time, and first-rate trackers. One's known as Fox—and a fox he is, if one judges by his cunning—the other hasn't a name, so far as I have ever gathered, so he's 'Bill' to me, and answers the name promptly. They ain't much good at talking, either of 'em, though they can speak English. I've known them sit all day long round the fire and not pass more than a dozen words between them; but clever trackers they are, and that's why I've brought 'em. Now, boys, something to eat, and then away."

By now the fire had been coaxed into a blaze, while a number of steaks which George had prepared overnight, and had already skewered, were soon sizzling over the flames. Tom came running back to camp from a stream to which he had been sent, and at once the kettle was hung in position. As for Joe, he felt a new lad indeed. He might never have come by an injury, though his head was tender enough when one touched it. He slipped from the camp with Jim, and the two, having walked a little way down the stream, stripped off their clothing and had a splendid dip.

"Regular dodge of an Englishman," grinned Jim, as he sat on the bank to allow the sun's rays to dry him. "Your Englishman comes to a foreign part and plunges right into the first pond he happens on. There's hardly another man that's so keen on bathing. But it freshens a fellow—eh, Joe? How are you this morning?"

"Hungry," came the prompt answer. "But I felt I wanted a livener, and that dip has done it. Suppose we shall ride right off as soon as breakfast is finished?"

"You've hit it; Peter and Mike has brought along some spare hosses. There was Peter's to begin with, and Mike's; then there was two in my rig and two in Jack Bailey's, making six in all. With the Indians we muster just eight, so two more hosses were wanted. You see, we ain't going to take rigs with us. They'd be in the way, most likely, especially in this sort of wooded country. We shall ride; Peter's brought along the saddles."

When they returned to the camp and were in the midst of their breakfast, the voluble Peter explained matters fully.

"Me and Mike hit right up agin one another last night," he said, "and in course we got to gassing. We allowed as rigs warn't no sort of use away up in the country to which this Hurley had made, so it war clear that extry hosses was needed. Wall, we fetched 'em. Hank Mitchell, one of the best fellows you could hap upon, lent 'em willingly, and he's coming to join us. He's bringing guns, too, for they're to come along in a freight train from Sudbury fust thing this morning; so's saddles and tinned provisions. Hank has also arranged fer two of his hands to come right along here and clear back with the rigs, fer it wouldn't do to leave 'em here fer more than a day or two. People's mighty honest in these parts, but there might arrive someone who was a stranger, and who jest happened to be in want of a rig same as one of these. So they'll be took back to the rail track, near Hank Mitchell's, and wait thar till we returns. Why, ef that ain't Hank hisself! He has been extry nippy."

A short, spare man came cantering up to the camp at that moment, his approach having been hidden from all by the trees which surrounded them. He dropped from his saddle with as much ease as the average man steps from one board to another, and walked swiftly forward.

"Hallo, mates, how'dy?" he said softly, as if he were afraid of having his voice heard. "My boys are close handy with the guns and sichlike. Which one's Joe, him as I've heard of?"

"Thar," cried Peter, grinning, and pointing to our somewhat bashful hero.

"Do yer drink?" asked Hank abruptly, stepping across till he was close to him, and regarding Joe with a pair of eyes which might be described as actually piercing.

"No," was the equally abrupt answer. Joe, in fact, stared hard at this newcomer. He didn't quite know what to make of him, though, to be sure, he rather liked his looks. Hank's nut-brown face, clean-shaven, unlike most others in those parts, with its deeply-lined forehead and the whisps of grey hair showing beneath his hat at the temples, spoke of one who had seen many years. But it was a kindly face, kindly and keen; that, perhaps, was the better description. Every movement of the little man was jerky. His lips, when he spoke, opened sharply and closed again, as if he were anxious to hide his teeth. His eyes blinked with spasmodic suddenness. He even seemed to breathe differently from other men.

"Smoke?" he demanded, firing the question off as if he were glad to be rid of it, and yet observing Joe all the while, as if he would penetrate to the centre of his brain and steal the very thoughts he was thinking.

"Sometimes," admitted Joe, somewhat guiltily; "not often; shall do later."

"Huh! Larned farmin' yet?" asked Hank, with comical shortness.

"Trying," grinned Joe, beginning to see fun in this catechism, and taking a decided liking for the newcomer; "but I ain't through yet. I admit that I don't know everything. There's a few things yet that Peter can teach me."

"Ha! Ha! Ha!" shouted the latter. "He's had you, Hank. He's always like this is Hank," explained Peter. "He don't 'low no one to be friends till he's sort of axed him all sorts o' questions. And guess he jest don't care much fer a Britisher as comes out here and knows most everything. Git ahead, Hank, boy," he bellowed. "Joe ain't one o' them. He's one of the right sort; he's a good plucked 'un."

"You kin shake," said Hank, his comical gravity unmoved, though there was just the suspicion of a flutter of an eyelid. "Lad, I'm proud to meet yer. The chap as could stand up to Hurley are worth knowing. Shake!"

Joe shook. He danced almost on the toes of one foot, for this lean little man had a hand grip of iron. His fingers closed round our hero's as if he meant to crush the very bones, while those curiously piercing eyes never left the young fellow he was addressing.

"I say," roared Joe, "now try again."

He offered his hand for the second time, while those who observed Hank saw distinctly a twinkle of his eye. He even smiled, a rarity with Hank, and responded at once to our hero's invitation. This time Joe returned the grip with interest. Some weeks of farming, of rough work in Peter Strike's service, had hardened his muscles, and anyone could see that he was filling out. Indeed, but for the fact that Hank had taken him unawares, Joe's fingers would not have received such a crushing. Now he let them close round the diminutive Canadian's like a vice, and fixed his eyes on those two piercing orbs which he found so wonderfully attracting. The two closed in to one another till but a short space separated them, and then and there exchanged a second grip, the grip which spoke of friendship, of strength, of firmness, of virtues which the man who lives his life in the open and meets danger and privation often enough prizes above all other virtues. As for Hank, the suspicion of a smile in his eyes went promptly. He was all seriousness. Indeed, all of a sudden he seemed to view Joe from an altogether different standpoint. A minute before he had been greeting a green lad, one who had shown pluck and deserved encouragement; but now he seemed to have dipped somewhat into the spirit which kept Joe going, which dominated every waking moment of his life, which made of him the youthful leader of that band of volunteers aboard the emigrant ship, and again urged him to stand fast in Tom's behalf in spite of Hurley the bully. Intuitively Hank seemed to guess that Joe had balance and grit, and promptly he acknowledged the fact.

"I'm fair glad to meet you," he said. "From now on you've a friend."

Then they sat down round the fire, while their comrades watched their faces for some few minutes.

"Hank ain't often done a thing like that before," Peter whispered to Joe a little later. "He's just the queerest bird I ever met, and don't never show no feeling; but he's took to you, jest as a duck takes to water. He's got grit has Hank. I've knowed him foller a chap as had robbed a widow woman, follow him for two weeks on end, and take him almost aboard the ship he had booked by. That meant determination, or grit if you like to call it so. But here's the men with the guns, and guess Mike's getting restless. Now jest take the word of one who's been out here a while and has met bad men. Ef you sight Hurley, don't stand hankey-pankey. Back in England you'd call to him and then give chase ef he didn't round up. Out here you kin call to him; but ef his hands don't go sky high above his head, and that in a jiffy, give him lead—lead, boy, or else he'll be putting daylight through your own valuable carcass. This ain't a game we're after; we're following a man that's murdered a woman, his own wife, and who's got nothing but the hangman's rope before him. He won't be over particular what happens to those who pursue him. Now, Mike, what's to do?"

"Fall in and arrange the order," cried that latter, swinging his leg across his horse. "First, Tom there, stamp out the embers of the fire. Things haven't got dried up yet awhile, for the weather hasn't been overhot. But it's always as well to be careful; a forest fire is something wuss than chasin' a murderer. Now, Fox and Bill go ahead. Ah, they're there already—that shows that they've had practice. Then I'll follow them close. Jack Bailey and George can ride along side by side. Jim and Tom can come along next, while I guess that Peter and Hank had best ride right in rear, taking Joe with 'em. It'll teach him a heap, ef only he keeps his eyes and his ears open. Boys, there's grub and stuff to bring along, so divide it up and drop it into your saddle bags."

Some little while before, Hank's men had put in an appearance, bringing stout saddles with them, all of which were fitted with two canvas bags. There were rifles also for each one of the party, as well as revolvers and the necessary ammunition. The provisions consisted of tinned goods, as well as the stuff which the thoughtful Jack Bailey had brought with him. It took but a little while to share out all the things, and very soon the cavalcade was mounted. Then, having seen Hank's men ride off with the rigs trailing behind them, the party set its face to the north and rode off in wake of the murderer. And a very formidable and business-like little band they appeared. We have already described the Indians known as Fox and Bill. They sat their horses bareback, as if they were part and parcel of their mounts, while not once had either addressed the other or one of the white men they were to lead, save in the case of Mike, when all that passed seemed to be a succession of incomprehensible grunts. For the rest, Mike himself made a fine figure of a horseman, and sat head and shoulders above everyone, for his horse was big like himself. Jack and George followed some ten paces behind him, boyish eagerness on their faces. Then came Jim and Tom, none the less eager, while in rear of all the lanky Peter bestrode his horse with legs swinging loosely on either side, while Hank sat his saddle for all the world as if he were a statue. The man was taciturnity itself. He was almost as reserved and silent as the Indians, and for watchfulness, there never was such a man.

"Guess them two Injuns has made a mistake," cried Peter, after a while, pointing away from the track they were following. "There's marks of hosses to one side. Hurley stopped jest here."

"And rested," agreed Hank, with brevity. "They ain't missed that. No Injun could. They've seed that Hurley rested there some while, and then went on agin. They didn't need to go and look; they kind of knew it."

"How?" asked Joe curiously, himself puzzled to see how the Indians could have divined such a matter.

"Simple," came the response. "We've been going this hour and more. Wall, reckon it war evening when Hurley abandoned the rig and pushed on. He travelled an hour, when it fell dark. He jest camped for the evening. That thar place was his fust stopping point. It ain't of no importance except to tell us that he's got so much start of us this morning, besides what he made by getting off before we broke camp. Young chap, this here's a sorter stern chase. Time's everything in it. Hurley's got, say, three hours' start, and the country ahead is wooded. Wall, we've got to make up that three hours afore we can come up with him, and stopping jest to see what sort of a bed he made last night ain't a-going to help us. See?"

Joe did; he smiled at Hank. "Never even crossed my brain," he said. "Somehow, when one tackles a job like this for the first time, one doesn't see things as does a practised hand."

"In course you don't," agreed Hank, winking back at him. "It's jest like the farming; some chaps think they know everything, but they don't. Most folks is bamboozled right from the beginning. They has to learn; and tracking wants learning jest like farming. Now, jest you see here; how should I know as Hurley warn't more'n three hours ahead?"

It was a conundrum. Joe puzzled and puzzled, and then gave up the riddle.

"Don't know," he said, disappointment in his voice. "How?"

"In course you don't know. How could you, youngster? But I'll larn yer. This here's a wooded country, as you've agreed. Wall, now, most all the time we're steering in and out amongst the pines, and every now and agin you or me has to separate because there ain't room. Hurley's got two hosses—don't ferget that— and he can't so easily separate, 'cos he'd lose a hold of the led hoss. So he has to ride round the narrow places or squeeze through. He squeezes through at times, and what happens? Jest this."

Suddenly Hank drew in his mount at just such a spot as he was mentioning, where the trees were grouped in a thick cluster, and the track led between two of them, both on the high road to become giants. Hank leaned from his saddle and pointed to a spot on one of the trees about the height of his stirrup iron.

"Hurley barged through that 'ere place," he said, "and, so as his leg shouldn't get jammed, he pushed his foot out and rid the hosses as much to the other side as he could. Wall, his thick, hob-nailed toe came agin this tree and chipped the bark. I've seen a dozen similar places."

Joe regarded the spot closely. It was evident, now that the fact was pointed out to him, that Hurley's toe had been responsible for the injury.

"Wall?" demanded Hank. "See?"

"The place he's left? Yes," assented Joe; "but——"

"Jest so—wants larnin'," asserted Hank dryly. "Now, see here. This aer a deepish cut, and a jagged one. It's bleeding; there's gum oozing from the place, and it aer fresh and sticky. That shows as the wound was done not so long ago. Ef it was last night, then the gum would have balled down below, while the surface of the wound would hardly be sticky, but gettin' dry. Now, how do I know as Mike or his Injuns ain't done it passing along?"

"Because the gum has balled to a certain extent already, while I see it oozes very slowly from the wound."

"Good fer you," cried Hank, evidently pleased with his pupil. "That's a fust lesson. That there gum ha' balled jest a little, as you've said, and there's some of it still oozing. Wall, now, it stands to reason that a man don't go riding around in a wood like this when it's dark, fer he'd get knocking his ugly head agin the branches. So he either lies down and sleeps, or dismounts and leads the hoss. This war done by a mounted man, and sense it ain't been light more'n three hours, and Hurley couldn't ride during the dark, why, there's my question answered. Even ef we hadn't seen the place where he camped, this here wound in the pine would ha' told us all the story. Jest you put that in yer mouth and chew it."

Joe did with a vengeance. The two rode on side by side for three hours, hardly exchanging another syllable; but all the while our hero was observing. If he had imagined previously that he was a fairly lively individual, quite wideawake and aware of his surroundings, he was beginning to discover, particularly in the company of this sharp little Hank, that he was by no means a marvel.

"See whar Hurley stopped fer a bite?" asked Hank one time, as they pressed along across a more open part of the forest. "You didn't? Wall, jest ride back a pace and take another squint. It aer fairly talking to yer."

They returned some twenty paces, and Joe looked about him eagerly. But not a sign did he see to convince him that Hurley had pulled up and eaten. Hank grinned, one of those irritating and superior grins. His dried-up face became seamed with subdued merriment, while Joe went the colour of a geranium; and then, when in the depths of despair, he of a sudden made a discovery. "Ah!" he gasped.

"Jest so," said Hank encouragingly.

"He hitched his reins over a branch, and the horse jerked his head and pulled the limb off the tree. There it is. There's the place where it broke, and, by jingo! there's gum below, slightly balled already. Besides, there's a piece of paper a little to the side. Probably it contained the food he was eating, while underfoot there are horses' hoofs in all sorts of positions."

Hank grinned the grin of a man who is elated. "That 'ere Mike'll have to look to hisself, and so will the Injuns," he said. "Soon we'll have you leading this here party. But you have got the hang of the thing now, lad. Never get tired of looking about you. There's tales to be read in most every spot. P'raps it's a bear that's passed. Then you'd see a footmark same almost as ef it was a barefooted human. Or you may drop on the splayed-out markings of a moose. That's the thing to fire the blood of a hunter. Maybe there's not a sign, but only trees and rocks and stones that seems to tell nothing; but there's always something to be learned. A wolf has had his quarters here, fer there's a hollow, and there's bones in heaps all round. Or there's been a prospecting party through the place, fer there's stumps that has been cut with an axe, and not broke off rough as ef the wind had done it. Tracking aer a game that don't tire, never! It's a thing that a man aer best at ef he's been born to it; but it can be learned, same as farming. You ain't too old to start, not by a long way."

Not till the sun was directly overhead did the little band come to a halt, and then only to allow them to eat a little, while girths were loosened to give the horses every chance of resting.

"Steady and sure does it," said Mike, as he smoked his pipe and leaned against one of the trees. "Of course, we've got to push the pace whenever we're able, and I reckon we've been doing that all along. Anyway, we've made up some of the distance, for single horsemen can get along through these trees quicker than a chap who's got one to lead. It's when he gets to open country that he'll make the most of the hosses; for he'll be able to change over, and that means a heap, don't it, Hank?"

"A heap," answered that individual jerkily. "But he has to sleep, Mike. That's where we'll have him."

"Eh? How's that? I ain't followed."

"Jest like this. He's fresh now we'll 'low, and ef he's able he'll push on all through the night. To-morrow he'll still be going; but when night falls he'll be wanting a rest, and so, you may say, shall we be. Now, ef half this outfit pushes on, Hurley has to move ahead, and it'll be slow travelling. Our chaps'll go afoot, so as to rest the hosses. At dawn the rest of us rides along the trace after 'em, and can cover the ground mighty quick in comparison, seeing that it's daylight. Wall, we leave half the hosses with the fust party, who're resting, and push ahead. Our chums gets a four-hour sleep and comes along after. Both of us is fresh that night, while Hurley can't hardly keep his eyes open. It aer as clear as daylight."

The little man shut up like an oyster. He drew a pipe as diminutive as himself from an inner pocket, crammed it with tobacco while his eyes rested dreamily on the forest, and then struck flint and steel with such unerring skill that he soon had the weed smouldering.

"It aer as clear as daylight," he puffed at the company. "Ef things goes in the ordinary way, Hurley'll be taken just when I've hinted, and he'll be in jail come the week-end."

"And supposin' they don't go along in the ordinary course?" asked Mike, who, from his experience, thought highly of the taciturn Hank. "It ain't of much use to set out follerin' a criminal and expecting him to do jest as you want him to. You've got to make allowance fer all sorts of strange turns. He's making north; he might fall in with some wandering Indians, or a prospecting gang, and get off along with them because of their help."

"Yep!" answered the usually silent Hank, with accustomed brevity. "Guess he might. Even so, we ain't done with him. This outfit's out to catch a ruffian who wants catching badly."

"You bet!" agreed Peter, with a quick shake of his head.

"A brute who's been and murdered his wife," cried Jim, his face flushing.

"The sort of bully whose capture we must make our duty," declared Jack Bailey, not the least enthusiastic of the party.

"Yep!" responded Hank. "So it comes to this, Mike. Supposin' he does do something we can't yet guess at, why, where's the odds? We still goes on after him. And sooner or later, barrin' regular bad luck, we'll have him. That's what I'm out fer. Guess it's the same with you and the other partners."

All that afternoon they pushed on through the forest, sometimes pressing their way through closely-grown pine trees, and then through thick masses of maple, of spruce, of birch, or of the scarlet sumac. At times streams cut across their path—for Canada is a well-watered country for the most part—and more than once had to skirt the edge of great lakes. But always Fox and Bill went ahead without hesitation. Not once had they met with a break in the trail. Their ferrety eyes hardly seemed ever to look to the ground. It seemed, indeed, as if they followed the trail of the murderer by intuition alone. When night came pine stumps were set fire to and the chase continued.

"You kin say as we're making even way with him," said Hank, who still rode with our hero. "He's got to find his way amongst the trees, and he's walking, I guess. Wall, so are we. But we've pine knots to light us, and kin follow the trace easy. It's to-morrow night that'll be the teaser."

The early morning found the devoted little band emerging into a stretch of open country. But there were trees again in the distance, and always the tracks left by the fugitive went due north.

"A child could follow all the way," declared Hank, as they went on at a steady walk, sometimes trotting to change the monotony. "This here's grass country, and no man can ride through it at this season without leaving a trail. I wonder he ain't tried some tricks to throw us off, sich as droppin' into a stream and riding down along the bed; but he ain't, and it begins to look as ef he knew there was someone after him and was feelin' hustled. All the same, he's 'way ahead; you can't get a glimpse of him across the open."

Halting for meals, and to give the horses a rest, the band had reached wooded country again that evening, and about eight o'clock came to a halt.

"Here's where we camp," said Mike. "Now we'll divide up. Some of us has a feed and a smoke, and then goes on ahead on foot; t'others has a sleep along of the hosses, and then rides on at the first streak of dawn. Who's going on?"

It took but a little while to settle this point, and since it was agreed to by all that young fellows like Joe and Tom needed sleep more than did older men, and, moreover, had harder work to do without it, these two remained in the camp, Hank and Peter staying with them. Fox and Bill, with a curt grunt, assented to the fact that they should proceed at once. Mike, of course, was one of the forward party, while George and Jack Bailey and Jim completed its numbers.

"Reckon you ain't got no great need to hurry," said Hank, when the meal was finished and pipes had been lighted, while a tin pannikin was being passed round with an allowance of whisky for all who cared for it. "Guess Hurley'll think we won't be out to-night, and he'll take things easy. In course he might camp too, when you might drop nicely upon him. Jest hold yerselves in, for it's little sleep you'll get till we have him."

About an hour later the little band selected to move on in advance left the camp in Indian file, Fox leading, with Bill immediately behind him. They left their horses with their comrades, so as to give them a good rest.

"Yer see," explained Hank, "hosses is queer cusses. They kin stand a deal of gruelling work ef they're fed right, and most of these here is corn fed. But you can't drive 'em too hard. There's no other animal that breaks his heart sooner, and that's a fact. They're that game, they'll keep on till they're ready to drop. Therefore, you've got to save 'em, particularly seein' as Hurley has got two to our one, and so kin rest 'em in turn. Now the sooner we get stretched out the better."

There being no need to set a watch, all who were remaining in camp at once wrapped themselves in their blankets and threw themselves upon the beds already prepared—consisting of the leafy tips of small spruce trees, than which nothing can make a more comfortable couch—and, needless to say, their eyes closed almost at once, for they were weary after their travels, and they slept till the first streak of dawn awakened Hank.

"Up you gets, one and all," he sang out. "Jest give them hosses a mouthful of water, and then we'll ride. Time we come along with the others we'll feed, and then away agin."

That was Joe's first experience of working on an empty stomach, and truth compels us to add that he found the experience a trying one. He felt hollow and sickly. The sharp morning air made him ravenous; he simply longed for the hour for breakfast.

"Guess you do feel holler," laughed Hank, when our hero told him of his feelings. "I mind the time when I was jest a slip of a lad and felt jest as you do. But I was away huntin' with my father then, for he made a tidy pile of dollars by gettin' skins and selling 'em in Montreal, and sometimes over the border in America. Wall, he were a hot 'un. He never seemed to want to eat, only when he was set down to it—gee!—he could put away double as much as the average man. It was then that I used to get that sinking sensation. We'd be out at daylight winter mornings, with the thermometer 'way down below zero, and the air that crisp it made you jest long for a bite. And I've been two days and more without a trace of food. That's mighty hard, you'll believe me. Howsomever, you stick it out this time. You'll soon get used to waitin'."

However, when three hours had passed, during which the party had made very rapid progress through a country thinly covered with trees, the famishing feeling with which Joe had been assailed had worn off to a considerable degree.

"Feel as though I could go along comfortably all day without food," he told Hank. "I'm not nearly so hungry."

"You jest wait till you smell a steak cookin'," came the laughing rejoinder. "Gee! Won't yer mouth water jest! But we're mighty near them folks now. Seems to me as ef I could smell a fire burnin'."

A mile farther along they came upon their comrades camped in a little clearing. Mike at once came towards them.

"He was camped sure enough last night," he said; "but Hurley's a smart 'un. He heard us comin', and streaked straight off; but he ain't far. We've picked up a heap of lost way, and to-night we'll nab him. You ain't fed?"

"None," answered Hank, dropping from his horse. "These here lads is fairly shoutin' fer food."

They made a cheerful party round the fire, and Joe sniffed expectantly as George skewered some steaks and set them to frizzle over the blaze. And oh, the enchantment of that open-air meal and this camping life! Joe revelled in it. Never had he tasted such juicy and succulent meat. Never before had steaming tea seemed so very entrancing. And think of the future! The excitement of this chase had grown upon him. In a measure he was sorry for Hurley; but then he was a brutal murderer, and such people must not expect anything but strict justice.

"We'll have him come to-night," said Mike, with assurance, as he led the way to the horses. "You folks had better see to yer guns. There's never no saying when this Hurley won't stand to his ground and put up a fight. Ef he does, wall, things will be flyin'. He ain't likely to be so careless as to miss a chap who stands out clear under his sights, as ef he was askin' fer a bullet."

The announcement sent a flush to Joe's and to Tom's cheeks. They rode forward eagerly, wondering when the silence of the forest might be broken by a rifle report, and whether, supposing that event happened, either one of them would drop out of his saddle.

"Makes a chap tingle all over," Joe admitted to Hank. "But I ain't going to let this Hurley scare the life out of me, not by a long way."

"Good fer you," came the answer. "I ain't afeard of his bullets, only lest he should beat us and give us the goodbye. That'd be tarnation bad fortune."

The result of this long chase was, in fact, still very much in the balance, and it remained to be seen whether Joe and his friends would yet lay their hands on the murderer, and if so, whether our hero would be fortunate enough to recover his dollars and that vastly important letter.

CHAPTER IX

Lost in the Forest

"Them 'ere Injuns has stopped, and the hull crowd of us is collecting together," suddenly exclaimed Hank Mitchell, when the party of pursuers had marched steadily throughout the day till evening was approaching, and were in the depths of a forest which, for three hours past, had been getting denser and denser. "I've seed myself signs that told as Hurley wasn't so far ahead, and I'd reckon that Fox and his friend have seen something more than warns 'em that things may be warmin' up in a little. There's Mike beckoning."

It was not an easy matter to see far in this thick forest, even when the light was at its best, which was not the case now that evening was approaching. But it happened that Mike and the Indian trackers had come to rest at a spot which gave the others a clear view of them, so that as those marching in the rear came up, they were able to see the comrades who preceded them gathering into a circle. Mike addressed Peter and Hank immediately on their arrival, speaking in subdued tones.

"He ain't got much go left in him," he said excitedly. "Fox reckons as he went right off to sleep in his saddle hereabouts, and happenin' to ride under a low branch, got swept off his horse. See here."

He had halted his friends a little to one side of the track followed by Hurley, a track easily to be distinguished; for the two horses the murderer had stolen trod down undergrowth at every step, leaving a trail which even Joe, with all his inexperience, could have followed. Some yards ahead it was evident that something unusual had happened, for the undergrowth was trodden down in a wide circle. Hank, his head down, his eyes glued to the trace, sniffing as if he were a dog, at once shot from the circle and, taking pains to tread outside the trail, inspected every part of it.

"Huh!" he grunted, with satisfaction which was evident. "Hurley ain't the man that can put up with much loss of sleep. Besides, he's been bustling these many hours, and that makes a man tired. You kin see what happened. Of course, Fox and Bill were bound to notice it. Reckon he carries a gun slung over his shoulder, and that was the cause of his tumble."

Joe looked the question he would have dearly loved to ask, and Hank, happening to catch his eye at that moment, beckoned to the lad.

"You come along over here and keep right clear of the trace," he said. "Now, I know what you were about to ask. How'd I know as he had a gun slung over his shoulder? Wall, here's the answer." He pointed to a low bough which stretched right across the trail, and at once Joe's eyes searched it. There was a small gash on the side from which Hurley must have approached the branch, and the gash extended underneath for some little distance, perhaps for a matter of three inches, while right at the end a piece of bark had been torn out.

"Plain, ain't it?" said Hank. "You could draw his picture, ef you had a pencil and paper and was a hand at sich things. Just tell us how it was."

"Fast asleep and bending forward," ventured Joe.

"Jest so. Bendin' forward, 'cos that's the way with a man that has dropped off in his saddle. Wall?"

"Gun slung over his shoulder—right shoulder, I should say."

"Why?" snapped Hank. "No guessin', now."

"Because the gash on this side of the branch slants in that direction, looking at it from below."

"Good fer you. Get ahead!"

"I shouldn't have guessed that the gash was caused by a rifle, though," admitted Joe, with candour. "You told me that part of it. However, I think the gun was over his right shoulder; the muzzle caught the branch and swept Hurley backward till he toppled out of his saddle. I suppose he awoke with a start and made a frantic effort to keep his seat. That's when the muzzle—perhaps the sight of the rifle—dug deeper into the bark and ripped a piece away."

"You aer gettin' along fine," said Hank encouragingly. "What next?"

"There's where he fell," said Joe, pointing to the trace. "His fall startled both horses; one went to the right and the other to the left. They were roped together in all probability, or they would have gone farther apart. Hurley picked himself up, scrambled on one of their backs, and went ahead."

"Cussin' at bein' so shook up," grunted Hank. "That's a fine tale, and you've told it well, young chap. But next time you must be the fust to spot things like this without gettin' hints from anyone. Mike," he called softly, "what'll you do?"

"That's jest what I'm wonderin'," came the answer. "How'd you fix it?"

The shrewd and sharp little Hank had no doubts on the matter; in fact, it was clear that he had come to a decision promptly, the moment he had seen what had happened. "There ain't two ways for it," he said crisply. "Hurley's 'way ahead, and not so far, neither. Most like, ef he feels as we're close on his heels, he'll choose a likely spot and turn. Now we don't want to let him feel anything of the sort, and so it's up to us to creep on without a sound. Ef I war boss here I'd send three or four of the party 'way ahead, t'others to follow, and be ready to dash along up ef there was a call. But four ought to be enough to collar Hurley ef he was without a rifle, while the same number kin easy round him up and hold him till t'others arrive."

"Then that's jest what I was thinking," cried Mike, looking across at Peter.

"Same here," nodded that individual. "Hank aer the boy fer jobs of this sort. He's had experience, while chaps same as I am can't hope to know much about tracking, when the best part of our time's spent on our sections. Ef he says go ahead like that, why, in course it's up to us to do it."

"Then we'll send Fox along," said Mike. "I'll go ahead too, and Hank with me. Who else?"

"Why not Joe?" asked Hank suddenly. "He's cute, he is, and he ain't likely to get scared. You could shoot, lad, ef this Hurley turned and fired in amongst us?"

"I would certainly," admitted Joe. "Of course, I don't want to have to, for I should hate to kill or injure a man; but then he's a murderer."

"He's that," agreed Mike, with energy, "and he don't deserve soft treatment. Still, ef he'll come in quiet, he shall be treated fair; ef he don't, why, then, it's his own lookout. Best go afoot; eh, Hank?"

"Sure! We can move jest as fast, and we shan't make anything like the sound. You get ahead with Fox, Mike; I'll take Joe and larn him a little as we go."

At once they handed over their horses to their comrades, Joe passing his to Peter.

"You're in real luck, you are, lad," whispered the latter, as he took the bridle. "I ain't never seen Hank take so much trouble with anyone, least of all a green 'un lately out from the Old Country. He aer fair took to you, and Hank aer one of them queer cusses that when he's fixed a thing in his own mind he don't never alter. So you've a friend there as you kin count on."

Slinging a bag across their shoulders, and packing a tin mug and some provisions, the quartet took up their rifles, saw that they had sufficient ammunition, and then strode off through the deepening gloom of the forest, the silent and ever-watchful Fox in advance, with Mike close behind him; at a little distance in the rear came Hank, with Joe beside him.

"Jest you watch this," whispered the little man. "That there Fox don't make a sound as he goes, nor Mike neither, and he's a big man. Wall, see how they tread: always with caution; always lookin' first to see what's underfoot. And ef they can't see, as'll be the case afore long, why, then, they bends down and feels. You've got to be wary all the while, I tell you. Supposing as you go you swung the butt of your gun agin one of these tree trunks, wall, a man as was listening could hear the sound half a mile away, for a forest carries sound; then, supposin' you was to step on a piece of fallen branch, fallen perhaps last year and dry as tinder now, why, it'd break with a crack that would make you think someone had fired a gun, and that 'ere Hurley would hear it whether he was listening special or not. So go carefully, whatever you do; silence aer important."

Joe found the task he had undertaken one of the most fascinating he had ever attempted, for he was aware that the other three who formed the party were experienced men, and unlikely to do anything to cause an alarm. It was with himself that the danger lay, and he determined then and there that he would return Hank's kindness in asking for him to be one of the band by taking every care to avoid noise. Yet it was not by any means an easy matter, for Fox pushed the pace. The lean Indian strode forward with a long, stealthy stride, making not so much as a sound. His head was bent towards his chest, his back bowed, while the inward-pointed toes of either foot seemed to be able to see every twig beneath them, and avoid them as if they were so many tinned tacks, liable to cause a spasm of agony to the one who trod upon them.

The huge and bulky Mike, contrary to one's expectations, followed the Indian with fairy-like footsteps; for the policeman was possessed of a wonderfully springy step, which carried him silently through the forest. Hank's method of progress hardly needs description. The little, lean man, whose features expressed his character so faithfully, strode along in silence, and with such apparent unconcern and carelessness that one would almost have expected him to trip over some rotting stump, or in other way create some sound liable to reach the ears of Hurley. But that was Hank's way. As a matter of fact, the little fellow might be said to be all ears and eyes. He never seemed to step aside, or to alter by the merest inch the length of his paces; and yet contrast his movements with those of our hero. Joe was in a fever; his eyes were glued to the ground, while his legs were flung this way and that; for every second he seemed to see some lurking twig, the smallest pressure upon which would send an alarm ringing through the forest.

Two hours later the light had failed to such an extent that it became difficult to see the underwood, and the whole party was forced to proceed as best they could, an occasional sharp crack showing that one or other had stepped on a branch.

"Seems to me as ef we was coming somewheres near water," said Hank, after a long silence. "Somehow the air feels moister, and I've heard tell as there are big lakes in this direction. What's that 'ere Injun stopped for?"

"Men been here before," exclaimed Mike, who had halted beside the Indian as Hank came up. "Fox has found trees cut down; lumbermen perhaps have been in this direction."

"Seems to me as ef we was nigh clear of the forest too," said Hank. "I've kinder felt water this past half-hour, and ef we pushes on a few yards, seems to me we'll sight it. Ef so, Hurley aer closer than we thought, for he'll have had his way stopped, and will have had to turn. Let's git on."

They proceeded again, but this time with added caution, and within a little while suddenly broke their way out of the forest on to the bank of a lake which seemed to be entirely surrounded by dense tree growth. It was almost too dark to distinguish the size of this lake, though Hank declared that it was very large.

"What's more, we're at the far end of it," he said, with conviction, "and ef I'm right, this Hurley ain't had to go so far out of his course. He'll have cut to the right a little, and then straight north again. I kin see his game too. He aer making for James Bay in the hope that he may hit upon one of the Hudson Bay steamers going north. It aer a long journey, but ef he could win through he'd be safer than anywhere else. See here, he's gone right as I said he would."

They turned along the trail again, this time in the gloaming, their eyes now and again turned to the surface of the lake afar off, where the rays of the setting sun were reflected. Not that they could see the sun itself—that orb was entirely hidden by the trees—but perhaps its light reached the water by way of some huge gap in the foliage at present unseen by the little party.

"A hut, 'way over there!"

It was Mike who brought all to a sudden stop by this information, sending them one and all to their knees, so as to make themselves less visible.

"Not as it aer likely as he could see us any more'n we could see him," said Hank. "Still, it aer always wise to take precautions. Now I guess there is jest one thing fer us to do. We want to strike right off into the forest and skirt round till we're closer to that 'ere hut. Of course, Hurley mayn't have stopped there; but then he may. Ef so, like as not he'll be watchin' the trace he's left, and ef we continued to follow it, he'd see us in half a jiffy."

"Then let's get moving," cried Mike impatiently. "I'm for taking Hurley the very first moment we can. But we shall have to rush him; he's not the sort of fellow to give in without a struggle, and he'll kick hard, you may say for certain."

"He's bound to put lead into someone or sommat," agreed Hank dryly. "We've got to get him cornered, and then attract his attention in one direction while some of us rushes him from the other. Now, boys."

"This way." Mike led the way beside the Indian, and once more the little quartet dived into the forest, where giants towered on either hand. Not that your wooded country in New Ontario can show such enormous trees as are to be found much farther west, on the far side of the Rocky Mountains, in British Columbia, to wit. For there a favourable climate and a wonderfully fertile soil has caused monsters to rear their heads to enormous heights, while the girth of some is stupendous. But New Ontario can show some arboreal development that is not to be despised, while in parts timber groups itself into great forests, some of which have perhaps never yet seen a white man, though the majority have by now witnessed the arrival of prospectors, and may even have echoed to the ring of the lumberman's axe.

Threading their way amongst the trees, and now and again having to clamber over some fallen giant—for here, on the edge of the lake, the trees were more exposed to winter winds, and some had suffered in consequence—Joe and his friends gradually worked their way along till opposite the part where the southern bank of the lake turned abruptly north. Following this new direction, and creeping with the utmost care through the undergrowth, it was some little while before they were within sight of the hut which they had viewed from their first position. It stood down by the water, thickly surrounded by undergrowth, though the trees which had at one time no doubt reared their heads there had been felled. It was just a small shack built of logs and roofed with strips of bark.

"Nigh falling to pieces too," whispered Hank, who had wonderful eyesight. "Guess a lumber gang was 'way up here some little time back, and that's where they worked and lived during the winter. The question now aer this. Where's Hurley? Ef he's hidin' there we have him. Ef he ain't, why, lookin' at the hut don't help us any, and merely lets him get farther off."

"We'll send Fox forward, then," answered Mike, his mouth close to Hank's head, "unless you think that you——"

"No, I don't say as I couldn't get there and back without even a Redskin hearin' or seein' me," said Hank; "but then I might fail. And it's jest sense ef you've got an Injun to make use of him. The critters is that cunning, they'd nigh creep into a house and be sittin' down beside you before a man was aware that they was there. They're the silentest and the most cunnin' fellers as ever I did set eyes on. Ef it wasn't that Hurley might be over yonder, I'd tell yer a yarn of how a Redskin crawled into my camp one night and as near killed me as possible. But send him off, while we lie down close."

Sinking their bodies in the undergrowth, they lay still for some twenty minutes, during which Fox was away from the spot. He went off towards the hut with merely a low grunt to show that he knew what was expected of him, and though Joe did his utmost to follow the man's track, there was never a sound, never a waving bramble to show where Fox had gone. Then, quite suddenly and unexpectedly, our hero discovered the Indian crawling in behind him.

"Shucks!" grinned Hank, watching Joe. "I was wonderin' when you'd get wind of him. That 'ere chap could ha' knifed or tomahawked you easy. How did I know that he was comin'? That's what you're trying to ask. Jest this way—you heard a frog croaking a while back?"

Joe had; he had wondered where the beast was, and had listened to the call three or four times repeated. He nodded in Hank's direction.

"Wall, that war this here Injun cuss. It was jest his signal to let us know as he was comin', so that we shouldn't get blazing into the bush and shooting him. Seen anything?" he asked, swinging round on the Indian, who, now that his task was accomplished, was seated nonchalantly behind Mike, not venturing to give his news till he was interrogated.

"Seen the man," came the curt answer. "Tracks lead right to the shack. Hurley lying down asleep, I think. Horses hidden in the forest to the left."

"Ah! Then this chase is drawin' to a close," said Mike, satisfaction in his tones. "Hurley's there, fast asleep, perhaps. Seems as ef he must have made up his mind that we'd stopped for the night. Guess we can walk right in and take him—eh, Hank?"

"Shouldn't, ef I was you; Hurley aer as cute as a hull bag o' monkeys. True, he aer dead sleepy, onless he managed to get some sleep on his hoss, which ain't altogether onlikely. Only he got knocked out of the saddle, as you might easily expect. Supposin' he ain't asleep, but aer lyin' hid there, you ain't going to take him so easy. Seems to me the fust thing's to make sure of the hosses; then you kin creep in, and ef you still ain't certain whether he's awake or asleep, why, one of us kin kick up a rumpus close handy. That'll bring him out, when t'others can jump on his back and take him."

"Then Fox will see to the horses," declared Mike promptly. "We three will creep up close to the house. As soon as Fox sends us his signal we'll get closer, and if there's no sign of our man, we'll send Joe out to draw him. Savvy, lad?"

"Quite," said Joe. "I'll strike a blow with the butt of my rifle on one of the trees and then sit down close to the trunk."

"And keep out o' sight," advised Hank. "That ere the hull ticket, Mike. There ain't no use waitin'. Jest now there's a little light; in half an hour a fellow will want a pine knot flaring before his face ef he wishes to know where he's going."

Once more the little party was set in motion, Fox detaching himself from the others. As for Joe, he crawled after Hank, every muscle of his body vibrating. Every now and again his eyes went to the hut, now easily distinguishable; for though it was dark within the forest, there was still some light over the lake, while the hut itself stood silhouetted against the fast-failing rays of the setting sun as they fell aslant the water. Perhaps it took the trio ten minutes to reach the shack. Perhaps the minutes were even shorter, though to our hero the time seemed terribly long. His patience, indeed, was badly strained before he had taken up what was to be his position. As for Hank and Mike, they were lying down within ten feet of the shack, on that side away from the door opposite which was Joe. It now only remained for Fox to send his signal. As for Hurley, there was no sign of him. He might have been a hundred miles away. Suddenly there came a loud neigh from the depths of the forest, followed by another, and then a whinnying which told of the presence of horses. Joe heard the beasts stamping as if they were frightened, or as if the arrival of the Redskin had caused them pleasure. In any case, the noise came to the hut distinctly. A second later Joe imagined he heard a sound from within. It was followed by the sudden appearance of a figure, bent almost double, and rushing out into the open, as if some force were behind him and propelling him. Indeed, long before our hero could lift his weapon or could shout, Hurley—for he it undoubtedly was—had bounded across the narrow open space about the shack and had dived into the forest.

"After him!" bellowed Mike at the top of his voice, as he plunged through the bushes. As for Hank, no sound left his lips. The little man trailed his rifle and went off after Hurley with his head down and his ears pricked, and eager to catch every sound. Need the reader feel surprised that Joe followed suit. Recovering from the utter astonishment into which the sudden manoeuvre had thrown him, he gripped his own weapon and darted after his comrades. He could hear them directly to the front, and dashed headlong after them. Then his already-wounded head came into somewhat violent contact with a branch, and Joe sat down rapidly. But he pulled himself together after a while, and, with his brain dizzy and buzzing, thrust his way onward through the dense growth of trees and underwood. How long he continued the effort he never knew. Suffice it to say that he made a desperate endeavour to keep up with and gain upon his fellows. Then, of a sudden, he discovered that there was not one single sound to direct him. A minute before he had imagined he heard the crash of men dashing through the forest; now there was a deathly silence all about him. He stood still, panting, endeavouring to silence his own breathing and to still the thud of his throbbing heart. No, not a sound but what was made by himself. He shouted—

not an answer; not a shout in return. He called loudly on Hank and Mike to tell him of their direction. Then, as the minutes passed and silence still surrounded him, he pushed valiantly on amongst the trees, hoping every half-minute that there would be a signal. Whether he went directly forward or retraced his steps, or faced the east, the west, the south, or the north, Joe was entirely ignorant. He was lost, in fact. The knowledge after a while drove him frantic, so that he plunged aimlessly to and fro; then, fortunately for him, perhaps, a second collision with a tree knocked him senseless. For the moment his troubles were forgotten, though his plight was still the same; and the plight of a man lost in the backwoods of Canada is often enough desperate. Indeed, many a poor fellow has gone, never to be found again, swallowed by the trees which, as the years roll on, are felled to form the log huts of the settlers crowding into the Dominion.

CHAPTER X

A Hand-to-hand Encounter

While Joe lies senseless in the depths of the forest, lost entirely to his friends, and in as desperate a condition as he well could be, it will be as well to follow the footsteps of Mike and Hank as they dashed away in pursuit of Hurley. Both were well accustomed to the muskegs and the timbered lands of Canada, and, if only the truth were known, had before now been engaged in a similar expedition. But following a murderer during the daytime through such a place, and at a sedate pace, was entirely different from the same attempt at night, and all the while at such speed that precautions could not be taken.

"Ef that ain't the third time I've barged into a tree trunk and near had all the breath knocked out of my body," growled Mike, when he had progressed a mile, and was still well behind Hank. "Seems to me that we should ha' done better to sit down and wait till morning, or lit pine knots and then followed. Hank may do it; I shan't. This forest fairly beats me."

But Mike was a man possessed of wonderful perseverance and tenacity, and, in spite of the numerous occasions on which he blundered into trees, he held to the chase till he also, like Joe, lost his comrade. He stood listening for a sound to tell him where Hank was striding between the trees, then, hearing nothing after quite a long wait, the wary and experienced Mike sat down in the most comfortable attitude he could assume, dragged his ever-faithful pipe from his pocket, and, having filled and lit the weed, puffed away philosophically.

"Hurley ain't got nothing to fear from me, that's certain," he told himself, not without some amount of disappointment and bitterness. "But Hank is the boy to keep him running. The little chap is that hard, he could keep at it all night and right into to-morrow, and he'll stick to his man unless something clean throws him off the scent. For me, reckon I'm trapped here. I'll have a smoke and then a sleep. Early in the morning I'll consider things, and then push on or make back to the hut, as seems best."

Meanwhile Hank slid through the forest as only a practised hunter could have done. It was on this night expedition that he proved his worth, as also the value of an early training. For while Mike dashed so often against a tree, and we know that Joe had done so to his own injury, Hank seemed intuitively to know when a low-hung branch stretched across the path he was following. More than that, somehow he contrived to keep directly on the trail which Hurley was making.

"I'm getting closer," he told himself, when a whole hour had passed. "Any time now Hurley'll turn, and then, ef he don't climb down and cry out that he's beaten, I'll have to put lead into his carcass. That's him 'way ahead, making as much noise as a bull would ef he was gallopin' through the forest."

Loud bangs and crashes indeed told of Hurley's presence, for the trees carried every sound, and accentuated most. It may be imagined, therefore, that the sudden cessation of all noise astonished Hank considerably.

"Eh?" he asked himself, coming to a halt and standing perfectly still so as to listen the better. Not that Hank's breath was coming fast, as in the case of our hero; no, he was not even panting. His heart beats were scarcely increased in number in spite of his exertions, which only went to prove that constant training, correct diet, a good digestion, and a happy and contented mind are advantages possessed by men such as Hank who live their lives in the open.

"Not so much as a sound," he told himself. "Now, what has happened? Seems to me likely that Hurley aer turned and ha' got his gun ready fer shootin'. Wall, an old bird same as me don't get frightened jest because lead may be flyin'. It wants a clever or a lucky man to make a hit in the darkness, specially when there's tree trunks all round to give a fellow cover. I'm going to move forward."

He drew back the hammer of his gun, for Hank was a conservative little fellow. "None of yer new-fangled guns fer me," he had said more than once. "Mind you, I 'low as the new 'uns is fine, and has many advantages. A chap can load and fire twenty times perhaps while I am fiddling with this trigger. 'Sides, I've one myself, and know 'em well. But ef there ain't likely to be quick firin', give me this old thing."

Gripping the weapon in one hand, he bent double and went on stealthily, and in five minutes he had gained some fifty paces. But of Hurley there was no sign. The murderer gave no signal which told of his whereabouts, and though Hank stole on farther, still there was nothing to indicate where Hurley had got to.

"Fair beats the band," growled Hank, beginning to doubt his own powers of trackin'. "I'm past the spot where I last heard him, and I'm dead sure he ain't been within ten yards. Hurley aer a town man, and I'm game to say as he couldn't have sat so still as I should miss him. This fair puzzles me—oh!"

His keen ear heard something towards the left, then again there was silence, save for the murmur of the breeze playing amongst the leaves overhead. Hank slid in that direction promptly, only again he gave a gasp of astonishment, and finally one of extreme annoyance; for it seemed that he had missed Hurley's new path by but a very little. It is not to be wondered at that he had not always been able to follow the exact steps which the fugitive had taken, for he was tracking now not by signs conveyed to him by leaves and sticks and bushes, but by sound alone—the noise of the murderer as he broke his way through the underwood. When that had ceased, Hank had lost direction slightly. He had turned just a little to the right, whereas to the left, where Hurley had passed, there was a curious clearing. It was a broad glade, in fact the same through which the falling sun had sent its glancing rays to the surface of the lake. Clear of trees, thickly covered with grass, it offered a carpet which deadened all footsteps. No wonder that Hank had heard nothing. It was a fortunate matter, indeed, that some slight sound, perhaps his boot striking a pebble, had shown Hurley's position. Hank bounded into the glade as if he had been shot out of the forest.

"Thunder!" he growled. "Ef that ain't the cutest move of any as he's practised! He's made back towards the lake, that's fer certain. There ain't no use in waitin'."

Once more his gun was trailed, and this time, bent less low than formerly, the little hunter went speeding off in the direction Hurley had taken. Nor did the darkness trouble him, for whereas amongst the trees it had been intensely dark, here in the glade it was comparatively light, and a man with eyes such as Hank possessed could detect every obstruction.

We will leave him in pursuit of Hurley, and, having already shown Mike calmly smoking in his leafy retreat, will once more visit our hero. Joe was in a sad way, and it was, without shadow of doubt, a boon to him that collision with a tree knocked him senseless, for but a few moments before there had come to him that stupid, senseless frenzy which comes to those who are lost. Even the brave man is not proof against that frenzy. Sudden, nameless terror snatches at him; the very silence mocks him, while calmness and reason, virtues of which he may well have been the proud possessor earlier, leave him as if he were a leper. Distraction, desperate and hopelessly unavailing effort follow, and finally there comes exhaustion. The unhappy wretch who is entirely lost may become calm when strength has left him, and die merely from want of food and water; but more often madness is the enemy which finally accounts for his ending.

It was as well, therefore, for Joe that a severe blow on the head drove all sense and knowledge from him. He lay like a log for hours, and if we describe his condition faithfully, we must declare that the blow was not entirely responsible. Joe was fagged out with his long efforts; it happened, therefore, that a deep, refreshing sleep followed upon the unconsciousness produced by collision, and carried him well on into the morning. The shaded rays of a risen sun were streaming in upon his leafy prison when he finally opened his eyes.

"Hallo! Hank!" he called, and, getting no reply, turned to stare about him. "My word, don't my head hurt just! Now, how's that? Why, if—— Where am I?"

His brain was still muddled, though wonderfully refreshed, and for quite a little while he sat thinking, trying to remember exactly what had happened. Then the knowledge of his true position came to him—he was lost in the forest.

"And made a fine ass of myself, to be sure," he cried, remembering his fears of the previous evening.

"Lost my head; got scared at the silence, and then went barging right and left. This is the dickens of a muddle. Here am I, goodness knows where. Anyway, in Canada, I'm dead certain."

That set him laughing—for Joe was a merry fellow—moreover, the warm rays of the sun streaming down upon him, together with the fact that the past few days had accustomed him to his surroundings, cheered him wonderfully. He began to whistle, an old habit, and then recollected that he was hungry.

"I'll be better for some food, that's certain," he told himself. "I can't think properly as yet. But there's one thing I am sure of—I behaved like a child of two last night. I clean lost my head, and am jolly glad there wasn't anyone else here to watch me. My, how Hank would laugh, and Fennick too! Wonder how he and his wife are doing, and Jim and Claude too. Wonder, also, whether Hurley's captured."

Quite accidentally his hand fell into the bag which he had suspended over his shoulder, and it was with a gasp of pleasure that he remembered that provisions were inside. Joe dragged them out, and, just to show his independence, gathered some sticks and lit a fire. Water was what he wanted now, and a search for that commodity told him still more of his own condition of mind on the previous evening; for his way took him along the track he had himself formed, and presently he came to a part which looked very much as if a circus horse had been driven there, and forced to carry out all sorts of evolutions. Tracks led through the underwood to right and left, crossed one another, and joined sometimes so that two or three were side by side. In one he came upon his rifle, a find which caused him pleasure; but where the outlet was, in what direction he had been coming when he reached this spot, Joe could discover not the smallest inkling.

"Anyway, there's water," he said, filling the kettle which he carried slung to his belt, and which had received a sad battering in the forest. "Jolly glad I've got the tea—that'll put life into me—then I'll have to think this matter out; shouldn't wonder if a shot wouldn't bring an answer."

It was a brilliant idea, and cheered him wonderfully. Let us say, too, that Joe needed cheering. In spite of his undoubted courage, and of a naturally cheery disposition, the terror of the intense silence of his huge prison sometimes almost got the better of him. It was with an obvious effort that he beat down the feeling. Retracing his steps to the fire and busying himself with his cooking preparations helped him wonderfully, and when at length he had swallowed a hot cup of tea and had eaten a couple of grilled slices of meat he felt distinctly better.

"I'll try a shot now," he told himself, "then I'll think matters out. I wonder in what direction I came—beats me hollow."

He was in the act of loading, for he had withdrawn the cartridge popped into his gun on the previous evening, when a sound suddenly reached his ears and caused him to sit bolt upright.

"Eh?" he asked himself. "Hank or Mike or Fox perhaps. Hope so."

There it was again, the noise made by a man thrusting a way through the underwood. Joe gathered up his belongings, stamped out the fire, and went off in that direction. Bang! Crash! He heard the noise time and again, and getting nearer. It seemed, indeed, as if someone were coming towards him. Perhaps five minutes later, when, convinced of the fact, he had thrown himself down to wait and watch, the figure of a man came into view, seen somewhat indistinctly between the maze of leaves and branches.

"Mike!" thought Joe. "About his size. No; too small, though it's a big man but less bulky than Mike. Can't be Hank. Then who is it? Hurley!"

The knowledge that the murderer was actually before him sent a rush of blood to Joe's head. His ears throbbed and buzzed, his pulses beat spasmodically, while his heart thundered against his ribs.

"Hurley!"

Joe climbed silently to his feet and raised his rifle. He now could see the man approaching him better, and could no longer have any doubt as to who it was. It was, without a question, the murderer whom he had fought outside the shack in defence of Tom, the very man Hank and his fellows, with Mike, the policeman, had been following now for such a time.

"Hurley! Still escaping! Then Hank failed to get him! Where's his gun?"

Joe peered through the leaves and branches, and presently caught a glimpse of the weapon which it was known the murderer carried. He bore it before him, fending brambles away with it as he went. That gun, no doubt, was loaded, and Hurley still able and willing to slay anyone who dared to intercept him. What was Joe to do? Let him go? Funk the business, or call to him and chance a bullet?

"Nasty thing if he hit me here; nobody would know. I might be badly wounded and help never reach me. Rotten that, very!"

Joe shivered. We are describing his feelings and his actions with the utmost truth and fairness, and truth compels us to say that he shivered. He looked about him doubtfully, seeing nothing but leaves and waving branches and underwood, with the figure of a man he knew to be already a murderer breaking a path through the forest quite near at hand, while a rifle was borne prominently before him. Bear in mind, too, that Joe had had a terrifying experience already, that he still bore a wound given by the bully, while his scalp was sore and his brain still dizzy with the collisions he had experienced on the previous evening.

"He'll miss me by fifteen feet," said Joe, measuring the distance with his eye. "If I like to stay quiet he'll be by in a jiffy, and then—then I'll be safe!"

He could have kicked himself for the thought; the blood flew to his cheeks again and shamed him. He clenched his teeth and bobbed his head higher.

"Frightfully tempting to funk the meeting," he told himself wrathfully; "but I'll not be such a coward.

"Hurley!" he shouted.

The man stopped abruptly, his eyes shooting into sudden prominence.

JOE SURPRISES HURLEY

Page 174

JOE SURPRISES HURLEY

"Hands up!" bellowed Joe, keeping well hidden. "Hands up or——"

There was a loud report which reverberated through the wood, while a rattle overhead told its tale unpleasantly. A shower of severed leaves sprayed on to Joe's head, while he listened to a curious click with which soldiers are familiar.

"Loading again—might get me next time. Shall I plug him?" he asked himself.

Very cautiously he lifted his rifle, and with it his head, which he had ducked at Hurley's shot. But where was the man? There was no sign of him. He had disappeared entirely.

"Dropped down where he was, and is waiting and watching. Dead certain he isn't moving," said Joe, "or I'd hear him. I'll wait and watch too."

Presently his patience was rewarded. A black sleeve came into view—only a tiny triangle showing—then the muzzle of the weapon. Joe levelled his own on the sleeve and called again loudly.

"Drop that gun, Hurley," he shouted roughly, "or take the consequences!"

The answer came so swiftly that he was astonished, and once again our hero had the unpleasant feeling of a bullet passing within close distance of him. Under the circumstances it required nerve to kneel a little higher, take aim just a foot below the spot where he had seen that sleeve, and press his own trigger. Then, like a dart, he sprang away, and within a moment was located behind a stout birch tree, which gave excellent cover.

"Got him, I think," he gasped. "There was a shout directly I fired. Wonder if I killed him?"

The thought set his ears tingling and a nasty cold feeling down the centre of his back. Joe wasn't bloodthirsty by any means. He hated the very thought of killing a man; but here it was decidedly a case of Hurley or himself. Softness and pity would be thrown away on such a villain; the smallest advantage allowed would certainly end in his own undoing. It was with the utmost caution, then, that our hero peeped out from behind cover, while his fingers were busily employed in thrusting a fresh cartridge into his rifle. Moreover, he listened eagerly for any sound which might tell him that Hurley was moving. Joe had, in fact, an artful and cunning foe to deal with, and quickly found that he was very far from effecting his purpose, also that the murderer was by no means likely to give in without a struggle. For as he peeped from behind the shelter of his tree a figure rose suddenly, a weapon was fired, and at the same instant down went the figure.

"Thunder!" he exclaimed, using an exclamation which Hank was in the habit of employing. "That was a near one; chipped a nice little piece out of the bark of the tree and—yes, perforated the butt of my rifle."

Very cautiously he peered round the tree again, and then, with a sudden feeling of elation, caught sight of a black object slowly rising above the undergrowth. Joe dropped his sights on it and pressed the trigger steadily; but, to his amazement, the black object continued to rise for the space of a few seconds, then it dropped just as suddenly out of view.

"Huh!" he grunted. "A decoy! Lifted his coat on a stick and drew my fire. Two can play at that game."

But even if he were to follow Hurley's example, caution and cunning were still required. Joe dropped on to hands and knees and then spread himself face downwards on the ground. In that position he wormed his way along some three yards to the right, where he again took cover behind a tree, and on this occasion he lifted his head with the greatest care.

"He'll be watching the tree where I was located," he told himself, "and if I wait a little he'll show himself, seeing that I don't put in an appearance. Then will be the time to aim straight, for I am sure that if I don't take the fullest advantage of every opportunity he will shoot me down."

"That 'ere young cub that was the cause of most of my trouble," growled Hurley, as he lay on the ground awaiting developments. "Wall, it might ha' been wuss; I kin knock him out easy ef I'm just ordinarily cautious, then there won't be no one in the way. I'll double the hull way back—that's what I'll do—get along to the railway, and board a freight train. Down by Niagara Falls there won't be no difficulty in hoppin' across the suspension bridge, and afore these fools is much the wiser I'll be hid up in Buffalo."

His keen eye detected Joe's new position, and, watching closely, he soon saw a portion of the latter's clothing projecting from behind the tree. Up went his rifle, and an instant later the clothing fell to the ground. With a shout of triumph, Hurley stood to his feet, only to drop back again like a stone; for Joe was undamaged. He had merely played Hurley's trick upon himself, and now that the opportunity had come to him, he stood out from cover and fired direct at the man. Unfortunately, however, he was too late, his bullet tearing on through the undergrowth.

"The young cuss!" growled Hurley, startled by his narrow escape. "But I'll get even with him yet. Ef he can play a game same as that, see me foller."

He thought it all out as he lay there in the underwood, and then once again selected a suitable portion of a fallen branch. This time it was his wide-brimmed hat which he raised slowly above the leaves and ferns. But though Hurley peered from amidst the tangle of boughs and leaves, he could see no sign of our hero. It was an intense surprise to him when there came a flash and a loud report from the left, from an altogether different position, while his hat twiddled round on the branch he had thrust into it.

"Jingo! He's shootin'!" he told himself, with a growl. "Lucky my head warn't in there. But I ain't done, not by a long way. I'll try the trick agin, and then I fancy I shall have a surprise fer that 'ere Britisher."

Very slowly he proceeded to elevate his hat again, and this time so soon after the last that he guessed that Joe would hardly have had time to change his position. So that it was again a shock to find a bullet swishing rather from the right. However, Hurley was a man with an iron nerve; moreover, he knew what awaited him should he be captured. Straightway leaping to his feet and trusting to Joe not having had time to reload, he dashed into the bush and, seeing our hero, threw himself upon him furiously. Nor did he deign to make use of his own weapon. Dropping it as if it were no longer of use, he gripped Joe with both hands and, swinging him aloft as he had done once before, he prepared to hurl him against a tree. Indeed, he almost carried out that intention; but Joe managed to curl in his legs and so escape.

"You're jest about dead this time," gasped Hurley. "You'd have done far better to have stayed right at home with the kids, which are yer place, than have come out here to take grown men. That'll finish it."

But the second swing he gave didn't finish the matter. Joe was a tougher foe to deal with than Hurley imagined, for, locking his arms round the murderer, he defied his every effort to lift him. But all the while he was conscious of the fact that the man was a great deal stronger than he, and that unless he could deal him a vital blow, his own chances were far from good. It was at this critical moment, when the two were once more struggling fiercely and had rolled to the ground, that a man came darting through the underwood. Dashing up to the combatants, he placed the muzzle of his old gun against the murderer's head and called loudly on him to surrender.

"You may jest as well throw it up, Hurley," he said, with wonderful coolness, "fer I guess you're cornered. 'Sides, ef you're troublesome you're like to get the sort o' dustin' a feller don't take to kindly. So jest turn it up. Joe, get a hold of his rifle. Now, my man, you stand there agin the tree and don't try hanky-panky. I ain't particular whether it's the law that deals with yer or me. Savvy?"

Hurley did; he unloosed his grip of our hero promptly and, now that the tables were turned, stood cowed and subdued in front of Hank, eyeing his old muzzle-loader askance. As for Hank, he grinned at Joe.

"It war a near call, lad," he said. "Strange that it should be you as really cornered him. But keep yer eye on him and yer finger on your trigger. There ain't never no saying when he'll be up to games, though it won't be often he'll play 'em once Mike's up. He could lift this hulkin' feller as ef he war a baby, and my, wouldn't he give him sauce!"

Some twenty minutes later Fox put in an appearance, and after him Mike. Hurley was promptly secured, his hands being bound behind his back, for Mike had lost his handcuffs, while a stout cord was passed from the lashings and secured to Fox's wrist. Then the party wended their way through the forest, and in a wonderfully short space of time came to the hut in which Hurley had taken refuge. Here their comrades joined them in the evening.

"It war a close call," said Peter, when he had heard of Joe's adventure; "but I ain't quite clear as to how it come about that you was out there in the forest all alone. Spin us the yarn."

"I was lost, that's the simple explanation," answered Joe, telling them how he had dashed hither and thither in a frenzy, and how a collision with a tree had in the end sent him senseless to the ground. "And a mighty big bump I've got to show for it," he added ruefully.

"You're jest mighty lucky to have one to show at all, young feller," growled Hank. "I ain't been in these parts without meeting with similar cases. I've known young fellers, and oldish men too, go off into the timber and never come back. I've seed a ghost of one crawl back after a week, and he as mad as a hatter. What's more, I know what the feelin' of bein' lost is. An old hunter same as me don't never feel like that. When I war young it war different. Nowadays I could find my way out anywhere. I'd do as you did, doss down fer the night— so I reckon that blow you got war lucky,—then, when morning came, I'd watch fer the sun, and I'd go ahead always in one direction; but it seems to me as ef supper war ready."

"One moment," said Joe. "How was it you came upon the scene so opportunely, Hank?"

"How? Jest like this, and simple enough. This 'ere Hurley give me the slip, and shot out into a glade. Wall, a bit of a rattle as he passed over a stony patch told me the direction he had taken, and precious soon I had picked up his traces again. Seems he took to the lake, straddling a log he found there and pushing out. But the wind war on this shore and brought him back. Early this mornin' I dropped on his traces and found as he'd turned south. Mike come along with Fox at the same moment, and reckon we set out fer all we war worth. It war then that we heard a shot, and then others. That set me movin', and—wall, that's all."

He closed up like an oyster, and actually blushed when Joe continued. "Not all, Hank," he said earnestly; "you saved my life. I'm grateful."

"Gee! Ef I ain't that hungry!" shouted Hank, springing to his feet hurriedly. "George, ain't you got them steaks frizzled yet?"

"Ready," came the answer, while George held a stick to which the steaks were skewered aloft.

"Then we'll eat," growled Hank, as if he had recently had a quarrel with our hero; "and mind, there ain't no more gassin'."

"He aer fair set on you," whispered Peter, after the meal, taking Joe aside. "He knew you was in trouble, and I tell you he wouldn't rest. All night he war searchin' for your traces, and ef he hadn't bustled, guess he'd have reached you too late. Hank aer the queerest little morsel as ever I set eyes on."

"He's a fine fellow," declared Joe eagerly. "Some day I'll get even with him."

The following morning they mounted again, and in due course reached the settlements, where the party divided.

"Hank's comin' along to stay with us," said Peter. "How's that, young 'un?"

"Ripping!" Joe meant it; he had taken a huge fancy to the little hunter, and hoped, if he were lucky, to learn a great deal more from him.

"You'll do that right enough," laughed Peter, when our hero told him. "Hank aer a troublesome feller. It ain't often that I hear of him that he ain't been in some adventure. Jest you watch to see that he don't drag you in too. I don't altogether trust the little varmint."

"Drat the man!" exclaimed Mrs. Strike. "Joe was a steady worker afore he came here; but now, bless us! he's always wantin' to be off into the wilds and forests."

And go Joe did. He worked all through the summer and autumn, helping Peter to get in his harvest, and learning much about farming; then, leaving Tom, the lad for whom he had fought, as Peter's man in his place, he packed his bag and rode off with Hank on a prospecting expedition.

CHAPTER XI

Investing Hard-earned Dollars

Barely six months had passed since Joe Bradley took passage to Canada and became one of the ever-growing army of immigrants who yearly ascend the mighty St. Lawrence river and are scattered throughout the provinces of the Dominion. The days had flown since his landing, and but for that long chase of Hurley, the murderer, scarcely an event had happened to break through the orderliness of his day's duties. No longer was he a greenhorn, either. His knowledge of farming as it is practised in England may be said to have been still extremely small, but of farming in the Dominion he knew almost enough to manage a quarter section of his own.

"Not that I advise it," said the cautious and knowing Peter. "You're over young yet to face the worries which must come to a landowner, and you could do with more capital. So you take the advice of one who's tried, and go as a labourer a bit longer. Meanwhile, you could put that 'ere money you've saved into something likely to make it grow whilst you're prospecting with Hank."

Joe had, in fact, saved quite a respectable amount, for it must be remembered that his personal expenses were extremely small, while his wages were good. Moreover, the dollar bills which Hurley had stolen from him had been recovered when that individual was captured, though the precious letter left him by his father seemed to have been lost for ever.

"It war a piece of luck, I do declare," said Peter. "Ef he'd gone off along the railway there would have been a different tale to tell. Joe aer fortunate to have come out of that mess with his life, and still more lucky to have got back his dollars. As to the letter, there ain't no saying if it war valuable. P'raps not; least, that's what I'm hoping. And now the thing's to invest his savings so as they'll grow while he's away prospecting. Seems to me, Hank, as ef this here place, as well as the settlement right up agin the railroad, might soon get big. The land's good for working. The crops this year has been first-class, and some of our boys has won prizes for their wheat. There's Jim, fer instance. His was nigh the heaviest yield per acre that there's been recorded, while the grain weighed mighty heavy to the bushel. In course the papers prints and publishes all these things, and people gets to know. There's been strangers hereabouts looking fer sections to take up come the summer. Wall?"

Hank was not the one to give an opinion offhand. He cogitated a great deal, and as a rule his faithful little pipe helped him considerably, or rather it appeared to help him, for it was his invariable custom to fill it on such occasions, set fire to the weed, and sit crouched into a ball, holding the pipe between two of his shapely fingers while he stared into the open. In this case there was no open, for they were seated in Mrs. Strike's parlour, and Hank had perforce to stare into the open stove, which is part and parcel of every settler's dwelling.

"Never did see such a man!" exclaimed Mrs. Strike impatiently. "He's all movement, you tell me, when he's off in the forest; but here, when you want his advice, he jest sits down and blinks, till you feel as ef you could shake him. I ain't got no patience with the man."

Peter grinned widely; he was accustomed to his wife's ways—and Joe also—knowing well that it was all playfulness on her part. As for Hank, the little man whom nothing daunted, as a rule, he pulled heavily at his pipe and looked as if he might take to his heels and run away. He glanced askance at Mrs. Strike, till the good woman smiled at him.

"I'm only teasing you," she explained, with a laugh. "But, dear, dear! you do amuse me. Seems to me as ef I shouted you'd be scared almost out of your life."

That set Hank grinning also—a nervous grin—then he became solemn, for matters which concerned the welfare of Joe needed the utmost attention.

"I'm with you, Peter," he said at last. "Down by the railroad things'll move soon. A few dollars laid out in town plots wouldn't come to harm, while ef we was both to apply for quarter sections right here, we could sell 'em at the break of winter to new settlers anxious not to be too far out. What about Hurley's, by the way?"

"That aer fer sale now," came the answer. "He didn't do much to it, and there don't seem no one wanting it just now, which are natural, seeing that winter's here. Come next spring it'll be asked for."

"Then there's Joe's chance. Ef he ain't got enough dollars, I'll chip in with him. Eh?"

"Ready and willing," agreed Joe. "I like the idea immensely. Hank and I are off into the woods prospecting, and we're not likely to want much cash. Seems to me it's a wise thing to put what I have where it may grow during my absence. I'll apply for a quarter section right here. It's a condition of the Government that all settlers shall fence their sections in a given time, and break so much of the virgin ground. I can't do that now, as we have hard frosts, and things are too cold for working. In the spring, if I like to, I can tackle the job. If not, I can sell; then I'll buy Hurley's if I can, and sell that again also."

Buying and selling is the life and soul of Canada. Land speculators purchase from the Government with the sole idea of selling to those who follow, and see in the land for sale something with greater attractions than that offered free by the authorities. Again, men must fail in such a country, and here and there are always to be found those unfortunate enough to have to offer their sections, on which they may have expended much toil already. Whereas a quarter section of virgin land, extending to one hundred and sixty acres in all, may be of little value when unbroken, broken and fenced it is almost always of considerably enhanced value; for breaking and fencing mean the expenditure of labour, and labour is terribly hard to come by at times in the Dominion.

"We'll go along and see into the matter to-morrow, then," said Peter, when the question had been further discussed. "Jest throw on a log or two, Joe; it's cold enough to freeze one even inside the shack."

Those few days which followed gave our hero some idea, though not a complete one, it must be acknowledged, of the life of settlers in Canada during the long and severe winter which visits the land. There are those who dread the winter. One meets occasionally a man who has returned to England because of the Canadian winter, because of the inertia it brings to great stretches of the country, stopping all outside work, and, on the farms, cutting off neighbours from intercourse with one another. At other times it is the loneliness and silence of the life which send would-be settlers away; but not very often. There are scores and scores who put up with the winter as we in England put up with decidedly dispiriting weather, resting tranquilly and passing the idle hours as best they can, knowing well that a glorious summer will surely follow.

"Not that there's fogs and suchlike," explained Peter, when telling Joe of the life. "Most days its beautifully sunny and bright, though the thermometer may be down below zero. And as to stayin' indoors all the while, that we don't. Most of us has knocked up runners, on which we put the rigs when we've stripped the wheels from 'em. Jim down below thar being a bachelor, with plenty to spend, and being also a good bit of a sportsman, has dogs, and his team drags him from shack to shack, specially round about Christmas. Even the school children get to school on their snowshoes. There ain't no difficulty about that neither, onless the weather's too altogether bad, for the Government build schools fer each settlement. There only wants to be a matter of seven children, and up goes a stone-built school, and a mistress who's properly trained for the job gets a lodging in the nearest shack, or in the school itself, and starts off to teach the youngsters. As to work, wall, I finds heaps. Winter's jest the time for papering the walls of the shack or fer doing a bit of painting. There's furniture wants making, and last winter I and the hand that stayed with us built a new stable. This time I'll whitewash all the outhouses, as well as the fowlhouse."

"And for me there's enough and to spare to keep me from being idle or from grumbling," interjected Mrs. Strike. "There's the house, in the first place, with the beds to make and sichlike. There's food to be cooked fer all, including the chickens, which have hot stuff every day through the winter. And ef I'm dull with looking at Peter there, I've only to go to the telephone and ring up Mrs. George Bailey. A real nice woman that, Joe. She's a help to her husband, she is, and that can't be said of every woman who's come out from England and has lived her life till then in a villa just outside London, with never any greater difficulty to provide for her family than that of stepping along the street to the nearest shop. If they was all like her, there's many settlers would be more successful."

It was clear that Peter and his wife could have kept on discussing this theme for an hour or more; and to those who knew them it was equally certain that these two worthy souls practised exactly as they preached. They had faced the difficulties and the privations often met with in greater number by early settlers, and they had succeeded. Peter was a man who, thanks to hard work and a genial temperament, had made a success of his quarter section, so that the land which had lain bare for centuries before was now entirely tilled, and yielded handsomely to his efforts. In fact, from the position almost of a pauper, the man had advanced to a point where he earned a handsome income that was more than sufficient for his needs, and allowed him to put by many dollars during the course of a year.

"And it ain't finished there," he told Joe and Hank gleefully, when dilating on the subject. "There's the quarter section. It's worth a tidy heap of dollars—more'n a thousand pounds in English money—and that's what I could get any day of the year. But I don't stand still, not never."

"I've had my eyes around, and have gone in as a partner with a brother of mine who came out to Canada at the same time. We worked together for a while, then he went west into British Columbia. Wall, he took up fruit land when irrigation wasn't much more'n dreamed of and, with dollars I put to his, bought two sections close handy. They're gold mines. He's been able to get labour, and seeing that he has a large family of sons and daughters able to work and help, why, it's only needed honest work to tickle the soil and put in the trees to turn over a fine penny; the land does all the rest. It's that fertile it grows astonishing crops of apples, while peaches, strawberries, and sichlike do thundering well. Tom—that's my brother—was mighty wise and lucky too; he took up ground within easy reach of Vancouver, so that he always has a close market for his goods, putting aside the fact that it allowed him to watch things going on, and buy other bits of land when he thought they were likely to go up in value. That's where some of my dollars has gone. Me and the missus will be sellin' up one o' these fine days, and going west where it's warmer."

Joe was bound to admit that the cold did not trouble him. Not that the winter had as yet set in in full severity, though there had been heavy frosts and a fall of snow; but, as Peter had told him, he always found work to do. Even those few days before departing with Hank were strenuous ones. There were logs to saw for the stove, for the huge iron thing which warmed the shack, and which is essential to a Canadian winter, ate timber wholesale. Then there were the cattle to be tended to—for they required feeding, since they could not graze for themselves—there were the pigs also, while always water was wanted inside the shack, and must be drawn from the well which had been one of Peter's labours.

Of an evening, too, while the weather was so open, George and his brother, Jim and other neighbours would drive over, and there would be a jovial supper, followed by a dance, when Mrs. Strike bustled Joe tremendously, till the rough furniture was cleared aside and the boarded floor made ready for the dancers. Then it was Hank's turn, and sometimes Jim's, though Hank was the one who usually obliged. Seated cross-legged in a corner, his face as serious as if he had an army of Redskins after him, the curious and lovable little fellow would bend over his concertina and send forth such notes, that dancing became easy even to the most clumsy.

Those were jolly days. The jovial and friendly fellow who had come out from England had found not a set of desperadoes in the settlers of the Dominion, but men and women just as he had known at home, with only the difference which climate and environment necessarily bring. Hard workers, they liked Joe because he was like them in that, and because of his modesty. They liked him, too, because of his open admiration of the country of his adoption and the life he led.

"Ef they was all like you there never wouldn't be any squabbling," said Peter; "but Canadians is getting to understand the Britisher better. He's coming out in greater numbers now, and sense he and we are the backbone of the country, why, we're fools if we ain't friends."

It was on a bright, clear, frosty morning that Hank and Joe climbed into Peter's rig and, with that worthy driving, set off for the nearest station. Mrs. Strike wiped her eyes as they went, for she was genuinely fond of them, while Tom shook Joe's hand as if he would wrench it off and hold it as a keepsake. An hour later they were aboard the train, and could see Peter driving back home to the settlement.

"Guess he's a good fellow, and deserves to succeed," said Hank, settling himself into a corner. "When next we see him it'll be spring or later hereabouts, and things will have changed wonderfully. There'll be a pile of people here compared with what's settled now. That's always the case; every year makes a huge difference. Shouldn't wonder if the plots you've bought didn't bring you in a small fortune; but of course it's a toss up."

Joe watched the surroundings as they pulled out of the station, noting the many shacks in the distance, and the fact that nearer the railway some of the older settlers had replaced their log dwellings by neatly-boarded houses. It was close to some of these that he himself, with the advice of Hank and Peter, had purchased certain portions of vacant ground in the hope that, as time passed, a township might spring up, and thereby make his purchases more valuable. As to Hurley's quarter section, the winter being on them, it happened that there was no one who cared to purchase, and Joe had picked it up at a very modest figure.

"You jest forget all about them things and set yer mind to the expedition we're after," said Hank, after a while. "Fust we goes along to Sudbury, where we can buy all that we want; then we sets off for Fennick's. Guess we'll put in a week with him, and then strike off for the country we're after. Maybe we'll get a bit of huntin', and seems to me we should be wise, for a pelt or two will be useful for bedcovering. Of course you've got to be able to stand the cold, youngster. There's lots would think this job but madness. But a man can easy stand the winter ef he's in hard condition, and particularly ef he's in amongst the forests. As to bear, why, seeing as they hibernate, there ain't much chance of meeting the beasts, though it do happen sometimes that one of them gets disturbed, and then, ef he ain't too sleepy, jest you look out fer ructions. I don't know of any animal that's so tarnation dangerous as a bear, 'cept perhaps a caribou, and he's jest every bit as bad as, they tell me, is a rhinoceros. Ever hunted, lad?"

Joe was forced to admit that he had not. "Never had the chance," he answered. "Minding a cycle shop for Father didn't give one opportunities of going hunting, and besides, there isn't much to be had in England, not of the sort you mean."

Of a sudden, as they sped along in the train, his thoughts went back to the little township in which he had spent his boyhood, till the moment had arrived for him to emigrate. He could not help but contrast his condition here in Canada with what it had been there, and with what it might have been had he remained. Travel and the wide expanse of New Ontario lands had broadened Joe's mind, as it is bound to broaden the outlook that any traveller takes of the world. Joe was, in fact, beginning to realize that there is some truth in the statement that travel is one of the finest educations.

"In course it is," asserted Hank, when he broached the subject, with the idea of starting up a conversation with the little hunter. "How could it fail to be? Don't I know the lives of them stay-at-homes. They work hard, no doubt. They does their whack of toil that helps to make the earth turn round, as you might say, and keep things hummin'; but, 'cept for the papers and sichlike, they ain't got two ideas as to what other people's like, what they does with themselves, and how they lives. And there's more, too, ef I could tell you. Stay-at-homes is sometimes narrow-minded. Narrow-mindedness gives rise to suspicion, so that it follows that men who are ignorant of one another's affairs and of all that concerns 'em is often not too good friends. That's how it is with nations. One don't know the other, and suspects all sorts of things. Wall, see what's happenin'. The railways and the steamships and them motor cars has made a deal of difference. People move about a heap these days and see other people. So they get to understand 'em, and, understandin' them, they see as they ain't much different to themselves; also, they see that their intentions are just as friendly as their own. And what follows? Why, better understanding, and the way is paved to international friendships. Dear, how jawin' do tire a man! I'm on fer a smoke."

He shut up like the proverbial oyster, leaving Joe to go on immersed in his own particular brown study. He was wondering now what the Fennicks had been doing with themselves, for though he had had a few lines from them, he had had but the scantiest information; he had heard, in fact, that they had settled, and that was all. Whether they had been fortunate in finding exactly the class of surroundings they desired, and whether the land they had chosen was rich, he had no idea. This he knew, they were a two-days' march from the railway, so that he and Hank had a long step before them.

"Guess we'll fill up at Sudbury," said Hank, after a while. "There's a gun wanted fer you, and ammunition for both of us. A shooter, too, ain't out of the way. We shall require warm clothing, too, though we'll trust to our shooting to get us pelts and make the most of those. A kettle, a fry-pan, and a few sich trifles will fill our kit, and then we'll step it to the Fennicks'. Guess we ain't so far from Sudbury now."

They found all they required in the town to which they had booked on the railway, and laid out quite a number of dollars in buying necessaries for their journey; for Hank insisted that salt, sugar, coffee, and tea were as necessary to them as were bullets. Each bought three pairs of thick socks, as well as roughly-fashioned fur gloves. The cooking equipment presented no difficulties, while neither bothered to buy extra boots.

"They'd load us up, that's all," said Hank; "besides, they ain't no use with snowshoes. You wait a bit till we're well away. We'll bag a few beasts that will give us skins, and then ef Hank can't make moccasins and caps and sichlike, why, all his eddication in the woods is lost. We've got enough as it is to carry, and come the time we reaches up at Fennicks' we'll be sorry we brought so much."

"What about some sort of covering for the night?" asked Joe, who was as yet ignorant on such matters.

"Coverin'?" asked Hank, scratching his head.

"Yes; surely we shall need it. It'll be frightfully cold, that is, if the story I have heard is true."

"True enough, lad," agreed Hank; "only, yer see, you and I'll be movin' every day, and exercise on snowshoes warms a man's blood. I know lots of young fellows who go off from their farms when snow's lyin' everywhere and the thermometer is 'way down below zero; but their shirts is open in front jest as ef it war summer, while they ain't got no use fer gloves. We'll be much the same, while at night a lean-to—a double lean-to, you understand—made by driving two forked sticks into the snow and laying one across the forks, with others leaning up agin it, will give us a crib that couldn't be beaten fer warmth. I kin hear folks that stays at home always shiverin' talkin' of rheumatism; but there ain't nothing of that. A man who starts healthy through a Canadian winter can keep healthy. Of course there's blizzards, and nasty, dangerous things they are! I've laid in one of them lean-to shacks as I've mentioned fer a week together till the snow was piled deep over the top, and would ha' broken through ef I hadn't crawled out every few hours and beaten it down. Cold? It warn't! It war hot inside that 'ere crib. As fer lonely, wall, to some folks it might be, but to me and mates like me—no, not bit! There's always a gun wants cleaning; logs has to be broke and the fire kept going, and there's tea and sichlike to prepare; while in between a man's got his pipe, and can smoke and think. Thinkin' ain't bad fer a man, nor fer a woman, ef it comes to that. There's many a time 'way back in my life when I might ha' done different and better. Wall, then, rememberin' that aer good; it's a sort of eddication. Then there's friends that you've knowed and had high times with. Guess it's when a man gets stuck up in a blizzard, with only his pipe to smoke, that he gets thinking of his old pals, wondering what they're doing, where they are, and how the world aer going fer them generally."

"But what about frostbite?" asked Joe, for that was a bogy which had been presented to him in glaring colours.

Hank laughed, a silent little laugh which shook every inch of his frail body. "Them old woman's tales was invented to scare new folks out from home," he said. "There's frostbites and there's frostbites. I ain't saying that they don't exist, but a hunter don't often get 'em, unless he's held up somewheres and can't get cover. His blood runs strong and hot most times, and the frost don't touch him. But it's the man who ain't used to the cold, and who huddles up in a shack most of the day, that gets bitten. Ef he's sensible, or has sensible friends, it don't make much harm to him. Ef not, like as not he loses a toe or a finger, or maybe a foot, though it's rare, so far as I'm able to reckon. You ain't likely to get bit; a chap same as you, who's always on the hop, gets his blood runnin' all the time. Don't you give a thought to it, Joe."

Having stayed in the town sufficiently long to complete their equipment, Joe and Hank finally took the track for that part of the country in which the Fennicks had settled. The weather was still quite open, though cold. But the bracing air agreed wonderfully with them both, and though there was not the smallest need for haste, they stepped out strongly, sending the miles rapidly behind them. It was some distance outside the town that they came upon a party of travellers riding in, and recognized Mike, the policeman, as one of them.

"Hallo, Mike!" sang out Hank. "Been after more of them 'ere murderers? How'd the case go with Hurley? This here Joe ha' been waitin' case he should be called for evidence; but he heard a while ago as he warn't likely to be wanted."

The face of the huge policeman, already tanned a deep colour, went red under his tan, while an expression of annoyance flitted across his features.

"We made a muss of that 'ere thing, Hank," he declared. "Joe wasn't called for the simple reason that the folks who'd taken Hurley in charge let him give 'em the slip. He got clear away, and I'm jest now returning after a chase. He's gone—where, I don't know. But he's got clear, which aer a bad nuisance. Jest you mind that you don't come up agin him. He's not the one to forget old scores, and he'd rub it in ef he'd the power. Wall, so long! I must get back and report; someone's going to get trouble over this business."

They parted where they had met, Hank and Joe pushing onward still at a sharp pace.

"I'm jest sorry that Hurley got clear," said Hank, after a while, as if he had been thinking the matter out. "He's a bad man aer Hurley, and bad men away in the wilds are apt to bring trouble to people. I've knowed one who took up with a party of Redskins wandering in the forests, and, gee! he didn't stop at anything. He'd made bad trouble before the police rounded him up and shot him down. Let's hope we shan't knock across this Hurley. Now, lad, guess we'll do another mile or so and then fix our camp fer the night. Looks ter me as ef it might snow, so we'll be wise to make all snug and tidy."

They came to a halt finally beside a small wood, and, penetrating to a part where the trees were of considerable size, deposited their belongings on the ground.

"Don't do to camp where it's damp, in the fust place," explained Hank. "Where there's muskegs the trees soon rot, and ef a wind springs up you might have the trunks coming about your ears, to say nothing of rotten branches. This place is high and dry, and the trees, being stout and well inside the wood, will stand up to a gale. Now fer that shack I was talking about. Look out fer a tidy long-forked stick, and fer other straight ones to lay across."

Hank was evidently a past master at all that appertained to camping, for even without Joe's aid he would soon have erected the shack. Taking two forked sticks, he drove the straight end in each case as deeply into the ground as he was able; a third was laid over the forks, and then a number were allowed to lean against the one laid horizontally. Thus a species of *tente d'abri* was constructed, and a roofing quickly put to it, by the simple means of slashing off spruce twigs and branches and laying them on top.

"That ain't always enough," explained Hank. "Ef there's a bad wind, it would blow all them branches away. But it don't take long to cut turfs or to peg the branches down, whichever you've a fancy for. Seein' as the ground in here ain't over-hard, we'll take turfs; the wind won't hurt 'em, and ef it turns to rain instead o' snow, why, not a drop'll fall through. Now fer a bed—one between us, mate, for we'll be companions in every way. A pile of these spruce twigs will suit us well; then we'll light the fire and get the kettle going. A pot of tea with a morsel to bite won't come amiss after our march. How do yer think you'll like prospecting?"

Joe did not think; he was emphatic about the matter, for the farther they went the better he enjoyed the trip. He busied himself now with the fire, for, during the chase of Hurley, George Bailey had taught him much that concerned the culinary portion of a camp. Then he produced a small loin of pork, and, cutting portions from it, soon had them sizzling over the flames.

"My, what with the smell of these here spruce boughs and that 'ere pork, it makes a hunter's mouth jest water!" declared Hank, sitting down to watch Joe, and smoking the pipe which he loved so much. "See here, youngster, while you're gettin' supper ready I'll collect a few more logs. There's never any sayin' what sort of weather we may have, and ef we was short of firin' we'd have to eat cold grub, which ain't over fanciful, I kin tell you."

By the time he was back in the camp Joe had a number of pieces of pork cooked, and was fain to admit himself that the smell of cooking them was most appetizing. Then, as the shades of night drew in, he and Hank—as strangely an assorted couple as one could well come upon—sat down in the entrance of their humble shack and, wrapping blankets about their shoulders, ate their supper, enjoying every mouthful of it as others cannot do, even your gourmet set before the most recherché meal that was ever invented; for an active open-air life gives zest to everything. Your traveller does not complain of the toughness of his steak or of the weakness of his tea. He is thankful for all that is set before him, and with appetite sharpened by exercise, and tastes unspoiled and unpampered by a multiplicity of viands and etceteras, eats heartily, thankful that there is food to be had, mindful perhaps of other times when he went hungry.

"Wind's turned," stated Hank, as he rose after supper. "It's got away round, and we're in for a north-easter. That mostly brings snow, so I shouldn't wonder ef we was buried nigh the mornin'. That means snowshoes, and it aer a lucky thing that I brought all the fixings. There's many as buys their snowshoes. I ain't one of them. Ever sense I was as high as a table I've made 'em myself. Throw on another log, Joe, and let's get snug down inside. And jest for a moment have a look at our shack. You can see that I've faced it so that the opening looks west and south. Ef there's snow from the north-east it won't enter so easy, though, in course, there'll be eddies in here amongst the trees, and some of it'll be blowed in."

Tossing branches on the fire, Joe soon joined his comrade, when the two wrapped their blankets round them and were quickly asleep; but at midnight they were awakened by noise without, and crept to the exit of their shack.

"Blowin' moderate," said Hank, "and my, ain't it snowin'! Lucky there's a moon. It makes it look as ef the weather wouldn't be outrageous."

Joe was enchanted when he looked out into the forest. It was his first real taste of a Canadian winter; for here, besides the cold blast which whistled amongst the trees, there was snow. Flakes eddied and twirled everywhere. They came sidling down upon the shack as if afraid to disturb the campers. They had already formed a white carpet over the ground, while many a branch was groaning beneath the added weight. Under the rays of a pale, wintry moon the scene was simply enchanting.

"Beautiful!" declared our hero. "And just fancy being in camp at such a time! It would make them all sit up and have fits away back in Old England."

"It'd make men of some of them that needs changin'," grunted Hank. "You jest wait a tidy bit. This ain't nothing to what we'll get before we've done with the winter. But let's creep back agin'. It ain't too warm outside, and reckon the inside of that 'ere shack aer as comfortable as a feather bed under the roof of a palace."

It was, in fact. Joe's head hardly touched the heaped pillow of twigs when he fell asleep, and slumbered on, oblivious of the increasing sounds without and of the silent snowflakes settling overhead.

CHAPTER XII

The Canadian Winter

"It aer jest blowin' an almighty gale, and there ain't nothing to do but feed and make our snowshoes," said Hank, when early on the following morning he and Joe looked out of the shack. "It aer a lucky thing fer us that we brought a tidy-sized piece of pork along with us, 'cos this gale might last fer days. Not as I think it will, but it might; and ef we hadn't had plenty of grub, gee! it would ha' been a bad case."

Such a prospect met Joe's gaze when he stood to his full height and, having helped to throw the snow away from the entrance of the shack, peered over the white edge before him! The trees on either hand were heavily laden with snow. Branches here and there had crashed to the ground and lay in an unrecognizable heap, save for a twig here or a stronger bough there thrusting a way upward into the light; for all around everything was covered, smoothly clad in an all-pervading vestment of white. Gorgeous blue shadows lurked here and there, the faintness of the colouring adding to its beauty. Long icicles, beside which those to be seen in England were but babies, hung from branches already overweighted, one, a ponderous fellow, drooping to within a few feet of the shack; for the heat of the fire had melted the snow as it fell upon a branch above, and had produced this monster with the help of the frost.

"You kin get in at breakfast," said Hank, looking about him with the manner of a man who saw nothing extraordinary about the transformation which had arrived since the day before. "The fire's been out this two hours, so you'd best start another."

Joe showed his want of experience at once, for he began to rake away the snow, so as to get down to the ashes of the fire he had built on the evening of their arrival. But Hank stopped him with a merry guffaw.

"That ain't the way," he said. "You start buildin' yer fire right here on top of the snow. It'll eat its way down. Yer see, ef you was to begin right down in a hole, there wouldn't be any sorter draught, and how's flames to get in at the damp wood ef you don't have draught to help 'em? But once they get movin', and things is hot, why, in course the fire burns its way slowly downward to the ground level, when there ain't sich draught required."

It was one of the sort of things Joe and many another new to this country, and to such quaint surroundings, would never have thought of, though he was quick to see the reason in Hank's explanation. He arranged his logs, therefore, on the top of the snow, and then removed them once more.

"Wall?" asked Hank, who seemed always to have one eye for our hero, whatever he happened to be doing himself. "What are the game now?"

"Too much draught, that's all," grinned Joe, blowing on his fingers, for an icy wind whirled the flakes about him. "Too much of it, Hank. Blow the fire out or set our shack alight. Fine that'd be—eh?"

The little hunter grinned widely and nodded vigorously. "Good fer you," he shouted. "I've knowd chaps as would ha' taken a month o' Sundays ter spot that. There's some as is jest almighty windbags, and go about talkin' so much that they can't think, let alone allow others that has a mind to. There's something in bein' silent at times, Joe. A man ain't a fool 'cos he stays quiet takin' in things as they happen."

He sniffed the air as Joe's pork steaks began to frizzle, and looked up from the work he was engaged on when the kettle began to send out a merry tune, heard in spite of the howling wind. Steam whistled from the spout, and was the signal for Hank to step across to the canteen and extract the tea leaves which were to form their staple beverage during the trip.

"Tea aer comfortin'," he had said many a time, "and tea aer sustainin'. There ain't a one as I knows of that don't drink tea and feel better fer it. In course there's a few as is ill and find it hurts 'em, but, gee! you get to thinkin' of all the old ladies who swears by a cup! As fer hunters and prospectors and sich-like, tea don't hurt none of 'em. Summertime, when it's cold, it quenches thirst better nor anything I've met. And winter, when it's that cold you can't feel yer hands, why, a tin dish of the stuff warms yer right down into yer boots and sets toes and fingers tingling. Pitch in the dose, lad. I'm that set this mornin', seems to me I could eat all you've cooked single-handed, and a tidy slice more in addition."

It was all good-humoured fun, and Joe found that Hank was a splendid travelling companion; for he had proved time and again now that he had a means to get over more than ordinary difficulties, and that whatever the times, pleasant or foul, he was genial and bright, always looking on the right side of misfortunes.

"Now, jest as soon as you've cleaned up these here things, we'll finish off the shoes and try 'em," said Hank, when they had eaten their fill. "I brought along these two sets of frames from home, they being the ones I made this four year back. The strip to go across 'em war to be had back there in the settlement, and all we've got to do is to bind it on. Ever been across snow afore, lad?"

Joe had to acknowledge that he had not. As he melted snow in his kettle and washed the few tin utensils they carried with the resulting water, he watched the busy fingers of the hunter threading raw hide strips through holes bored in the tough, bending wood which formed the frames of the snowshoes. Then he was shown how to lash them to his feet, while a little later he essayed to test them, and, clambering out of the hollow which they now occupied, joined Hank on the snow. But Joe did not remain long there; a projecting bough brought his attempt to a sudden ending. One shoe caught badly, and before our hero knew precisely what was happening or where he was going, he took a header into the soft snow, till Hank could merely see a pair of shoes waving wildly above it.

"You jest try agin, and take care of snags comin' up from below," he cautioned our hero. "This here snowshoein' ain't really difficult. A fellow soon gets the knack or hang of it, and then he can go across frozen and snowed-under country quicker'n he could walk ef the ground was hard and he jest in boots. You stick to it, mate; nothing was ever larned but what caused trouble."

Joe did stick to it, in spite of the wind howling about him, and though he took many a tumble, there was nothing in that soft, unfrozen snow to do him injury; and in course of time he became more handy.

"You ain't done badly fer one lesson," said Hank encouragingly. "Best give in for a time now and go inside the shack. It aer snowin' a trifle harder, and sense it's gettin' dark too, it seems to me as ef the wust war before us. We'll smoke and sleep; a long rest won't harm either of us. 'Sides, there's heaps we could do. Now, see here, Joe. I don't rightly know much about England, nor more'n a little bit about Europe. Jest you get in at the job and tell me about it all. When you're tired I'll yarn to you all about the other provinces in Canada, for I've been in most of 'em. It might turn out handy for you, for one of these days you may be going west. They say out here that a settler in Manitoba or Ontario stays jest so long as is wanted to make enough dollars, then he streaks off west and takes to fruit farming, or settles nigh to Vancouver. In course he goes so as to have more folks about him, and also because the winter is a good deal less severe. Fer me, give me this sort of thing; I ain't afraid of winter."

Hank was a cheery individual to have to deal with and Joe found him, as one might have expected, a most attentive and intelligent listener. It was well, too, that they got on so easily together, for the gale lasted some twenty-four hours longer, though snow ceased to fall long before the wind had subsided. This change was followed by a sudden rise in temperature and then by a fierce frost.

120

"Couldn't have been better fer us," declared Hank. "That 'ere thaw made the snow soft and sloppy on top. Now it's all ice, and it aer likely we shall be able in parts to walk without snowshoes. In any case, the shoes will hold us up over the deepest drifts, seein' that there's now a firm skin all over. Guess we'll move come mornin'."

Busy always, for he could not sit down, in spite of his own statements to the contrary, and remain idle, Hank that evening, with the aid of a torch of the yellow birch bark, instructed Joe how to fashion moccasins, the soft leather socks and boots combined, with which all trappers and hunters are shod. Using some of the same hide which he had employed for the snowshoes, he laid out a pattern in a few moments, and then, with the small blade of a knife to bore the holes, and a thin lace of the same material, laced the sides of the sock together.

"In course, like that it ain't waterproof," he said, "and though trappers ain't so very careful, yet ef you've to march miles in moccasins, and has to sleep in 'em during the night, you might jest as well have comfort and dry feet. We'll march along in these to-morrow. It'll be easier than using snowshoes, for the surface is nice and hard. Soon as we kill a beast or two we'll make ourselves an extra pair, so as to have a change."

A brilliant wintry sun flooded the landscape as the two emerged from the forest on the following morning, and Joe got some idea of Canada's appearance once winter has set in. Everywhere a mantle of snow covered the ground, while trees, bushes, and rocks were clad in a thin coating of ice following the thaw. As for the surface of the snow, it was harder than that so much in request for skiing in Switzerland. The sharp thaw had liquefied the surface for a depth of perhaps half an inch, and this was now frozen hard.

"Likely as not there'll come another thaw," said Hank, "and in a jiffy almost all this snow'll go, and the country be jest as it war before. But that won't last long. Now that November's set in, we soon gets winter fer good, and then it ain't till late March that there's a sign of its ending. Sometimes it's later; sometimes earlier. But once the snow's down, we gets bright days same as this often enough, and though the thermometer may show thirty and forty degrees below zero, one don't seem to feel it. Now, lad, put yer best foot forward; we ain't goin' to fetch up at Fennick's to-night. This here snow'll delay us; but ter-morrer, somewheres about noon."

With their packs slung over their backs, and each one using a strong stick, the two went away on their journey, sometimes travelling over a smooth expanse which must have been the surface of some frozen lake, of which there are many in that part of Canada, and at other times plunging into forests. The backwoods, in fact, extended as far as the eye could reach, with open spaces here and there.

121

Joe enjoyed the journey amazingly. Think of the delights of such a new experience. Well clad, and in suitable clothing, he was as warm as a toast, while the unwonted exercise and the crispness of the frosty air made him step out as he had never done before. Hank even was hard put to to keep up with his young comrade.

"Blest ef you won't tire me one of these fine days," he cried, calling for a halt. "It's them long legs of yourn; they takes you along over the snow quicker'n mine. Do yer feel lonely, lad?"

Joe shook his head with marked emphasis. "Not a bit," he said, "though if I were by myself I might very well do so. But there's something new to look at all the while, and the sun is so jolly. Still, I can imagine a farm hand, stuck away in some place right away from the villages or townships, eating his heart out if he had never been used to the wilds."

"Jest so; and that's why it is that bad tales of Canadian winters gets out of the Dominion and reaches the ears of those thinkin' of emigrating. It stands to reason that ef you take a young fellow that's lived in a thickly-populated town all his life and plank him away right in the wilds, he aer likely to feel lonesome come the winter, specially ef he ain't got move enough on him to find a job or so to occupy his time. He'll get thinking of the picture palaces and sichlike he might be able to see ef he was back in a town, and he gets grumbling. Even married folks do. I've knowed a chap go half crazy long afore the winter was ended—but then, there you are!"

He raised his eyes significantly, for Hank had experience of what every old settler has seen amongst newcomers. The life in the Dominion is new to them. The winter is cruelly hard, without a shadow of doubt; but grumbling does not help matters. Those who are ready to grumble at their surroundings find the winter more than trying. Those who have their hearts in the new life, and the firm resolve to persevere and be successful, make the most and the best of what cannot be avoided, and in place of longing for old conditions, for the amusements of a town, settle down to find tasks to occupy their attention. As Hank had told Joe before, and Peter also, there was always furniture to be made for the shack. The winter months, when the shack was as warm as possible, was just the time when papering and whitewashing could be done. There were, in fact, a number of jobs to keep idle hands busy, to help pass the time, and to aid settlers to happiness. However, if the winter were hard elsewhere, Joe found this, his first experience of it, most exhilarating. He trudged along blithely, whistling often. It was a couple of hours after noon, when they had eaten and were on their way once more, that something occurred to interrupt the journey.

They were thrusting their way noiselessly through a wooded glade, when Hank brought his companion to a stop.

"There's been moose hereabouts," he told Joe, pointing to the snow. "You could tell it blindfold, for though there ain't no footmarks, there's deep holes. Yer see, a moose is that heavy and his feet so small comparatively, that the hard crust of snow that's frozen ain't strong enough to hold him up. He goes through deep ef he's making a new track, while ef he and his mates has been along afore, there's a deep hard path that there ain't no mistakin'. There's been jest one along here; it's likely they has a yard 'way up here."

"A yard?" asked Joe, ignorant of what that might be. "What's a yard?"

"Jest a place to which moose flock every winter almost. In course it's more or less open ground what's known as a 'barren', and there is always heaps of the class of trees and moss on which they feed. They congregates and treads the snow flat, and lives there till their food is eaten; then off they goes to form another. Jest you slip along easy, lad; a bull moose ain't the sorter fellow one asks to come up aginst."

A mile or so farther on it was evident that the moose whose tracks they were following, and who happened to have preceded them in their own direction, joined a well-worn track which plunged at once into forest. It was then that Hank again came to a sudden halt.

"Did you hear that sort of cough?" he asked. "That's a bull moose fer sure; 'praps we'll come in fer some shootin'. Anyway, reckon we'll get our guns unslung and ready in case."

Slipping cartridges into the breaches of their rifles, the two proceeded cautiously, and before many minutes had passed heard a succession of sounds which puzzled Joe immensely. Someone might have been thrashing the trunks of the trees with a heavy stake; at times the sounds were almost metallic, while now and again an angry cough came to their ears.

"It aer a moose bull fer sure," whispered Hank. "Yer see, the wind's fallen and there ain't a breath, else he'd have scented us long ago; what's more, there's been something happenin' to upset his temper. Bull moose aer the angriest, fiercest things as ever I clapped eyes on. One moment they'll run at the very shadow of a human, and next they'll charge with their heads up and their spreading antlers ready for the enemy. Hark there, he's 'sounding'!"

When our hero had the latter term explained to him, he gathered that it meant that the moose, scenting an enemy or a rival bull moose, perhaps, had halted and was thrashing some tree stump with his antlers, till a succession of blows sounded through the forest, for all the world as if lumbermen were at work with their axes. Then followed a series of lower-toned noises.

"He aer fairly working hisself up fer a fight," whispered Hank, crouching behind a trunk. "That 'ere bull moose aer laying into the trees with his fore hoofs, and lucky we are that it ain't us. Their fore hoofs is just edged as sharp as any axe and would cut badly, while a dig with the antlers would kill a man. You kin lay it as sartin that there's another bull moose around. Mayhap there's been a cow moose a-callin'. That's brought two of the others along, and now, ef I ain't altogether mistaken, there's likely to be an almighty ruction, for it ain't in reason fer one moose to give way to another; they're terrible fighters. Jest about this time o' the year they're in grand condition, and fights take place constantly. I ain't never seed one, but I've come up to moose as was in them as was nigh killed. Come along quietly; we may have a peep at what's happenin'."

Creeping on through the wood, the strange sounds which they had heard were for a time altogether absent. But it was not for long, for a dull croaking cough suddenly reached them from an opposite direction, and was followed instantly by loud and furious "sounding" and by a huge clatter that told of falling branches. Ten minutes later Hank put up his hand and slank in behind a thick mass of underwood.

"Look away over there," he whispered hoarsely. "He aer hidin' jest in amongst the trees, and another challenge from his rival will bring him out. Ain't he layin' into the trunks and sichlike?"

The noise made by the furious beast became in fact even greater, while there was a commotion amongst the branches and withered leaves which still clung in places. A second later there came a croaking roar from some point to the right, the trees in that direction were thrust asunder, while a magnificent beast pushed its way into the clearing. Joe's eyes opened wide in amazement, for never had he beheld such a sight. There, standing erect before him, was one of the wonders of the Dominion; in fact, one of the deer tribe peculiar to Canada, which, unlike ordinary deer, noted for their timidity, was obviously the reverse. A coat of shimmering black clothed the beast, setting off a neck and shoulders which were decidedly massive; huge palmated antlers of enormous breadth crowned a head which was large, like other portions of this animal, and extremely fierce in aspect. Grand upper limbs supported on slender lower ones, both streaked with orange lines, were finished off by shapely hoofs, which, as Hank had said, could be extremely dangerous. The animal made a truly magnificent spectacle, and Joe could have continued gazing at him for a considerable time. However, there was more to come yet, for of a sudden the leaves away to the right parted, and a second moose bull, bigger if anything than he who had already appeared, came striding into the arena.

"It'll be a fight that'll be worth watchin'," whispered Hank, his face set with excitement, his eyes blazing. "See 'em charge."

It took perhaps less than a minute for the two rivals to take stock of one another. A glance at either showed that their courage was raised to the highest and their tempers ferocious. Then they charged furiously, their heads down and their formidable antlers to the front. The shock of their meeting could have been heard a mile away, while Joe could easily hear their loud hissing breathing. Rising very cautiously so as to obtain a better view, he looked on spellbound while the two massive beasts fought for the victory, sometimes with their antlers locked, and then, separating for a little space, only to dash forward once more and come into contact with a crash which vibrated through the forest. It was at one of the moments when they withdrew from one another, as if to gather strength for another charge, that the brute Joe and Hank had first come upon suddenly threw up his head and gazed in their direction, causing both of them to crouch lower; then there came a bellowing roar and a commotion there could be no misunderstanding.

"He's scented us and is charging," cried Hank, leaping to his feet. "There ain't nothing for it but a tree. Quick, Joe; climb into one!"

So sudden had been the change, that our hero was altogether taken aback and, as it were, robbed of his energies. He could be quick enough at other times, but now, when there was urgent need for haste, his feet seemed too heavy, while as yet he had hardly taken in the danger of the situation. It was when he saw Hank's active figure already shinning up a tree that Joe awakened to his own position. By then the moose was within some ten yards of him, its head down, coughing and bellowing angrily.

"Dodge him! Dodge him!" shouted Hank, now astride a branch and looking as if he were about to leap down to aid his comrade. "Don't try to climb, or he'll cut you to pieces with his hoofs. Dodge him, lad!"

Joe heeded the warning, and, darting to one side, took cover behind a slender oak which happened to be there. But if he thought it would protect him he was much mistaken, for the moose charged madly, and, striking the tree with head and antlers, broke it off short at the bottom, sending the other portion and our hero flying together. In fact, the whole thing was a huge surprise, and might well have been expected to rob Joe of his wits altogether. But a sharp pang in his shoulder as the trunk struck him heavily seemed to sharpen his energies, and, leaping to his feet, he raced at once to another tree and sheltered behind it. Then began a chase that was anything but amusing, for the moose bull struck repeatedly at him, making the tree shake, and sending the sound of his blows echoing and reverberating through the forest. He rose on his hind legs and slashed fiercely with his fore legs, ripping long strips of bark away. It looked, in fact, as if any one of his rushes might take Joe unawares, and that his dodging behind the tree might come to a sudden ending. As for Hank, he was entirely helpless, for it was this selfsame tree in which he had taken refuge, while his own and our hero's rifles lay behind the thick underwood where they had been hiding. However, the little man was not the one to give in without a struggle, more particularly when Joe's life might depend upon his efforts, and presently a brilliant thought came to his aid.

THE MOOSE CHARGED MADLY

THE MOOSE CHARGED MADLY

"Jest keep dodging him," he sang out encouragingly. "Ef he ain't reached you yet he ain't likely to. Jest keep well clear of his hoofs and out of sight of the brute as much as you can. He ain't as fresh as he war, and that'll help us."

The cunning hunter rapidly unwound the long piece of raw hide that he had cut for use on the snowshoes, and which, having more than he required, he had carried with him since, in case of renewals being wanted. Perhaps he had as much as eight feet, perhaps there was less; but, in any case, it was as tough and strong as any rope ever constructed. While Joe continued to dodge the angry moose, now escaping his attacks with comparative ease—for he had regained his coolness—Hank made one end of his rope fast to the tree, looped the other, and then crawled out on the branch.

"Jest get him to come dodging round this way," he said hoarsely. "Ef I hooks him, you make a run fer one of the guns, and then climb into the nearest tree. This rope won't hold him overlong, but it'll do to let you get clear. Now, I'm ready."

Joe merely required to show himself plainly for the maddened moose to come dodging after him. The huge antlers, as hard almost as steel, struck the tree a resounding clang, then the fore feet were used till strips of bark were flying. Slowly Joe edged round the trunk, luring the animal after him, till a lucky move brought the moose directly under Hank.

"Git ready!" he shouted, at the same time dropping one foot and kicking the antlers. Instantly the beast raised his head, and like lightning Hank slipped his noose over one of the broad branches.

"Run!" he bellowed. "Don't ferget the gun, or we'll be both of us fixed for days together."

It may be imagined that Joe did run. He dashed across the open space to the spot where their rifles were lying, turning his head to see what was happening. If he had felt less confidence in the little hunter, there is small doubt that he would have neglected to pick up a weapon; for the fury of the moose on seeing his movement was terrible. It lowered its head and dashed after him, till the strong hide rope brought it up with a jerk that threatened to snap the noose. Then began a mad struggle on the part of the moose for freedom. Rearing up on its hind legs, it struck out with its fore feet, almost reaching the bough on which Hank was seated. It backed and tugged, it fell to the ground, trusting by those means to tear itself free; then it dashed this way and that, arrested on each occasion with a mighty jerk that actually shook the tree.

"Even a chain wouldn't stand much more of such tugging," shouted Hank, watching Joe anxiously out of the corner of his eye. "You be slippy with that gun, lad, or else we'll lose him. Ah, that's a relief! He's into a tree. Now, wonder what sort of shooting he'll make. Say, lad," he called out loudly, "take him when he lifts his head, and put a bullet into his shoulder jest about where the neck joins it. Steady, Joe; you're puffed. Pull yerself together."

If our hero had attempted a shot then, there is little doubt but that he would have missed entirely, for what with the active movements of the moose and his own trembling fingers, a sure aim was more than difficult. However, he did as he was ordered. Bracing his legs round a branch, he brought the butt of his weapon firmly to his shoulder, then, choosing a moment when the animal lifted its head, he sent a bullet crashing into it. A yell from Hank told him, even before the thin cloud of smoke had cleared away, that he had been successful.

"Good fer you! Killed him dead!" Joe heard, and, looking down, saw the huge bulk of the animal stretched on the snow, thick steam still issuing from the nostrils.

Let us be strictly truthful again with regard to our hero. Joe was shaking in every limb as he dropped to the ground and stood over the fallen animal; for excitement had told upon his nerves, as yet unaccustomed to such strenuous moments.

"You don't need to be ashamed," said Hank, seeing that Joe looked downcast. "I've seen many an older chap all of a shiver with excitement when the thing was over. The main thing aer that you kept your head and held your sights straight when they was wanted. This here exhibition will have given you a good idea of the moose that roams about Canada, and next time you meet one don't wait too long for his charge. I've known a man to be skewered on those antlers afore you could shout, and killed jest as dead as possible. Reckon we'll skin the brute and take his head. It'll be a fine gift for the Fennicks."

They spent the remainder of the day in skinning the moose and in removing the skull and antlers. Indeed, they camped beside the carcass, not troubling themselves about the other brute, which had retreated at the very beginning of their adventure. That night, for the first time in his young life, Joe cooked moose steaks over the fire and ate of meat of his own getting.

"Prime, ain't it?" grinned Hank, as he devoured a savoury morsel. "But you wait; there'll be more huntin' before we've done with this here expedition."

CHAPTER XIII

A Co-operative Proposition

It was rather later than they had anticipated when Hank and Joe arrived at Sam Fennick's shack on the following day; for again a thaw had set in—not the "silver thaw" so much prized in Canada, which they had previously experienced, and which, by freezing the upper layer of snow and, as it were, laying a sound crust upon it, had enabled them to make good progress, but a thaw unaccompanied by change, or, to be exact, not followed by a succeeding frost. They finished their journey, therefore, through a snowy slush, sinking often above their knees, while their moccasins and their feet were wringing wet and very cold.

Shouts greeted them.

"Why, if it ain't Joe!" came from Sam heartily, in his well-known bellowing tones, while the ineradicable cockney accent was obviously there; in fact, it was an accent of which Sam was proud. It was something never likely to leave him however long he remained in Canada, and however much he interlarded his conversation with Americanisms. "Missus, it's Joe!" he shouted, turning his head over his shoulder. Then he dashed forward, seized our hero's hand, and squeezed it till the latter almost winced.

"Howdy?" he exclaimed, swinging on Hank. "Introduce us."

"Hank," said Joe shortly, "hunter and trapper, a friend of mine. Hank, this is Sam Fennick; but——"

"In course I knows Sam," cried Hank, stretching out his wiry little paw, but one, nevertheless, which could give a grip that would make a strong man squirm. After all, outside the polite society of London and other large cities, where very vigorous handshaking is not looked on with favour, men often enough, the rough men of the plain, the prairie, the backwoods farm, and of the forest, exchange greetings with an earnestness there is no denying. Such men do not simper and dangle nerveless fingers before a stranger. They stand facing squarely, looking closely into the other's eyes, and when their hands meet, and their fingers grip the other's, the firmness of the grip, its vigour, its unflinching support of the return pressure somehow conveys something of the character of one man to the other. Hank had treated Joe in that way. To a man such as Hurley, whom he did not like, whom he suspected to be a craven, Hank merely waved or nodded; for he had his own views of what was proper, and they were far more exact and far more straightforward than one would have imagined.

"What! You, Hank—me old pal!" shouted Sam, delighted beyond measure, and almost hugging the little hunter. "You along o' Joe? How's that? He been doing something fer you, same as he did fer us?"

Hank asked an abrupt question. "What?"

"Ain't he never let on about the fire aboard ship, the rumpus there was, and how he led the volunteers?"

"Nary a word. Peter—Peter Strike, that is—did tell me a tale, but he warn't too sure of it. The young cuss is that silent when it comes to hisself. But he's been doing well. Sam, let's get these wet things off us, and something hot inside, and then we'll gas. Gee! Ef that ain't Mrs. Fennick! Howdy, maam? Here's Joe."

The good woman almost embraced our hero, for she felt like a mother to him.

"Come right in and let us hear all about you and your doings," she cried. "And Hank Mitchell too! I'm that glad to see you both, and Sam has been waitin' these many days for you to arrive. He's got a scheme for the winter."

The grinning master of the shack accompanied the visitors into the interior of the shack, and there stood, first on one leg and then on the other, while Joe and Hank looked keenly about them. It was to be expected that a man of Sam's energy, a Canadian settler who liked things to be right, should have erected a dwelling which should be fitting for his wife. Besides, there was reason for even greater magnificence.

"Guess you've been hard at work," said Hank, looking about him with twinkling eyes that nothing escaped. "This here shack's meant to last."

"It's that and more," cried Mrs. Fennick, pride in her tones. "Sam has built for a purpose. This shack's too big for what we want; he planned to have an office."

"Eh?" asked Hank, turning on the grinning owner, who had flushed to the roots of his hair for all the world as if he were a schoolboy. "What's this?"

"Part of the scheme, lad," came the answer. "Jest you two get seated and pull off those wet moccasins; then, when you've got dry socks to your feet and has had a bite, I'll get to at it. It's a fine yarn; I've dreamed of it this past five years."

No amount of persuasion would drag from Sam what his scheme was till Joe and Hank had eaten, and the latter had lit up a pipe.

"You kin fire in at it, Sam," said Hank at length, in the crisp little manner which was so distinctly his own. "I kinder gathered from this here Joe that when you came along up here prospecting it warn't with the idea of the ordinary farm. Maam, it's plain to see as my old friend has nigh worked his fingers to the bone."

Once more the little hunter's eyes went round the large parlour in which he and the others were seated, while Mrs. Fennick and her husband followed his glances with frank pride staring from their own eyes. Nor could Joe help but admire all that he saw; for he and Sam had been parted but a matter of a few months, and in the course of that time the latter had pitched upon a suitable holding for his farm, and had cut the timber for his shack, besides erecting the house. As to the latter, it was far bigger than the ordinary shack erected by the settler. There was a parlour, a kitchen, and three bedrooms, while attached at one side was a large office.

"Where we'll have the telephone afore you kin look round," declared Sam. "It's jest like this. Me and a mate or two agreed to go along together into New Ontario and pitch upon a spot that was likely to open up. Wall, we took the line the branch railway was following, though there's not one save those in the know behind the scenes, who kin say exactly where it'll run. Still, me and the others prospected a heap till we came along here. What with the difficulties of rocks to the south, and big, straggling elevations, it was clear as the rails must follow the valley, and there warn't more'n one for 'em to take. So we prospected along it till we came here. You jist come outside the door and you'll see what I'm after."

He led the way to the door of the shack and pointed to the north across a narrow stretch of country bounded on either hand by elevated land, and seamed along a straggling line running a little to one side of its centre by a thin strip of blue which, here and there, was entirely covered with snow. As for the landscape itself, it was difficult to tell its aspect exactly, in spite of the thaw, for snow lay deeply in most parts.

"Wall?" asked Hank curtly, looking about him and taking in every feature. "It's the top end of the valley, I kin see that. Rails running north kin easily pass out, seeing that the two ridges on either side don't run together. But they can't cut off to right or left. Ef the rails comes along this way, why, in course they passes right through this location."

"Along by the river," said Sam quickly. "Hank, it's an easy rise all the way. The river ain't got no current to speak of, which tells the tale easily. As to the rails coming along into the valley down south, why, that is almost certain, as sure as one can take it. Anyway, me and my mates agreed that it was more than likely, and so we arranged to take up holdings here. There's four of us already, Claude and Jim and Joe makes seven, and come spring-time there's nigh twenty more married men to join us."

"Wall?" asked Hank, not as yet clear as to what was Sam's meaning. "Where's the difference between this and other settlements? You takes up land, and the rails come along. Good! Up goes the value of the land, as it aer sartin to do. You get a reward for foresight; after that, where's the difference?"

Sam had evidently sought for the question, for he rubbed his hands together eagerly and gripped Hank's sleeve.

"Jest here," he declared with enthusiasm. "Instead of some twenty of us starting to work our sections separately, and going mighty slow in consequence, we're forming a corporation. Each man who takes land will pool money with the corporation. With that money we buy implements, horses, cattle, everything that's needed. We divide our numbers into parties, and come the spring one of 'em sets to work to build the shacks, another does the ploughing, while a third'll get to at the irrigation channels."

"Ah!" gasped Hank. "This aer new."

"Sam worked the scheme out all alone," declared Mrs. Fennick, with energy, causing her lord and master to blush again.

"It sounds just splendid," cried Hank. "Wall? What more? I kin see that there's an advantage in working ground on the corporation system. If you've got the timber cut already, it stands to reason that ten men working on a shack can put it up more'n ten times quicker than one man all alone. If there's twenty shacks wanted, ten men can put 'em up heaps faster than twenty fellers working on their own. And irrigation too! That sounds fine; it's doing well elsewhere."

Hank spoke but the truth there. A far-seeing Dominion Government and an all-powerful railway company have already seamed portions of Canada with canals and ditches with which water is borne to lands hitherto useless. Their forethought has converted, and is fast converting, barren soil into country which in parts already bears smiling crops and happy homesteads. As for the corporate system, if the Dominion Government has not attempted that—and one must admit that it is a question more for individual settlers—it has at least other worthy schemes. A would-be settler can now sail for the Dominion, to find there a quarter section prepared for his coming, with the shack built, the well dug, and some forty acres broken and seeded. For this he pays a reasonably small sum down, and the rest by small instalments. Think of the huge advantage of such a system. In place of finding naked soil, and having first to build a shelter and then break the land, a settler finds a home in readiness and crops already sprouting. Then consider Sam Fennick's proposition.

"It aer bound to go with a bang," declared Hank, pushing his skin cap to the back of his head and scratching his forehead. "It aer jest tremendous."

"It'll work, I think," agreed Sam, with the natural modesty of the inventor of such a daring scheme. "Anyway, we've got the party together, and there'll be money in abundance. Each man will own his own taking, and ef others come along and settle nigh us, why, we're prepared to hire ourselves out ef there's a call and we've the time. As for implements, me and a few of them has talked it over, and come the spring there'll be two steam agricultural motors up here, in which we kin burn wood. They'll each do ploughing at three to four acres a day, and will draw the reapers and binders when it comes to harvesting. There won't be no need to wait for a threshing gang, 'cos the tractors will drive the machine we shall buy. They kin do wood sawing too, and a hundred other things, besides hauling the stuff to market."

"Ah!" gasped Hank, for this was a proposition which rather took his breath away by its novelty and its possibilities. "But——"

"Yes?" asked Sam, bracing himself, as if to face any awkward questions the little hunter might fire off at him.

"There's the winter," said Hank. "Your corporation comes to an end when the snow comes; you ain't thought of that."

But Sam had; he wagged a knowing finger, while Mrs. Fennick giggled. Indeed, it must be admitted that this cockney settler, who had come from London and done so well in the Dominion, had proved himself more than astute. Perhaps he had thought the whole matter out during some past winter in Canada. In any case, he had been wonderfully close where his scheme was concerned, for never once had he more than hinted at it to Joe. However, the question of work in the winter had not escaped him.

"You listen here," he said, shaking Hank as if he were a dog. "Come wintertime east of the rockies things mostly closes down in Canada; even in the towns there ain't too much work. There's men wandering to and fro searching for jobs, whereas, most times and in most places, when there's spring and summer, there's more jobs than men."

"Guess that aer so," agreed Hank, sucking hard at his pipe.

"But there's work in Canada that starts in the fall, and only then—eh?"

"Lumberin'," suggested Hank.

"Lumbering it aer," cried Sam, drawling the words. "Up there beyond the break through which the railway'll pass, ef we've any luck, there's land that's heavily timbered. Wall, it's part of the scheme. You kin get a timber concession from Government by paying so much on the logs you cut, and me and my mates has taken up a tidy piece of timber country. There's a lake twenty miles and more north into which we can slide the logs, and there's another jest at the head of the valley. Way south there's a quickish fall, with water in plenty, and ef all goes well, and we kin make enough dollars, why, we'll start a mill there and saw our timber. The rails'll be close by then, and will take 'em on to market."

"My," cried Hank, "you've been moving!"

"We're only beginning," said Sam. "But we starts out for a lumber camp soon as the frost comes, and there we'll work till springtime. You axed what we was going to do in the winter. There's the answer."

It must be confessed that Sam Fennick's scheme was ambitious to the last degree. But then, if one analyses it, one can see the possibilities that Hank saw, for co-operative working is often enough wonderfully successful where the single individual fails. Again, in a country where labour is scarce, and profits often lessened because of the lack of labour at critical periods; where, in fact, a man who may have broken and sown his land with the greatest industry may see his crops rot in spite of his energy, simply and solely because of the lack of help to harvest them; there, in a case such as that, the co-operation of his fellows would be all in all to him. Indeed, with pooled labour, and a certain sum pooled by all the settlers with which to buy implements, it stands to reason that work could be done more cheaply, more expeditiously, and always at the proper season.

"It aer a grand proposition," declared Hank, when he had thoroughly considered the matter. "I kin see a big saving in more than one way, and one of 'em's this. Suppose there's twenty settlers in the combine. Wall, now, with ten ploughs and ten harrows and seeders you've tools to break the land. Supposing there warn't a combine; each man has his own tools. They ain't all in use together, so some of 'em's lying idle. That's gain number one, and don't you try to contradict me. And so you're goin' lumberin'?"

"We are that," assented Sam; "and seems to me you and Joe had better come along with us. You could put in a month or more, and then go along on prospecting."

It took our hero and his hunter companion but a little while to accept the invitation, the more so as Joe was already more or less one of the corporation Sam was forming.

"There's dollars in the scheme right through," Hank said, as they sat round the stove that evening. "Ef you'll have me as one of the band, I'll apply for my two hundred acres right off, paying for 'em, for I ain't able to take up more free land. Joe's in the same fix. But he aer got the dollars to pay. We'll come north with you and do a little lumbering. Afterwards he and I kin move on farther, for I've a proposition of my own to look into."

"But——" began Joe, who had been a listener for the most part up till now.

"Huh! He's agoin' to criticize the scheme and pour cold water on it," grinned Hank, swinging round on our hero. "Tell you, Sam, this here youngster aer had his eyes opened wide sense he came out, and he's turnin' into a business farmer. Wall, what are it?"

"This lumbering," began Joe diffidently, colouring at so much attention being attracted to him.

"Just you give 'em what you think and don't be afraid," cried Mrs. Fennick encouragingly. "The lad that could organize volunteers aboard ship has a right to speak. Sam, likely as not he'll show you and Hank that you've made a big error somewheres. Now, Joe."

"I was merely asking about the lumbering," said Joe. "I always gathered that lumberers were men who were more or less trained. They go out in gangs, don't they?"

"And so'll we," interrupted Sam, with eagerness. "But there ain't so many chaps out here that hasn't had a turn with the gangs some time. I've done a season; p'raps Hank has too."

"You bet," came from that individual. "I've done most things 'way out here, from gold diggin' to farming pure and simple. Huntin' aer my proper trade, but I ain't too proud to do anything. Even when I'm my own master I ain't above takin' on a job for someone else ef I've the time, and the money's good enough."

"Then there's two of us has done the work before," declared Sam. "Eight or nine of the boys I've fixed it with to join our corporation are already up in the woods, where we'll join 'em. They've a shack built this three months, and no doubt they've started in felling."

It appeared, indeed, as if the thoughtful Sam had made very complete arrangements, and there was little doubt but that Hank, as an old and experienced colonial, was delighted.

"It aer a fine proposition," he repeated for perhaps the twentieth time. "When other folks is buried in the snow, and only finding work with feeding the cattle and sichlike, we'll be cutting timber that'll bring dollars in the summer, and be back on our holdings time enough to plough and sow and make ready for harvest. Autumn will see us threshing, and by the time the grain is hauled down to the railway there'll be frosts. Then out we go again. Gee, Sam, this fair tickles me!"

A week later the little band of lumbermen was collected together, while Tom Egan, a sturdy settler some fifty years of age, had arrived from his own little shack across the valley and had taken up his residence at Sam's dwelling, where it was arranged that Mrs. Fennick should stay with Egan's wife and children.

"Yer see," explained Sam, "a lumber camp ain't no sorter place for a woman. It's rough living all the while. Men are packed together as close as sardines, and even then it's mighty cold. So the missus stays here with the Egans while we move on."

They slung their traps over their shoulders, and with snowshoes on their feet set out towards the north. The thaw of the past week had by now given way to severe frosts, while there had been a heavy fall of snow. However, none but a confirmed grumbler could have found fault with the conditions, for a bright sun flooded the landscape, shimmering on hillocks of snow, throwing long blue shadows athwart the hollows, and causing the millions of particles of ice to flash and scintillate. There was a dry, exhilarating crispness about the atmosphere that was typically Canadian, a bracing coldness that made the little band step out briskly, Hank at their head, Sam following; then Joe, and Jim and Claude, the two young friends he had made aboard the steamer, marching side by side. Dick Parsons, a lanky, bearded colonial, brought up the rear, a veritable grenadier in proportions.

They formed a merry party in their lean-to that night, and went on their journey on the following morning with undiminished vigour. Late the following day the crisp ring of axes coming to their ears through the tree trunks of the forest they had plunged into some hours before told them that the lumber camp was within easy distance. Shouts greeted them as they trailed into a narrow clearing, at the back of which stood a low-built shack half-buried in snow, and with its roof supporting a vast mass of that material. Smoke issued gently from a centrally-placed chimney, while the door was wide open. Hearty indeed was the greeting, then the hut swallowed the whole party.

"You've jest come along in time for tea," cried one of the lumbermen, a bearded giant even taller than Parsons. "Sit ye down right there and we'll give you a meal that'll show you how we've been living. Bill, you fish out that bear's meat you've a-stewing, while we others get the tea on the table."

The table, let us explain, was a mere apology for that article as civilized individuals understand the term, for your lumberman has no time to devote to the niceties of furniture construction. Joe indeed found himself marvelling at the crudeness of their work and yet at its obvious utility; for split stakes had been driven into the ground down the centre of the shack, and cross pieces nailed on top. More long split logs secured to these formed the top of a table some two feet wide. As for benches, they were fashioned in the same manner along either side, and were by now fully occupied. A huge enamelled-ware teapot was passing from hand to hand, while Bill, the cook to this expedition, was standing at one end of the table dealing out helpings of a savoury bear-meat stew that tickled the nostrils of everyone.

"What about sleeping?" asked Joe presently, when the meal was finished and the lumber gang had gathered round the open fire placed at one end of the table. "Is there another room?"

"Another!" exclaimed Harvey Bent, the chief of the party. "Young man, there ain't time fer buildin' luxuries when you're lumberin', and what's more, guess there ain't warmth enough. Time we turns in to-night there'll be jest about room fer the lot of us, and no more. The closer we are the warmer, and 'way out here, when the thermometer's down below zero, that means something to men who has to work."

Joe and his friends found that the sleeping accommodation was quaint in the extreme. Along one side of the shack a sloping platform had been built of the usual split logs, and piles of blankets lay upon it. Going to bed was a simple proceeding in this lumber camp; for men merely slipped off their boots and hats and wrapped themselves in a blanket. Then they lay down side by side, packed closely together, so closely, in fact, that to turn was an impossibility. But Joe and his young friends, who were novices like himself, discovered very soon that these old lumbermen were not without consideration. They allowed for the possibility of a change of position, and that very night, some time in the small hours, a hoarse command awakened them.

"Heave!" they heard, and promptly, more asleep than awake, the band of men rolled over on to the other side and once more settled into snores and slumber.

"It's a sight that'll do your eyes good," declared Hank, early on the following morning, when the gang had eaten. "You watch these fellers cutting down their timber. It ain't likely that you'll be wanted fer much to-day, and so we'll take a look at 'em and then see their mates. All of the gang ain't fellers. It stands to reason that someone's got to deal with the timber when it's down, and has to haul it out of the way to where the water kin deal with it. We're high up here, for we was climbing most of yesterday, and this here shack aer located jest at the top of a steep slope cutting sheer down to the lake that Sam mentioned. You come along with me; when we've had a look round we kin tackle a job with the others."

Donning their snowshoes and taking their rifles with them—for it was already agreed that Hank should hunt for the gang and procure them fresh meat—he and Joe went sliding off along the hillside, and presently, reaching a spot where the lumberman's axe had cleared the trees, were able to get a clear view of their surroundings. Down below them, two or more hundred feet perhaps, was a vast expanse of white, unbroken for the most part, though here and there there was a dark-coloured elevation denoting an island, the huge expanse being the frozen and snow-covered surface of the lake. Beyond there was forest, patched with snow, silent and forbidding. As for the steep slope at that part, it was scored with a hundred and more tracks.

"Where the logs slide down to the lake," said Hank. "Now we'll go along and see 'em at it. My, these trees are mighty big, and will saw into fine logs! Ef that railway comes up this way, as Sam believes, timber'll be wanted, and the work that's being done here will bring its own reward. Ah! there's axes! Jest you come and see how a Canadian lumberman tackles a forest giant, and can throw the tree jest wherever he wants."

Joe marvelled, indeed, at the skill and the energy of the lumbermen. Hearty, healthy fellows one and all, they went at their work as if they loved it. Cutting niches with their axes high up the stem of a giant, they drove wooden stakes into the crevices thus prepared, and soon had a platform built on this somewhat insecure foundation. Then came the ring of axes swiftly falling, a hoarse cry of warning, twice repeated, followed by a reverberating roar as the giant succumbed to human forces, crashing to the ground with a thud which shook the surroundings. Joe stood by as one of the biggest of the trees tumbled, and watched the lumbermen shredding the branches from the fallen timber. The naked trunk was then levered with crowbars, and with a final jerk was sent skidding and sliding down the hillside, to come to a halt at the bottom, perhaps on the frozen surface of the lake, or at any rate within a few feet of it.

"There's a couple of men working down there with a hoss," explained Hank. "They hitches on to the logs that don't reach the lake and drag 'em into position. Look away down. There's a hull crowd of timber waitin' for the end of winter."

"And then?" asked Joe, for he was ignorant for the most part of the work of lumbermen.

"Why, the ice breaks up," said Hank, "the logs gets carried into the lake, and the 'drivers' takes 'em in hand. A mighty hard and dangerous job theirs is, too. They has to be at it night and day, wet and fine. Each of 'em has a long pole with a spike at the end, and their particular work aer to send the logs down. Sometimes the stream carries 'em all right. Sometimes they gets hung up in corners and eddies, and the driver has to set 'em afloat agin. Then, down at the bottom of a lake same as this it ain't so seldom that logs and ice'll form a jam. One of the logs gets across the outlet, stuck up on a rock or two. Others piles up behind, with blocks of ice maybe, till there's ten foot high of logs and stuff, with a mass of water and ice and logs 'way behind. That aer a ticklish job to tackle, and many a driver has been killed or drowned. But they ain't never afraid, and there ain't much that they can't do. I've seed 'em hopping from floating log to log and steering a single trunk downstream, as ef they was aboard a canoe and not on top of a thing that'd roll over with the ordinary feller.

Now, we'll make right off out of hearing of the camp. Bill war telling me this morning that when that bear's meat aer done, there ain't nothing left but pork."

It was with the keenness of a schoolboy that Joe threw himself into the work at the lumber camp. That very evening he was told off with the hauling gang, and for a month and more assisted in dragging the felled timber to the edge of the lake; and never once did he find the hours drag or the work too heavy. As for the evenings, they were a delight to all; for your lumberman's camp is a veritable club. There, with the door shut and a hot fire burning, the men made a circle once their meal was finished. Pipes were filled, and clouds of smoke obscured the surroundings, dimming the rays from the single oil lantern hanging overhead. And what yarns those colonials could tell! Rugged, honest fellows, they spoke in a simple manly manner which was captivating. The boaster was not to be found amongst them; their tales were of deeds which had actually occurred, while the truth of their statements was apparent. As for chaff, they were never done with it. Harmless jokes and horse-play made the evenings jovial and merry. It was thus that our hero passed a portion of his first Canadian winter, revelling in the brisk atmosphere and in his work, boon companion to every member of the lumber gang. Then he and Hank bade farewell to their comrades and, shouldering their packs, set out for the north, for a country hardly ever explored, where danger and difficulty awaited them.

CHAPTER XIV

Moose Hunting

"I'm agoin ter tell you now what's brought me away up here through the backwoods of New Ontario," said Hank, the very evening he and Joe had left the lumber camp and their friends, amongst whom Sam Fennick was numbered. "I'm looking fer Beaver Jack."

"Beaver Jack! Who's he?" demanded our hero doubtfully.

"That's what I'm jest about to tell. Beaver Jack aer the cutest, quietest, cussedest Indian that ever you set eyes on, or that ever anyone else set eyes on either. He kin talk our language fairly well, and he war for three years or more along with me and my father. That's a time ago. Of late he's mooned about in the settlements during summer, not doing more'n a hand's turn, as is the nature of the Redskin. And winter's found him 'way up north, trappin' and huntin' fer the pelts that keeps him in food during the summer months. Beaver Jack and me's old friends, and with him to lead there's a chance of our striking a country I've heard of from mates of his. There ain't been much prospecting up in New Ontario, lad, but I've heard there's gold, and gold mines are worth finding."

So that was the secret of this expedition. Hank, a naturally silent man, had said little about his intentions up to date, and Joe had but a vague idea as to his real object. For himself, it had been sufficient that he was to travel through the Canadian wastes with such a pleasant fellow, and experience a life the very mention of which was most fascinating. It can be imagined, therefore, that he looked forward to the meeting with Beaver Jack with some anticipation, and hailed that taciturn Redskin heartily when, two weeks later, they came across him.

"You'd say as it aer fair wonderful that we should meet him right up here in the wilderness," smiled Hank, as he and Joe prepared for the night's bivouac. "But Jack aer a long-legged man, and, Injun-like, he turns his toes in. You could tell his mark in the snow amongst a thousand, and it ain't much altered even with snowshoes. See there—there's my marks, there's yourn, here's Beaver Jack's."

"With a longer distance between each one," agreed Joe. "And the back of each shoe seems to have been trailed along the snow as he went. There's a clean line every time. With you there's much the same, but the distance between the shoe marks is less, while mine are broken and the snow is irregularly marked in between."

"So as you could swear to any one of the three any day," said Hank. "Now, guess how it war that I steered a course so as to cross his tracks."

The question was one of greater difficulty, and Joe found himself unable to answer. However, the explanation was simple enough when it came to be given.

"It aer like this," smiled Hank. "Beaver Jack don't never come far into the settlements, and his line ain't never due north. Reckon he ain't fond of coming across other Injuns that way, nor the half-breeds that live up towards James Bay. So his line's always to the west. Ours being north, and cutting up through the country Beaver Jack crosses, why, in course we was bound to drop across his tracks. Had sport this season, Jack?"

The Indian turned slowly upon his questioner and straightened himself, for he had been bending over the narrow sledge upon which he was wont to haul his pelts when their number became too burdensome for carrying. The failing light of a midwinter day fell upon a scarred and seamed face that might have belonged to a man of sixty, of seventy, or even of eighty. The brows were drawn down over the eyes, the hooked nose approached closely to the thin, closely-shut lips, while even the chin, square and determined, and yet narrower than is customary with white men, appeared to turn up towards the centre of the face. But the eyes were the feature that attracted one. Small, and set wide apart, they flashed round at Hank and then at Joe. At one moment they looked severe, fierce, almost cruel; the next moment one could have sworn that they were twinkling. As for the remainder of this native trapper, he was clad in skin clothing of his own making. Fringed leggings covered his lanky lower limbs, while a shirt of leather, soft and wonderfully pliable and stained with much exposure, was over his shoulders, wide open at the neck, the sleeves reaching only down to his elbows. The man pointed slowly to his pile of pelts, and then, as if to speak would be to waste words, bent down over his sledge again and went on with the work that engaged his attention.

"He aer a rare 'un to talk," laughed Hank. "You get almost tired of hearin' his voice. But he kin hunt, and he aer the best man as ever I came across for calling up the moose. Know what that means, Joe?"

"Haven't an idea," answered our hero; for even now he was ignorant of the ways of hunters.

"Then we'll teach you, me and Jack," said Hank. "Jack, have you seen moose tracks hereabouts? If there's some of the beasts within twenty mile, you ain't likely to have missed them."

The mention of something to do with hunting brought the Indian to an erect position again with remarkable swiftness. He lifted an arm and pointed away to the west, to where the snow-clad landscape reared itself abruptly till, rising to a great height, it cut across the darkening sky in a succession of jagged peaks, upon which the rays of the fallen sun flickered, though the orb itself had long since disappeared from sight.

"Moose yard up there," he said abruptly; "plenty beast."

"Then to-morrow we'll see what we kin do with 'em," cried Hank. "We kin leave our traps 'way down here in this camp, and jest take our rifles with us. We ain't likely to be back before the night comes, and ef we're still out on the hills, why, in course we'll make a camp that'll keep us warm and right till the dawn comes. Now, lad, on with that kettle; it aer time almost for supper."

Joe's experience of moose hunting had not been so great up to this moment that he was not keen on a hunt. Once only, in fact, had he encountered this huge, fierce beast of the Canadian forests, and then the moose bull may be said to have hunted him. It was, therefore, with a certain amount of elation and excitement that he set off with his comrades on the following morning. Leaving their pelts behind in the lean-to—for Joe and Hank had trapped and shot many beasts during the last two weeks—and taking only rifles and ammunition and ready-cooked food with them—the three turned their faces towards the west, where the land reared itself up suddenly into a long chain of hills which might almost be described as mountains. Trudging along in front went Beaver Jack, as silent as ever, his face always to the front, never turning his head by so much as an inch, and yet seeing and remembering every feature of his surroundings. Joe noted the long swing of his lanky legs, the sliding stride with which he carried his snowshoes from one part to another, and the manner in which he kicked his shoes from time to time. Then came Hank, keen and energetic, his rifle across his shoulder, his shoes sinking hardly at all into the snow. However, Joe found walking on this occasion somewhat difficult, for the pace the Indian set was terrific, while a mild-tempered wind had softened the snow which clung to his shoes, making them ponderously heavy.

"Steady!" called Hank, after a while, arresting the rapid progress of the Indian. "This here pal of mine are puffin' and blowin'. Yer see, Joe, you ain't so used to snowshoein' as Jack and me, and when there's a thaw it aer heavy work. But jest you watch Beaver Jack. He gives a sorter kick every few steps, and so rids himself of the weight that you have to carry. We'll rest here a few minutes, and then you kin go in front and so set the pace."

An hour later they began to ascend a little, while within less than two hours the path they were making took them upward at a somewhat abrupt angle, which made the work extremely heavy. It was a relief to Joe, therefore, when Hank called another halt, and when Beaver Jack pointed away along the side of the mountain.

"We ain't likely to find moose much higher," said Hank, seating himself beside Joe; "not because it aer too cold for 'em high up, but because the stuff they feed on don't grow up there. Seems to me that we've a biggish wood in front of us, and we've got to make right through it before we shall come across their tracks. Even then there mayn't be any of the beasts, for ef they happen to have caught sight of us, or winded us, which aer far more likely, why, the hull crowd will have gone right off. You could shoot a charging moose, lad?"

"I'd try, anyway," answered Joe, mindful of his previous effort. "I think that by now I ought to be able to hold a gun straight, and if only I don't get too excited I ought to be able to hit a beast. I'm ready to move on if you are."

Once more they began their trudge across the sloping snowfield, Hank now leading, and presently he plunged into a forest clinging to the hillside. A wide space beyond was devoid of animal life, though Beaver Jack declared that moose had recently been across it. Then they dived into a narrow belt of trees, where the Indian came to a sudden halt.

"Try here," he said. "Not sure, but think beasts near; and if we go on, sure to hear us. Wait little—soon ready."

"Watch him," whispered Hank; "you'll see him set to work as only an Indian can. He's looking about for a birch tree, and with that knife of his will strip the bark in a matter of a few minutes. I kin tell you this, give a Redskin a knife and firelock and powder, and he kin go anywhere and make most anything in these forests. Birch bark aer the stuff he puts to roof his lean-to. A long strip cut from an extry big tree, and shaped and sewn, makes him a canoe that's better than any other craft known on any water; while, ef it's pots and kettles that's wanted fer cookin', he can fix the business easy with his knife, and so long as there's a tree of the right sort about. See him cut that roll free. Now, in a jiffy he'll have a trumpet."

Beaver Jack went about his work in a manner which showed that he was accustomed to it, and came back towards his comrades bearing a long strip of bark which he was slowly coaxing into the shape of a funnel. Then with his knife and a few strips of hide cut from the fringes of his leggings he tied the edges of the bark, so that the implement he had fashioned retained its shape. A little later he bent his lanky form, applied the smaller end of the funnel to his mouth, and blew heavily into it. The lines across forehead and face became even deeper. To look at the Indian one would have declared that he was in agony, and no doubt he was making a special effort. The result was truly wonderful. Joe had heard moose calling before, the sounds they made echoing through the forest. And here the calls were repeated, more loudly, it is true, since they were meant to pass to a distance, but wonderfully realistic and lifelike.

"Now listen," said Hank, in a whisper. "Ef there's a moose bull within two mile of this he'll answer."

The long, deep-toned call produced by Beaver Jack with the aid of his birch-bark trumpet was answered by a deadly silence that nothing broke, and though the call was repeated, it appeared as if the result was to be similar. But suddenly the Indian stirred, while Joe saw Hank's eyes concentrate themselves upon the forest. Then, far off, there came a dismal echo of the sound, as if the hillside were casting it back at the hunters. At once, without so much as a word, the Redskin slunk off into the forest, Hank and Joe following closely.

"You kin look for a burst of speed," whispered Hank hurriedly, turning his head. "There's a moose bull 'way ahead, and Beaver Jack aer going nearer so as to coax him. Jest make sure as you don't knock that rifle against the trees, or else there won't be much huntin'."

Silent after that, with hardly a glance to left or to right, the three pushed on through the wood, Beaver Jack choosing, as if by instinct, a path that avoided thick underwood, and allowed himself and his comrades to retain their snowshoes. Slowly the trees diminished in number, till they straggled out into the open in broken groups of two and three, and finally singly, scattered here and there over a wide field of snow that seemed to be unbroken and unmarked by beasts of any description. To the left the hills reared their heads abruptly, snow-covered to the summits, grey and forbidding, as if they resented the coming of these strangers. Ah! The Redskin had lifted a hand; he came to a halt.

"He aer going to call agin," whispered Hank, who seemed to be tingling with excitement. "Ain't that 'ere Beaver Jack clever?"

None but an expert could, in fact, have produced the impression this seamed and lined Indian contrived at. That long, deep-toned call, rising and falling in cadence and halting abruptly, as if only half-completed, went booming across the snowy waste, and echoed amongst the pinnacles above. It was followed by a second call, the tone of which was distinctly angry, as if the beast summoning its own kind were vexed at the want of an answer. Then, as the same faint response came to their ears—but this time distinctly nearer—a plaintive note crept into the summons which Beaver Jack produced with the aid of his trumpet, till one would have said that even the most heartless of listeners would have dashed forward promptly. But your moose is perhaps one of the wariest of beasts. Gifted with acute hearing and still more pronounced sense of smell, he is almost always suspicious. The least doubt as to the genuineness of a call, the faintest suspicion of the presence of others, will keep him sulking in the background, hidden by the trees, or will send him dashing off madly, his huge antlers steered with wonderful skill between the branches, so that not so much as a sound might help a would-be pursuer. It seemed as if the one in the far distance were of this character, as if he were suspicious. It made no difference to his movements even when Beaver Jack, working himself almost into a frenzy with his efforts, produced more mournful sounds, and then struck the tree trunk beside him heavily. Still the answering response was weak-toned and far off.

"He ain't coming, that's truth," whispered Hank. "We shall have to get along towards him, and this time we shall have to creep over every yard. Ef the brute does come, you shoot, Joe. I've had many a chance; so's Jack. Take him jest below the point of the shoulder."

Joe gripped his rifle with both hands, and saw that the safety catch was in position; then he fixed his eyes on his two companions. Nor was it long before there was a movement. Beaver Jack bent double and, thrusting the muzzle of his weird birch trumpet into the snow, sent forth a challenge which seemed to skim curiously over the hillside and burst into bigger volume in the distance. Then he dropped on to hands and knees, having already kicked off his snowshoes and slung them over his shoulders. A second later he was creeping away amidst the scattered trees, casting more than one glance over his shoulder.

"This aer a fair conundrum," whispered Hank to Joe, when the little party again came to a standstill. "I've hunted moose many a time, and, as a rule, ef there ain't no wind, as is the case jest now, and a hunter aer cautious, there ain't no great difficulty in coming up with them. Of course it isn't every Indian who can call, let alone a white man. A Redskin is kinder born to it, and most of 'em can call same as ef they was real moose. Guess Beaver Jack aer one of 'em. But look what's happenin' to-day. There's no getting nearer the beast that's answered. He's heard our call and has challenged back, but he goes off a bit every time we move forward."

"Perhaps there's something else disturbing him," ventured Joe, somewhat baffled for an answer, cautiously raising his lips to Hank's ear. "I notice that Beaver Jack has looked over his shoulder once or twice as if he thought there might be something behind us. Perhaps he's heard a call from that direction."

"Nary a one. Ef there had been I'd have heard it," asserted Hank, with decision; "but there may be beasts following. Ef it warn't fer the snow you could hear 'em by listening closely with an ear to the ground or placed hard up agin the trunk of one of the trees. But snow muffles most sounds, especially footsteps. Ah! That 'ere beast called from a point a little closer."

Whatever the cause of their want of success, Beaver Jack and Hank were not the men to give up the chase without a further effort, and without some show of that wonderful patience for which hunters are notorious. Time and again the Redskin repeated his call, and on a dozen occasions the trio went forward, crawling over the snow on their stomachs. At length, when Joe's small stock of patience was almost exhausted, the answering call came from a point distinctly nearer.

"That 'ere bull aer fair bothered," observed Hank, as Beaver Jack again buried the muzzle of his trumpet. "He aer been retreating all this while, and now it seems to me as ef he'd made up his mind that things was square, and had come towards us at a gallop. Ef he charges, don't wait too long. Give him a shot, and then ram in a cartridge."

It was perhaps some ten minutes later that the undergrowth clambering about the stems of a thick clump of evergreen pines three hundred yards from the hunters was suddenly rent asunder, and there emerged into the open two gigantic animals, the moose bull ahead and his consort behind him. As for the former, Joe could even at that distance see that his short mane was bristling, while his head was thrown upward, his antlers being carried high in the air, while one fore leg was poised, as if he were in the very act of galloping forward.

"Hah!" Joe heard Hank grunt. "That aer the meaning of the mystery. That 'ere bull has gone on retreating till he felt as ef he were bound to go no farther, as ef, in fact, he'd be a coward ef he didn't turn and face the danger. You kin look out for trouble."

Click! went the safety catch of Joe's rifle. He swung it into position and, taking careful aim, pulled the trigger. Almost at once there came a snorting grunt from the moose bull. The beast threw his fore legs into the air and stood there poised for the instant. A second later he had launched himself against the little group of hunters, and came charging towards them at a speed which was terrific.

"Agin!" cried Hank, his eyes gleaming, while his fingers closed round his own weapon. Up went our hero's gun again, and once more his eye ranged along the sights. But he never pulled the trigger, for, of a sudden, there came a loud report from behind him, while something struck the snow three yards in rear and ricochetting from the surface went humming and screaming over his head. Then came a second shot, falling almost on the self-same spot, while the powdered snow driven upward by the bullet swept against his face in a thick cloud which almost blinded him. Sweeping the crystals away with one hand, he

147

stared across the open, while Hank's sharp tones roused him from the form of stupor into which he had fallen.

"Git loaded," he commanded shortly, "and soon as you've given 'em a shot, run back where that 'ere moose has bolted. Reckon there's a pack of half-breeds after us."

The sharp snap of his weapon was heard instantly, and was followed by a shot from Beaver Jack's rifle. Then Joe, wrestling with the excitement into which this sudden interference had thrown him, levelled his own weapon at the foremost of two dog sleighs dashing across the open towards them, and steadily pulled the trigger.

"On snowshoes," cried Hank sharply. "Now, Beaver Jack, you kin take post behind us. You're the best when it comes to huntin', but when there's a ruction same as this is, guess Hank ain't in need of no coaching. Joe, you come second. Ef they gets much closer, you've to keep a tree between you and them most of the time, and ef they looks like heading us, why, in course we shall have to look lively to find a suitable place to hold, and must get to and fight 'em."

He turned without further warning, and with his rifle trailed in one hand dashed across the snow towards the thick clump of evergreens from which the bull moose had so lately put in an appearance. As for the beast and his consort, both had turned at the sound of that far-off shot and had dashed away at a pace which took them out of sight within a minute. It was but a few seconds later when the same evergreens closed about the figures of our hero and his comrades.

"We've got to search for thick forest all the while," called Hank softly over his shoulder. "Then those dog sleighs won't be able to make much pace, and so won't easily come up to us. Gee, this aer a do! I reckoned all the while as there was something queer happenin', something that that bull moose kinder scented and yet warn't sure of. This aer a fair business."

The sudden change in the fortunes of the little party was indeed extraordinary and inexplicable. Had either of the three been asked the question that morning, they would have declared that to the best of their belief there was not another living human being within a radius of perhaps a hundred miles. Yet see what had happened. Ever since an early hour that morning two sleighs, drawn by dogs, had been following their tracks up to the hills and along the elevated ground they had taken. Figures wrapped in skin garments much the same as Beaver Jack wore had trudged beside the sleighs, whirling their whips now and again above the heads of the teams they were driving. Then, coming to that open space across which the chase had taken our hero and his friends, these strangers had leaped on to their sleighs and had come across the frozen surface at a rattling pace that brought them within long rifle shot of the hunters as Joe was in the very act of achieving a triumph. When the latter turned, having narrowly escaped two bullets, it was to perceive the two sleighs being driven rapidly forward, one some ten feet in advance of the other. Instantly his eyes were attracted to the former; for in front sat a huddled figure, above whose head a long-lashed whip swirled and cracked, while behind there stood a burly man balancing himself wonderfully, and with rifle at his shoulder.

Who could he be? What was the cause of this sudden and unprovoked attack? From whence had come these men who had sprung upon the scene so unexpectedly? No wonder that Hank was troubled. Beaver Jack's seamed and heavily-lined face displayed not the smallest surprise or vexation; but Joe's features were a study. There was anger on his face; his lips were firmly pressed together. His bull-dog chin was, if anything, a little squarer than usual.

"Gee!" he cried. "Well, I'm jiggered."

CHAPTER XV

Pursued by Unknown Enemies

For the better part of an hour Hank led his two comrades across the snow-clad side of the hill, guiding them between the trees of the patch of forest land which they had now entered, and keeping always to the west. Then, without show of hesitation, he plunged into a wide-open strip across which could be traced, even at a distance, the tracks left by the two moose they had so recently accosted. Nor did he slacken his pace till a second belt of forest land appeared, and the trio had once more dived into cover.

"You kin sit down and rest awhile and get yer breath," he said shortly. "Me and Beaver Jack'll watch to see what's happenin' to them varmint. Gee! I'd give a pile of dollars to know who they are and for why they've taken it into their ugly heads to follow and attack us. You ain't got no notion, Jack?"

The Indian, who had already thrown himself down beneath an evergreen with his face turned in the direction in which they had been coming, merely grunted. It seemed almost as if he considered an answer superfluous. Then, as Hank repeated his question somewhat peremptorily, the Redskin swung over on to his right side and looked back at the hunter.

"Not sure," he said. "Bad men, anyway; half-breeds, p'raps. But want to kill us; maybe they think there is money."

"Then they're jest makin' an almighty error," grinned Hank, who seemed to be amused at the idea, and who, in any case, desperate though the position might be, seemed in no way put out or bereft of his usual cheeriness and assurance. "They're jest making a tarnation error ef money's what they're after, for Joe and I ain't got much more than the price of a tin of 'bacca between us. We've sunk it in land, Jack, land as thieves like them can't grab. But half-breeds they are, I'd guess; though why they should follow us beats me hollow. P'raps they're discharged servants of the Hudson Bay Company, and, happenin' to fall across our tracks, thought to knock us over the heads and clear all that we've got. There's two sides to that sort of business. I ain't never allowed people to give me knocks without rousin' trouble, and guess them 'ere varmint is in fer a little now. Joe, ha' you got any sort o' notion who they could be?"

Was it likely that our hero could have even an idea? After all, his experience of Canada was decidedly limited. It is true that the months he had spent with Peter

Strike had taught him a great deal, while his stay in the lumber camp, and the unending yarns of the men when gathered of an evening round the fire, had furnished him with many a little incident telling of the life of the settlers and also of old colonists. Indeed, there were men there who had passed to the north as far as Hudson Bay, and who, when pressed, had spoken of the long, dark winters, of the sparse population, of the half-breeds to be found at and about the forts erected by the all-dominating Hudson Bay Company. But search his memory as he might, there was nothing in those yarns to give him an inkling as to who these marauders could be; in fact, he had gathered that life was peculiarly secure even in the out-of-the-way parts of the Dominion. Why, therefore, should he and his two comrades have been so suddenly and unexpectedly attacked?

"Beats me, Hank," he exclaimed, shaking his head. "I got wondering once whether it could be Hurley, who somehow got to learn that you and I were off for a prospecting tour. But is it likely?"

The little hunter stuffed the bowl of his thin pipe with one firm finger tip, while he stared away across the open along the tracks which he and his comrades had made. It was clear that his eyes were hardly observing his surroundings. He was thinking deeply, and his coon-skin cap, though it was pulled low down on to his forehead, failed to hide the deep wrinkles which had suddenly appeared, and which even ran down over his brows to the corners of the eyes. He struck a match—for that was one of the luxuries of civilization which he clung to in the backwoods, though Beaver Jack was above such trivial help—and slowly lit the weed.

"I never thought o' that," he said at last; "but it ain't likely. You've got to bear in mind that Hurley ha got a rope round his neck every day of the week and every hour of his life. He aer likely to be informed against every time he sets his ugly nose near the settlements; and sense you may say as he's always in danger of being taken, it stands to reason that he ain't going to risk his neck jest for the sake of gettin' quits with two of the chaps who helped to chase him. No, it ain't reasonable. Seems to me as it aer likely that what Beaver Jack says aer right. Them 'ere skunks is half-breeds out ter rob. They've perhaps been huntin'. P'raps they belong to some station north of this, and has been sent along to get stores or to take a message, though as a general rule there ain't much of that sorter work done in the winter. Anyways, they dropped on our trace and, seein' as there was three of us, made up their minds to wipe us out. But ef they ain't mighty careful they'll come up agin bad trouble afore they're much older."

That was the utmost that one could say of this mystery. After all, what difference did it make who these strangers might be? It could not help Joe and his friends to be sure of their names, not in the slightest. But still Joe puzzled. Could it be Hurley?

"Nonsense!" he told himself. "Hank must be right. The man would never risk his neck just on the offchance of killing a couple of the men who helped to arrest him. All the same, I wish he'd never escaped, and in any case, I am awfully sorry about that envelope he took from me. I've bothered about it a whole heap; for though I feel sure that the contents were of no actual monetary value, yet there was some message of great importance which Father wished me to have once I had made some sort of a place in the world. What could it have been?"

What, indeed? Of what use to worry, seeing that Hurley had relieved our hero of the missive, and then, when that rascal had been captured, though his dollar bills were forthcoming, there was no trace of the letter? It was gone. Perhaps even Hurley was already captured, while the men following at that moment, and still out of sight, had undoubtedly no connection with the outlaw who had so nearly ended Joe's attempts at settling in this vast dominion.

"Guess they've been bothered by the trees, and has had to climb out of the sledges and walk quiet," chuckled Hank, when a quarter of an hour had passed without a sight of the enemy. "Now see here, mates, our game aer as clear as daylight. With this here snow all around we can't hope to smother our tracks and get clear off. Ef it war springtime, or summer, a babe could do it. There's fifty ways more or less. We could climb a tree, sneak along from branch to branch in a wood same as this and then drop into a river, takin' care to land somewhere whar there was rock. In course, ef it snowed jest now that'd help us. But then it ain't goin' to snow. There's nary a cloud in the sky, so it simply comes to holding them off as long as we're able, and this here aer jest the spot to work it. Guess me and Joe'll have a bite while Jack watches. When we've done, he can have a turn."

It was an excellent proposal on the hunter's part, and Joe seized upon the opportunity, for the brisk air and the excitement of the day had given him a keen appetite, and our hero had become somewhat notorious for that since he came to this glorious country. He and Hank sat down, therefore, and, pulling some of their ready-cooked food from their pack bags, made a hearty meal. Then Beaver Jack was relieved, while Joe took his place.

"Jest keep yer eyes skinned, and follow every inch of the line of the wood 'way across the open," said Hank. "I'm goin' to take a look round on either hand and in front. It wouldn't do to sit tight here waitin' and waitin', and have them skunks round us up and come along towards us from the opposite direction.

You kin never say what sort o' tricks a half-breed will be up to, so jest look lively."

He went off through the trees for all the world as if he were a ghost, his snowshoes making not so much as a sound. Joe lay flat on his face in the snow, taking the same position that Beaver Jack had selected. Placing his rifle a little to one side and somewhat in front, he stared steadily across the open, watching the edge of the wood from which they had themselves lately emerged, and then gazing to right and to left. But not yet could he detect the presence of the enemy, and since they were not there, he fell again to wondering who they were, from whence they had come, and for what purpose they had attacked a party of hunters who could by no possibility have done them harm, and who, in any case, could not be the possessors of great wealth. As to his own feelings on the question of personal danger, he had not so much as a qualm. Perhaps, if he had been warned that an attack was to be made, he would have been thrown into that curious condition which is neither caused by fear nor by anxiety, but merely by that natural agitation of spirit which comes to the average man when danger threatens. But here Joe had been, as it were, suddenly pitchforked into the midst of turmoil. At one moment he had been facing a charging moose, a situation requiring nerve, and the next he had found himself the object of bullets sent by an enemy from behind. Ah, there they were! The irregular line of the forest was of a sudden broken; Joe had been gazing in that direction but a second earlier and had seen nothing. Now, when his eyes swung once more to that quarter, two sleighs stood out prominently, their dog teams sprawling out ahead of them. The dark figures of five men moved about the sleighs, and it was clear from their movements that they had been marching through the forest, and were now about to mount their vehicles again.

"Slipping off their snowshoes and getting ready for a burst of speed across the open," said Joe to himself. "That'll be the time to read 'em a lesson, and seems to me they deserve one."

He turned his head for a moment and beckoned to Beaver Jack; then, picking up his rifle, he laid the sights on one of the sledges and waited for a forward move on the part of the enemy. Nor could it be said that our hero had the smallest doubt as to what his action should be, or the slightest compunction at the thought of firing on these strangers.

"It's they or us," he told himself, "and they have a bigger party. Ah! what's that? More of them!"

No wonder he gave vent to a cry of amazement, for a hurried inspection of the party aboard the pursuing sleighs had given him the impression at the beginning of this strange encounter that there were only four or more in the party. Now he knew that the sleighs bore five. But just as that number had embarked, he was thunderstruck to see four more dark figures issue from the irregular line of the forest and move out on to the open snow. At the same instant there was a slight noise beside him, so, turning his head, he found Hank had returned and had taken up a position. He lay full length, his rifle to his hand, his eyes glued on the enemy.

"The tarnation skunks!" Joe heard him growl. "I ain't surprised to see more of 'em. That jest explains why they've been so slow in following. The sleigh party went ahead, hoping to drive right up to us and finish the business. T'others followed afoot, and when the fust lot was disappointed, why, they halted for a while so as they could all come along together. This aer mighty awkward. Yer see, ef they breaks up into several lots, we can't hope to keep 'em back. There's enough hollows and trees out there in the open to give 'em shelter, and in course of time they're bound to close in on us. This aer a tarnation fix."

There was little doubt, in fact, that Joe and his comrades were face to face with a dangerous dilemma. For, as Hank was not slow to point out, if merely the two sleigh parties attempted a dash across the open, he and Joe and Jack might very well hope to pick some of the enemy off, and even to force them to retreat; but with four others added, and they on snowshoes, it would be next door to impossible to hold them at a distance.

"It aer come to a council," said Hank, scratching his head. "To me it seems likely enough that them cusses aboard the sleighs'll try a dash. Wall, that won't help 'em overmuch, for in a jiffy we'll teach 'em something worth learnin'. What bothers me is to say how we should work ef they makes across, taking advantage of every bit of cover. Where are we to go? We can't keep runnin' away for ever. 'Sides, I ain't so sure as I'm ready to show my heels to skunks same as these."

There was a resentful, threatening note in his words, and, glancing at the little hunter, Joe saw that his face was flushed, while his little eyes were flashing dangerously. After all, in spite of his somewhat diminutive proportions, there was quite a lot of the bull dog about Hank. Those who knew the hunter knew him to be a cunning and courageous tracker, a man to be depended on, a friend worth having, an enemy more than difficult to make—for Hank hated quarrels, and was for ever ready to forgive and forget—and yet an enemy to be duly feared and placated. Those who had been so unfortunate never to have had the opportunity of meeting this remarkable little man, save on one occasion, were none the less impressed. Hank's was a personality that bred confidence. Strength of character, honesty of purpose, bull-dog determination were written plainly on his face, even while it was wreathed with the most cordial smiles.

Joe had felt the very same about his friend. Hank had impressed him from the first. Sometimes he imagined that long acquaintance had disclosed all the hunter's points, good and bad, to him. But even now he had something to learn. He had never seen his friend in a similar position to this; he had never known him when he was the object of an unprovoked attack, and when the odds were opposed to him. But seeing his firm face now, the strong determination on every feature, his own chin took on something of the same aspect. Looking at the two as they lay side by side, one would have said at once that while the elder man could be relied on whatever the position, his youthful comrade was not one whit behind him.

"Wall?" came from Hank dryly, while the lock of his rifle clicked. "Ain't you goin' to speak?"

Joe looked sharply across at him. "Eh?" he asked. "I thought you were speaking to Beaver Jack and asking his opinion."

"And mighty nice of you, lad," came the answer. "I like to see a young chap as keeps his mouth shut till his elders has spoken. But there ain't too much time before us, and 'sides, I know that Jack would ha spoken already ef he had anything to say. What's your idea? You've reckoned the position. You ain't ready to go on runnin' away from a set o' skunks same as them, aer you?"

"No!" came emphatically from our hero. "Partly because I couldn't. I'd soon be done, for this snowshoeing is heavy work to one who is not hardened. Then I don't see why I should. Who are they that we should run from them? Let 'em prove that they are stronger."

"Gee! You'll do!" cried Hank. "That's the sort of spirit. Wall, now, you've some sort of idea?"

"None." Joe was bound to confess it. "But," he went on, "it seems to me that we ought to look out for some place which we can hold. Of course it could only be for a short while, as we have no large supply of food; but it would bring this business to a head. Perhaps these fellows would make an attack and give us a chance of beating them. If not, why—well something might turn up to help, and in any case it would be better than this constant running."

"And I'm with you," cried Hank; "only jest now there's not so much as the sight of a place where we could hold 'em, and till one turns up, why, in course, it's run we must. But we'll keep a bright lookout. See here, and jest you listen, Beaver Jack. We'll give them fellers a dusting ef they try to cross, and then we'll trail arms and slink off through the forest. Something'll turn up soon to help us."

It was perhaps two minutes later that there was a general move on the part of the enemy. The leading man aboard each sleigh was seen to stand, gripping the reins in one hand while he swung a short-handled whip with the other, one which boasted of an enormously long and heavy lash that even a moderately skilful operator could cause to crack with the sound of a rifle report.

"Ay, and more'n that," Hank had observed on one occasion. "I've known men who could swing a whip so as to cut in two anything that was anywheres within reach. One half-breed from 'way up north could stand on his head even and cut slick through a chunk of bread, while there ain't one of them that's used to the whip and has dogs to drive that couldn't set a pal up afore him with a cigarette in his mouth and jest flick the cigarette away as easy and as sartin as winkin'. Then, too, the cut of a heavy lash same as they use is that keen, they say some of 'em could nearly divide a dog with it, ay, cut him in two, while they'd easy whip a chunk out o' the poor beasts. Cruel! In course them whips is cruel, and so's the men. But then you ain't dealing with ordinary dogs; them critters is fierce, and ef they was hungry ain't above tearing a human to pieces."

But this was not the moment for discussing the pros and cons of dog whips, nor the prowess of the men who wield them; for the enemy were on the move. It seemed almost as if they had made up their minds to ignore all thoughts of danger; or perhaps they imagined that Hank had led his two comrades steadily forward, and was not lying beneath the trees beyond the open space waiting with loaded rifles for them. In any case, the drivers sent their whips cracking over their teams, while the dogs responded by leaping into their harness and speeding away from the irregular line of the forest. At the same moment the four men on foot, who were shod with snowshoes, shot out from the cover and, dividing till a wide interval separated each man, came speeding across the snow.

"Beaver Jack takes 'em to right," said Hank steadily, not a waver in his voice. "I take the critters in the centre; Joe pays partic'lar attention to the varmint on the left. Fire as you get 'em in line with your sights."

A spurt of flame issued from his own muzzle a second or so later, Joe peering out across the snow to see what effect the bullet had; and once more he was witness of the effect of a missile striking a glancing blow on the snowfield. A cloud of white particles suddenly leaped up in front of the foremost sleigh, hiding the men aboard it, while a shout came from the enemy.

"Missed 'em by a pip," observed Hank, ramming in a fresh cartridge. "You, Joe."

Our hero lined his sights on the second sleigh, followed the moving object for a moment, then pressed his trigger; and all the while as he aimed he was wondering at his own coolness. He might indeed have been firing at inanimate objects. The idea that he was aiming at living men hardly seemed to trouble him in the slightest, while if he had any qualms at the thought that his bullet might slay a fellow being, he never showed them.

"It's they or us," he repeated for the tenth time at least. "They've made an unprovoked attack, and must put up with the consequences."

Bang! His own weapon spat forth a bullet, while a cloud of white smoke belched from the muzzle, to die away at once. All eyes went toward the sleigh he had aimed at, and once again the tell-tale spray of snow showed exactly where the missile had landed, and precisely by how much it had missed the enemy.

"Not bad shootin'," said Hank. "Them sleighs is moving fast, and you want to give 'em at least a yard ahead when you're aiming. Beaver Jack, jest you see what you're made of."

There came a grunt from the Redskin. Joe watched the seamed and lined and strangely-impassive face of the Indian go down towards the butt of his rifle. He saw the hooked nose settle itself against the wood of the stock, while one of the keen eyes seemed to become rather more prominent. There came a sharp report, and almost at once an answering scream from the distance.

"Good fer you!" cried Hank. "Guess you got the man aboard the leading sleigh, and in falling backward he aer pulled the team in. Jest sit tight while I give 'em another, and you follow quick with your bullet, Joe lad."

In rapid succession the two shots were fired, and it seemed more than probable that they had hit their mark, for the men aboard the leading sleigh were thrown in great confusion. One was seen to stand and grip at the reins which his wounded comrade had allowed to fall. Then the team of dogs was headed round, the whip cracked, and in a trice the sleigh was being steered for the forest. Meanwhile a shot from Beaver Jack had caused one of the men gliding across the snow afoot to dodge suddenly to one side, and that, with the evidence the enemy now had that Hank and his friends had them under their rifles, sent the remainder of the band retracing their steps at a pace which was furious. Shouts escaped from them as they raced for cover, and in little more than a minute all had disappeared from view.

"That aer lesson number one," said Hank grimly, as he slid a fresh cartridge into position. "Ef them 'ere critters thought they was going to slit our throats without our kicking up a rumpus, why, they've found out the error. It'll make 'em a trifle more cautious now that one of 'em's gone under, and they kin see that we are able to shoot; but it won't turn 'em, I'm thinkin'. A half-breed ain't easily frightened, and ef it's gain they are after, why, this'll make 'em all the keener."

"What will they do, then?" asked Joe, who still lay on his face, his eyes glued on the distant forest. "It seems to me that if we can only stay here and hold them, they cannot get nearer. Of course, when night comes we shall be unable to see them, and nothing will prevent their getting closer."

"Guess that aer solid truth," agreed Hank. "But there's more besides. I've been takin' a good look round, and I've kinder put myself in the place of them critters. Wall, now, it aer clear that we can't climb over the ridge to our left. It rises quickly, and the snow lies in deep drifts; so we've got to go dead straight ahead or cut away down to the valley we left this morning. That being so, ef they believe we mean to lie here and hold 'em from crossing the open, they'll leave a man just to show himself every now and then, while the rest of the party strikes downhill and gets abreast of us. Then they'll come climbing up, and ef we stays they'll have us hard up agin the hill before we know what's happened. Leastwise, that's what I should do ef I was their leader."

"So you advise that we move on at once?" asked Joe, rising to his feet. "Perhaps farther along we shall come upon some place which would offer good shelter, some sort of natural fort in which we could take cover. I've an idea that——"

He came to a sudden stop and pointed out across the snow-covered ground before them.

"One of them critters," growled Hank. "Seems as ef I might be right. He's showing clear, and—yes, there ain't a doubt about it. He's got one arm hung in a sling."

There came an instant response from Beaver Jack, a deep-toned grunt. His keen eyes had evidently taken in all that was passing. "Same man as sit on the sleigh and tumble backwards," he grunted. "Not badly hurt. Bullet make hole through the arm, and that nothing."

"Only it jest makes him useless for the moment. See here," said Hank, "I'll move into the open and give him a shot. Likely as not he'll signal to his comrades."

On second thoughts the little hunter refrained from using his rifle. "I might hit him," he said, "and that ain't what I want. I'll jest let him get a squint at me, so as to make him feel sartin we're remaining here; then I'll hop back till he shows agin. Ah! Ain't that given him pleasure? He's gone into cover, but ef you look close you kin see him just inside the line o' trees wavin'. Gee! Don't they take us fer soft 'uns? As ef a baby wouldn't guess what was up."

There was no doubt now that the enemy, whoever they might be, had taken the course which Hank guessed at. Their design was clear and apparent, for the wounded man made repeated appearances during the next ten minutes, diving into the trees again on each occasion.

"You was sayin' that you had an idea," said Hank at length, stretching himself beside our hero. "What aer that idea?"

"I was thinking of the sort of place that would suit us," began Joe. "It occurred to me that there must be many little hollows which might serve our purpose, provided that they could not be overlooked; for it wouldn't do for these beggars to climb higher and pitch their bullets down upon us."

"That aer sense," agreed Hank. "Wall?"

"But——"

"There aer always a but," asserted the little hunter. "It aer there that gumption always comes in. Nothing goes right and straight in this world unless you help it. A man has to use his wits and his strength most always. What aer this but?"

"Just this," said Joe. "What's the use of a fort—a natural fort I'm meaning, though the same thing applies of course to one built by human hands—what's the use of such a place if you can't live in it?"

"Eh?" Hank pushed back his coon-skin cap and scratched his head. This argument was getting somewhat beyond him. He was a cute and cunning little fellow, stuffed full of worldly experience and of forest lore, but subtle argument was beyond him. "See here, Joe," he cried, somewhat testily; "plain words are wanted jest now. What's the meaning of this here fort that you've mentioned? Are you propounding a sorter puzzle?"

That set Joe grinning for the moment; but almost at once he became serious. "I'm in dead earnest, Hank," he said. "But this is what I'm driving at. We've no grub to speak of."

"Precious little."

"And no pots nor pans."

"I'm a-getting through with the argiment," declared the hunter.

"And it's likely to be mighty cold when we're cooped up in some hollow and unable to move about as we are now doing. In fact, blankets are wanted."

"All that aer sense," said Hank, jamming his hat back into place and staring closely at our hero. "Wall?"

"Well, my idea is this. Since we can't climb away to the left, as the ground rises so steeply, and as we can make the pace hot if we happen to be going downhill, why not strike in that direction at once, sweep to the right, and make back for our camp? That'll give us food and pots and pans and blankets. We'll be better able then to look about us for some sort of place that will give us cover. Tell you straight, Hank, I'm getting more worried at the thought that the supper'll be small to-night than I am at the knowledge that those rascals are after us."

Hank grinned widely; his queer little lips, usually pursed close together, parted in a capacious smile which he only indulged in on occasion. A deep-throated grunt came from him, and almost at once his rifle leapt across his shoulder.

"That aer solid sense," he cried at length. "Guess we'll make slick back to our camp, and then, when we've collected our traps and had a feed, why, we kin give some sort of attention to this other business. I'll step out agin so as to allow the critter yonder to see me. Then we'll face downhill, wait till the enemy ha' crossed in front, and go away over their tracks straight back to the spot where our traps are lying."

It was not by any means certain, of course, that this plan of procedure would improve their lot and aid them in escaping from the half-breeds who had so unwarrantably attacked them; but at least, if they were successful in reaching their camp, it would provide them with a hearty meal, and that was something.

"A full stummick makes a man look differently at troubles," observed Hank, as he slipped on his snowshoes. "Difficulties seem to slide away as soon as you've a good supper tucked behind your waistcoat. Joe, we'll reach the camp even ef there's a hundred critters between us and the place. Jest sling yer rifle, and don't forget, ef you hear a sound or see one of the varmint, jest drop as ef you was dead. Silence and cunning will help us heaps more'n bullets."

With rifles slung, and Hank in advance, the trio once more set themselves in motion. The little hunter went straight on into the wood till he was sure that none outside could see them, then he turned his face downhill, and, setting an easy pace, led his comrades towards the valley.

CHAPTER XVI

Choosing a Fortress

Barely ten minutes had passed from the moment when Hank led the way downhill, from the spot where he and his comrades had taken up their position and had repulsed the enemy, till the little hunter suddenly lifted an arm, bringing the party to an abrupt halt. Then he signalled to Beaver Jack, and with the lean, lanky figure of the Redskin beside him, stood listening intently. A second later all three were lying flat on their faces.

"You kin hear folks moving somewhars about," whispered the little hunter in Joe's ear, "but where they aer is more'n I kin say at the moment. Yer see, the snow makes things mighty difficult, while the tree trunks break up every sound and scatter it in all directions. But them critters is moving near. Seems likely they ha' halted for a while."

Tense silence fell upon the three, while each one huddled his body deeper into the snow, edging behind the largest tree and doing his utmost to make himself invisible. Hank, indeed, burrowed beneath the snow, and extracting huge handfuls of the white crystals, tossed them over his body.

"In course no half-breed and no Injun would pass us within a hundred yards and not see us," he said grimly. "But every little helps in cases like this. S—s—sh! Didn't I hear someone callin'?"

"Down there." Joe pointed eagerly downhill, hardly even whispering the words. And then, quite plainly to the ears of every one of the party, there came the note of a human voice, subdued and eager. Rising in cadence for the instant, it fell immediately and then died away altogether. Afterwards not a sound disturbed the ghostly silence of the patch of forest through which they were passing; that is, not a sound audible to our hero. Hank's staring eyes and the eager expression on the hawk-like face of the Redskin told their own story. They heard something. To them the presence of the enemy was evident. Ah! Joe buried his head still deeper, for away in the distance a figure came of a sudden into view sliding silently between the tree trunks. A second followed, muffled to the eyes; a third, a fourth, till eight in all were visible. Perhaps two hundred yards separated them from Joe and his comrades. Perhaps they were even closer. In any case, their proximity was such that the little party in hiding was in the utmost danger. One point, however, was in their favour. The enemy were facing the west, and were cutting across the line of flight which our hero had suggested. A minute passed, then two. It began to look as if the danger would be gone in a few moments. Then, of a sudden, that low-pitched, eager voice was heard again, and, raising his head ever so slightly, Joe saw that the enemy had halted and were now bunched together.

"Talking it over," he told himself, hearing voices. "They have an idea that they have come far enough west, and that now they had better cut uphill again, having got well behind us. Wish they had gone on another hundred yards or so, then there wouldn't have been any danger."

"The critters!" he heard Hank growl. "Ef they ain't turning uphill at this instant!"

That indeed seemed to be the intention of the enemy; for, breaking from the circle into which they had collected, they went off again in single file, one burly individual leading. As for the features of these unfriendly strangers, what they were like and of exactly what nationality, neither Joe nor Hank nor Beaver Jack had the smallest inkling; for the enemy one and all were thickly clad in furs, muffled to their eyes, and at that distance seemed to be merely grotesque bundles of clothing. This, however, was certain—they were adepts at the art of snowshoeing. Not one but was accustomed to the forest, for beyond a voice or two not another sound had come from them. Facing the hillside, they curled off in that direction and slowly moved upward.

"It aer a toss up," Hank whispered, under his breath. "Yer see, now that they've turned they gets a broadside view of where we're lying instead of a head-on view. See here, Joe, ef they spots us, jest get in behind a tree and pepper 'em; if they don't, be ready to move off the instant we're able. Seems to me as ef I've an idea that'll bother them badly."

The ten minutes which followed were trying, for once again the enemy halted, gathering together to discuss the situation. It appeared as if they were a little uncertain of their position, and at one moment they appeared to be on the point of proceeding in the direction which they were taking when first Joe and his friends saw them. But at last they went on again and slowly passed out of hearing.

"That war a near go," whispered Hank, with a sigh of relief, as he rose to an erect position. "Now fer that idea of mine. Yer see, we've got to bother 'em badly, fer it won't be long afore they comes upon the spot where we were lying. In course there'll be a hullabaloo at once, and back they'll come after us. Ef they're sure of the line we've taken they'll cut clear across for their sleighs, and then there won't be a dog's chance for us. Joe, look lively jest now, and see as you do as you see me and Beaver Jack doing."

He faced downhill without another word, while the Redskin fell in behind him. Indeed, the silent man seemed to have already guessed at Hank's intentions, or was it that the cunning learned by all hunters is of such a class that their minds move always on parallel lines, and difficulties are met in almost similar fashion? Whatever the reason, Beaver Jack seemed to have guessed intuitively what Hank's plan was to be, and fell in behind him without uttering a syllable. Then came Joe, watching closely, wondering what new tricks he would see put into execution.

"It aer plain," began Hank, when at length he had reached the track along which the enemy had so recently passed, "it aer clear as daylight that when them critters finds that we have moved, they will come dashing downhill as ef there was demons behind 'em. They'll come along in our tracks, and ef we was to cross their own here and cut a line of our own, why, in course there wouldn't be any need for 'em to wait to look about for the direction. So here we plays an old Injun game that ain't so often practised in these days—now!"

He swung round, and moving a few paces beside the track which the half-breeds had followed, joined it at an acute angle, making it appear as if he and his comrades were going in the same direction. Then the wily little hunter stepped out of his snowshoes and, reversing his own direction, thrust his warmly-moccasined feet into them in the reverse order.

"Yer catch the idea?" he grinned. "Now I walks along the way they came, but to look at the marks I'll leave you'd think I was jest going along with them. It aer said that a bear'll walk backward to his winter lair so as to deceive his enemies. That's what we're doing."

With shoes reversed, the little fellow set off at once, halting for a few seconds, once he had passed his comrades, so as to enable each in turn to step on to the track and face about. Then the three proceeded, the turning of their shoes making no great difference to their movement. As to the track they left, it was inextricably mixed up with the marks made by the enemy, and seeing that their snowshoes were reversed, it appeared that they were following the same direction.

"Not as a Redskin nor a half-breed wouldn't spot the thing right off," whispered Hank, "that is, ef it war a fresh track we was making; for it aer natural for a man to put his heel down heavily, even when carrying a snowshoe, and a practised tracker, same as these half-breeds, would see that the front part of our shoes is pressed into the snow. But here there's the marks of eight pairs of shoes already, and our three'll mix up nicely with 'em. Now, boys, let's git along slick; every second'll be of importance."

It was in silence after that that they thrust their way through the forest, and seeing that the direction the enemy had taken took the little party downhill, their pace was extremely rapid. Perhaps half an hour later Hank again came to a halt, pointing before him.

"Here we takes our own line," he said. "I guess those critters cut downhill amongst the trees yonder till they had got below a fold in the ground which would hide them. Then they swung straight across for our side, knowing that we couldn't see 'em. Wall, we'll do the same; we'll strike straight out into the open and, cutting away from their track, dive down the hill into the valley. After that we'll make a bee-line for the camp, and there make ready for the ruction that's bound to follow. Seems to me, Joe, as ef I'd already got an idea of a spot that would give us cover."

"Stop! Listen!" suddenly exclaimed our hero, raising one hand and standing in the position of keen attention. "I heard sounds from behind us. I feel sure that——"

"Yer ain't got no need to tell us what it aer," said Hank curtly, in the abrupt way he had when something specially stirred him. "Them critters has got to the point where they hoped to spring upon us and wipe us out, and they aer fair bustin' with rage to find that we've given 'em the slip. They'll be tumblin' downhill now as fast as their legs will bring 'em, and ef it warn't that we've put up a fine start and have left something behind to worry 'em a little, they'd be on our heels afore we could look round. Now, Beaver Jack, guess we've a long chase afore us; you kin take the lead and strike slick for the camp. I'll go behind and keep a weather eye open for them critters."

There was perfect order and coolness amongst the little party, though a glance at any one of the faces showed that all appreciated the danger of their position. No one, indeed, could have failed to gather that discovery of their escape would bring the whole pack of half-breeds chasing after them; the exchange of shots between the two parties, and the fact that the enemy had been the first to open fire proved, if proof were wanted, that a closer approach on their part would result in more shots, and in the slaying of Joe and his friends, if that were possible.

"But why? What is the attack made for?" Joe found himself saying under his breath again and again. "We don't look to be rich, I'm sure. We're just ordinary trappers or prospectors, and from what I have gathered such people don't carry much in the way of money with them. The rich prospectors, also, don't dream of setting out into the backwoods during the winter. They choose the spring and summer for two reasons, I guess. One, because then they can see the land, for there isn't any snow, and so can search for the veins of metal which attract them; and secondly, because they haven't severe weather to face. It beats me hollow; one would have thought that these men had been set upon us for some other purpose than that of robbery."

It was one of those questions, in fact, which would have taken a more worldly-wise fellow than Joe to answer; indeed, had he but known the true reason of this unlooked-for and undeserved attack, he would have been astounded. For the band then shrieking and shouting behind them, and at that moment dashing downhill on their snowshoes, had set out to search for our hero and his friends. They had hunted high and low for the trace of two prospectors, for the snowshoe marks left by Joe and Hank, and had fallen upon those marks prior to their joining hands with Beaver Jack. But the accession of one to the number of the little party made not the smallest difference. Why should it? There were nine in this gang, and only three in the other.

But Joe had other things to do than to worry his head as to reasons. After all, what did it matter who this enemy was? What difference could knowing make to our hero and his friends? For enemies are much the same all the world through. Once it is demonstrated that they aim at the slaying of those they follow, all come under the same heading. All are dangerous, and it behoves those who have to defend their lives to take the utmost precautions.

Beaver Jack therefore led the flight at a speed which suited Joe, who did not find it very hard to keep up, seeing that the way lay downhill. As for the Redskin, he might have been out for a promenade only; his shoes slid over the now hard-frozen surface with a queer little rustling sound, seeming to carry the user's legs rather than to require effort on his part. His head was sunk low down upon his breast, his hooked nose and upturned chin approximated. But nothing escaped this man of the woods, this child of nature, whose hearing and instincts were as developed as those of the wildest animal.

Hank made a pretty, if a rugged picture. The little man seemed almost to have his ears cocked backwards. In any case, they lay flat against his head, the coon-skin cap just dropping on to them. His head was erect, and even as he slid along over the snow there was little doubt that not a sound escaped him.

"Them critters ha' jest come to the spot whar we dropped in on their trace," he growled. "You kin tell as they're finely bothered. Seems to me they'll send a party forward and one along this way, and in a bit we shall hear a hullabaloo that'll be loud enough to scare the moose this side of the big lakes. You ain't tired, Joe?"

"Not I!" came the hearty answer. "Could go on for a while longer."

"Then you'll have need. There won't be so much between us by the time we reach camp; then it'll be a case fer thinkin'."

165

As if the question of their further movements bothered him, as indeed it did, his fingers slid up beneath his cap, a habit the little fellow had, and played with a loose lock of his thick hair; for Hank's hair was thick. Barbers do not live round the corner in the backwoods of Canada, and a long crop of hair is rather an advantage to a man when the temperature is below zero. It followed, therefore, that Hank's head was well covered, and Joe's also. Indeed, our hero showed a somewhat ungainly growth of fluff about chin and cheeks and upper lip, which, if it made promise of budding manhood, could not be said to be expressly elegant. But there again your backwoodsman shines. The man who carries all his belongings with him upon his back and sets off for a winter, meaning to spend it in the open air, subsisting on what his gun can procure for him, is not likely to be over-nervous as to his appearance. Hair will grow, and garments will become rent, even with the greatest care. Life also is too strenuous to make smaller things matter. Suffice it to say that Joe looked a gentleman in spite of his get-up, while already he had proved himself a jovial and boon companion, one ready to enjoy sport if it came, to take the rough with the smooth, and to face danger as if it were part of the day's happenings.

"Ha! There they go, yelping like a pack o' dogs," cried Hank, a little later, when shouts and yelps came resounding from the forest and across the snow-clad face of the hillside. "Let 'em yell! It don't do us no harm, and don't bring the critters any nearer.

"How far now to camp?" asked Joe, swinging his head round.

"Guess we're more'n halfway; in half an hour we shall do it. Suppose these fellers has been there already and has cleared all that we left."

The suggestion was disconcerting, for supposing the enemy had taken all the worldly belongings of this little party, how could they face a prolonged journey? In the summer it would make but little difference, for a stew-pan and a kettle are not absolute necessaries. Compared with the needs of the Redskins, they are merely luxuries, though long acquaintance with those useful articles has made white men find them an important portion of camping equipment. The habit of tea-drinking throughout the settlements and townships of the Dominion requires a kettle, and Joe doubted whether even the resourceful Beaver Jack could supplement such an article, however many birch trees there might be, and whatever his skill in fashioning the bark.

"Never cry till you're kicked," sang out Hank cheerfully, "and when you're kicked jest kick back mighty hard, ef only to show as you're still movin'. Ef they've took our kit, it's bad; ef they wipe us out clean, it's wuss. Let's put on steam a bit."

Beaver Jack seemed to understand the demand at once, for he broke into something resembling a jog trot, if there is such a thing when dealing with snowshoes. In any case, his feet slid over the snow at increased pace, and Joe found himself sweeping forward at a speed which set the freezing air buzzing against his ears, and brought a bright flush of colour to his face. It soon became evident, too, that the wily Redskin had noted every feature of the ground as he led his friends from the camp that morning; for suddenly, as the surface ceased to shelve and became almost level, he changed his direction. Nor did he join the wide track which presently crossed before him; he merely grunted and pointed.

"Half-breeds come along there," he said. "Go different way ourselves."

Joe looked closely at the trace they were crossing. There were the marks of the runners of two sleighs cutting through tracks evidently left by the dog teams, and on either hand, and mixed up with the former marks, were the impressions of many snowshoes.

"But—" he began, "if this is their line, and they followed us from the camp, as seems more than likely, why not take the same line back? They are sure to have come the quickest way."

"You bet; they jest followed our trace, and guess we came direct," said Hank. "Only you can't see our marks, as they've trod all over 'em. But you leave this here matter to Beaver Jack. He aer a cunnin' boy, and 'way back at the end of his head he's got an idea that'll knock fits out of them 'ere critters. I've half guessed at it already; you'll see. Seems to me we shall almost fly the last half of the distance."

"Eh?" Joe stared at the little hunter. He was quite willing to be led, and had implicit faith in his companions, but he was one of those inquisitive fellows who like to know the why and wherefore of everything. "But—fly!" he exclaimed.

"Ay—fly!" grinned Hank; "jest go along quicker nor a sleigh could take us. Ain't that it, Jack?"

Beaver Jack could enjoy a joke with anyone, only he enjoyed it in a manner peculiarly his own, or, one might more correctly say, in a manner characteristic of his people. His eyes were twinkling as he faced about, while his hooked nose and upturned chin seemed to have approached even nearer.

"It is well that the young men should know what is happening," he said. "They look to their elders for instruction, and in asking thus Joe shows that he is interested. It will also tell him the need there is always to watch the country he passes through. Listen: the land beyond falls very steeply. Leaving the camp, we passed to the right, so as to gain a track which was easy. To climb is hard; to descend is a different matter."

It was not all said in that fashion, for Beaver Jack's English was not of an advanced order. But a man of intelligence could understand him with ease, and, hearing what he had to say, Joe quickly realized what was about to happen. Also he remembered that the ground did rise immediately in front of their camp, and at such an angle that to climb it would have been almost impossible; but to descend would be easy.

"Easy as fallin' off a house," grunted Hank. "Jest sit down on your snowshoes and slide; sleighing won't be in it."

Speeding along now across a field of virgin snow through which an occasional tree cropped, the party were not long in gaining a belt of forest trees clinging to the hillside. Passing through these, they again emerged on to a space which was open, and over which the white winter mantle was spread, without so much as a footmark to mar its beauty. But the field seemed to end abruptly on that edge farthest from the summit of the hills, and striking out for the white line where sky and snow seemed to merge, the trio soon found themselves on the verge of a steep and smooth declivity. From it a splendid view was to be obtained, for the rays from the declining sun lit up a gorgeous landscape, swept with white from end to end, dotted here and there with darker patches, showing long shadows where the hollows lay, while patches of trees of larger and smaller extent cropped up everywhere. There was their camp, too, nestling at the foot of a clump of pines, while at its back was one huge expanse of white, unbroken, unmarked, bearing not even a shadow.

"A lake, and a big 'un, too," observed Hank. "Ef we'd looked that way this morning once we got on to the hill we might have seen it. But we was in the trees most of the time, and I expect that folds in the ground kept us elsewhere. Now fer a slide. Slip yer gun from yer shoulder and use it as a guiding stick. Yer see, it's mighty steep here, and though, ef you rolled from top to bottom, it wouldn't do no great harm—for there's drifts that would catch you—still it's nicer and better to go face forward. So put the butt in on one side and a little behind, and guide and brake with it."

That was a glorious ride down the hill. It carried Joe back to days, now so far off they seemed, when there had been a heavy fall of snow in England, and he, with friends in the little town, had rigged up a toboggan and had carried it to the hills. The speed then had been great; it was terrific here. However, there was no time for pausing; besides, the Redskin made nothing of it. This form of progress seemed to him to be much the same as any other. Without a word, with hardly a look at his comrades, he strode to the very edge, sat down on his snowshoes, and, thrusting the butt of his gun into the snow, pushed himself over the brink. He went whirling down before a mighty cloud of snowflakes kicked up by his shoes, and left behind him a track which a man standing in the valley below could have seen from a great distance. Once he swerved, and looked as if he were about to turn over; but the guiding gun held him straight, and in an extraordinary short space of time he was waiting for them at the bottom.

"Wall," grinned Hank, "you or me? Ef there was a chance of them critters coming along I'd say you."

"And I'd say you," laughed Joe. "I'd feel that I had to stay to protect you."

"Gee! Ef that don't beat the hull band," gasped Hank. "Protect me, you said! As ef I war a baby. Now, see here, lad; we'll make a race of it. You're heavier nor me, and so will have an advantage. At the same time, I'm that light I'll slide over the snow easier. We'll see who makes the quickest job of it."

"Agreed!" cried Joe. "Ready?"

"Ready it aer."

"Then off!"

They thrust themselves over the edge and went whirling down, huge clouds of snow spurting to either side of their snowshoes. Nor did Joe find the task one of the easiest. He swerved, and with a dig of his gun recovered his position. But the movement sent him twirling the opposite way. He made a desperate effort, and wrenched his body round again till he faced downhill; then, just as is the case with skis, something seemed to go wrong with his snowshoes. They displayed an unaccountable and all-powerful tendency to separate. No amount of effort would draw them together. The result was speedy disaster. Joe rose a little, struggling to regain equilibrium, but a curious thing happened. The very raising of his body proved fatal; for suddenly the shoes stuck fast, the toes entering the surface in spite of the steep slope. Thus arrested, our hero pitched forward on to his head, doubled up into a beautiful and most elegant circle, and went speeding down the hill like a ball, this time at an infinitely quicker rate. His antics, too, from that moment forward were more than funny, for he straightened himself out, with arms and legs widespread.

"I'll have the breath knocked clean out of my body if I don't come to a stop soon," he thought. "Ah! That does it; that's better!"

However, the relief was for the moment only. The pace lessened; he began to think that presently he would find a resting-place from which he might once more put himself in position for the remainder of the descent. But alas! he was to be disappointed. Shooting into a deep drift, he found himself buried beneath the snow, and expected to stay there. But the force of his descent carried all before it. His body broke through the mass of snow, and once more he was hurtling downward, falling this way and that, sliding, rolling head first sometimes, and at others the reverse. At last, however, he was able to arrest the rapid and exciting movement.

"Gee!" he cried. "That was a doer! Where's my gun? And one shoe gone also."

It happened that the lost articles had more or less kept him company. The gun, in fact, lay within a few feet of him, while as he turned there was the lost snowshoe descending in a dignified manner towards him. He snatched at it, donned it in haste, and once more prepared for the rest of the journey.

"Better luck, I hope," he said. "Ain't Hank grinning! The little beggar made a clean run right to the bottom."

On this second occasion Joe was more fortunate. He sat his shoes like a practised hand, and went hurtling down to within a few feet of his waiting comrades.

"You've come at last," grinned Hank, as Joe picked himself up and rose to an erect position. "Warn't it fair flyin'? Seemed to me as ef you was spreading your wings because you wasn't quite satisfied. But you ain't hurt, lad?"

"Not a bit; rather enjoyed it," sang out our hero.

"And ain't too much shook up? That sorter things kicks the breath outer a body."

"As fit as ever," grinned Joe, "and ready to continue. Where's the camp?"

"You're at the front door, as you might almost say," smiled the little hunter. "There it aer."

There it was indeed, almost nestling at the foot of the hill, and in any case within a few hundred yards. It took the little party but a few minutes to reach it.

"Will they have taken all or not?" asked Hank somewhat anxiously, as they came up to the place. "Ef so, it aer a bad lookout; ef not, why, things is beginning to move in our favour."

A deep-toned exclamation came from the Redskin, while his hawk-like face took on for one brief instant an appearance of sublime content.

"That's settled the matter," cried Hank. "You kin see as it aer all right, fer Beaver Jack stood to lose the hull of his pelts and the winter's work, which for him would be serious. He's seen that things aer all right."

"No take the pelts and the sleigh as they easy able to come back when they killed us," said Beaver Jack, his eyes twinkling.

"And so we'll take 'em," cried Hank. "But where? That do tease me more'n a trifle. Jest about here we ain't no better off than we was back up the hill, and men lyin' on the ridge above us could flick bullets into our camp every time. I ain't bad at some sorter conundrums, but here guess I've come to an end. Joe, boy, you are the youngest and brightest; what do we do?"

"Pack up at once, put all our things on Beaver Jack's sleigh, and make clear across the lake to that island," said our hero, promptly pointing across the smooth expanse of snow to where, nestling in the centre almost, was a prominence above which hung the heavily-weighted branches of a group of evergreens. "That'll be a fine castle," he said. "We've now grub with us, besides pots and pans; there'll be firewood yonder, and with that we'll be able to make ourselves comfortable. I'm for making for that island."

Hank gave a little exclamation, and struck himself violently on the chest as if in punishment for not having thought of the same movement, while the Redskin went to his sleigh, on which his store of pelts was still bound, and taking up the tow rope began to move away from the camp.

"It aer jest the very thing for us," observed Hank, with eagerness. "I war a thickhead too never to have thought of it. But lend a hand, Joe, and let's get the traps fixed and packed. Them critters ain't likely to be long now in coming."

Very rapidly but carefully they packed all their goods on Beaver Jack's sleigh, then, led by the Redskin, they stepped upon the snow-covered surface of the lake. And as they pushed their way across it the shouts of the enemy came to their ear, while presently they could be seen descending the hillside.

"They've seed what we're up to, and guess as they can't reach us afore we're at the island," said Hank. "So now they'll go back to collect their sleighs and dog teams. That'll give us time to breathe. We'll make our lean-to right off, and get a kettle of water boiling. A brew of hot tea won't come amiss after all this business."

They found, in fact, that cups of boiling hot tea, sweetened with some of the store of maple sugar which they had brought with them, was most reviving. It sent the blood surging through their bodies, and, had their courage been somewhat lacking, would even have restored that. But Joe and his friends had a deal of fight left in them yet. They hoped still to preserve their lives, and show these half-breeds who had so outrageously attacked them that matters were not all in their favour.

"We aer boxed in, more or less," said Hank, surveying his surroundings; "but they ain't much better off. The moment one o' the critters steps off on to the lake, we sees him. There'll be a moon to-night, and for a week almost, so night won't make much difference to it. Joe, I begin to think as this here island aer going to be the saving of us."

Whether or no that was to be the case had yet to be seen. It was fairly evident that the gallant little trio had a strenuous and exciting time before them.

CHAPTER XVII

Hurley's Conspiracy is Unfolded

Nowhere else in the vast territories of the Dominion of Canada could Joe and his two comrades have come upon a spot more suited to their purpose than was the tiny island which cropped out almost in the centre of the frozen and snow-covered surface of the vast lake they had encountered during their prospecting tour in New Ontario.

"It aer a fair treat," observed Hank, rubbing his half-frozen hands together, with a gusto there was no mistaking. "I allow that when we made back to our camp this afternoon things was looking uncommonly black, and ef we had found that all our traps had been taken or burned by them half-breeds, why, in course we should ha' been up a gum tree, as Australians is fond of saying. How do I know they're fond o' sayin' that, young feller?" he asked, with an appearance of severity he was far from feeling; for Joe had laughingly asked the question. "Jest fer this reason: there's Australians comes to Canada—not 'cos they don't like their own country, for I never heard of one as didn't swear by Australia; but, you see, things don't move quite as fast out there as they do here. This Dominion aer the place for settlers above all others for two good reasons. First, and it's a big 'un—the distance from the old country is so short, which makes the passage easy and cheap; and second, this here Government aer on the move all the time, more even than that over in Australia. Yer see, they've got the masses pouring in, and huge preparations has to be made. But we was talking of this island."

"Yes," agreed Joe, who long since had made a tour of the place. Not that that was a journey of vast extent or of difficulty, for the little heap of rock which cropped from the bed of the lake in such picturesque fashion was barely big enough to house three dozen men. That number would be uncomfortably squeezed together, as a matter of fact, and some would be pressed from the edge. Then, again, its outer edge was raised for all the world like the rim of a saucer, while the centre was depressed into a number of irregular hollows. "A fine place," admitted Joe warmly. "Shouldn't wonder if in summertime there is fresh water in these hollows. In any case, though, that wouldn't matter, for there is abundance of water in the lake. Seems to me we shall be able to make a fort here that will bother those people."

"What'd you do?" asked Hank, eager to discover the plans that Joe might have made. "Here you are with a couple of young fellers, me and Beaver Jack, to look after, and it aer up to you to protect us and lead us. What'll you do? No laughing matter, young feller—I'm serious."

It was hard to believe that, for never did hunter wear a more jovial expression. To be precise, that exhilarating flight from before the enemy, the discovery of their camp equipment undamaged, and then the gaining of this unique position had lifted the spirits of all three of the party wonderfully.

"It aer a regular nest, this aer," grinned Hank. "Wall? What do you make of it? Them critters is away over there talking things over, you kin guess. Havin' a bit of a pow-wow, as the sayin' is. They've seed us come away here, in course, for even now that the dusk are falling you kin follow the track we've left across the snow. It aer up to you, Joe, to fix a plan that'll save the lives of your two comrades."

There was a twinkle in the little man's eyes, and, looking at him, one would have said that he didn't care the toss of a button for the enemy, though, like a sensible and cautious man, he would neglect nothing which would give him an advantage over them.

"I'd raise this edge all round, first of all," said Joe, "and I'd make dummies to draw their bullets. We ourselves don't want to be perched high up, unless during the night, for when it's daytime one can see across the bare surface outside for a great distance; then I'd make openings close to the rock through which we could fire. It seems to me that by doing so we shall bother them, and make it difficult for them to pick us off as they advance."

"And how'd you raise the edge?" asked Hank, with interest. "Pile up snow? That takes time."

"I'd cut bricks of snow," was Joe's answer; "then, when they were built into position, I'd break the ice, if that's possible, and throw water on the outside face of the wall we've constructed. Talk about armour-plate on a ship! That'll convert our fort into a regular dreadnought."

Hank turned on an expansive grin for our hero's special edification, while even the austere Redskin smiled. "And these here snow bricks," said Hank, "you'd take 'em from where?"

"Just outside the island. That would leave a kind of trench all round, and so give the enemy a greater height to climb, supposing they got to close quarters."

"Which aer likely enough, seeing as they're so many, and kin scatter so as to make shooting extry difficult. Shucks, lad! Guess you've put the case nicely. To make good out here we've got to have protection more than rifles kin give us. We'll build that wall; seems to me it aer the first thing that's wanted."

Perhaps half an hour or more had passed since they reached the spot where they were now awaiting the enemy, and during that time the busy Indian had constructed a comfortable lean-to, while, as has been narrated, Joe had built a fire and boiled the kettle. There being no sign yet of the half-breeds, the whole party sat down about the fire to discuss Joe's suggestions, while that young fellow himself delved in one of the bags they always carried with them, brought to light a chunk of frozen meat which, in that condition, would have required a good-sized axe to cut, and placed it over the flames. Ten minutes later, when the frost was driven from it, he cut a number of slices, thrust his cleaning rod through them, and poised the rod upon a couple of forked sticks above the fire. As for the remainder of the piece of flesh, it was quickly frozen solid; for by this time the moon was up and the cold was intense.

"It aer nice to have a fire, and a hollow to sit in," admitted Hank, who, as a rule, seemed to be absolutely unaffected by extremes of temperature. Joe had, in fact, seen the little man cool and collected, and not inconvenienced in the slightest, even when working on the hottest day, with a swarm of mosquitoes about him; while the icy breath of this winter had passed unnoticed. "We aer in fer a cold time," said the little hunter, staring into the embers, "and seems to me that that 'ere wall aer wanted fer another reason besides fer keeping them skunks out. It'll make us as warm inside here as ef we was tucked in our blankets on the cosiest feather bed you ever thought of."

"While these men outside will freeze," added Joe.

"Not they!" came the instant answer. "Them critters is used to life up here. Wouldn't wonder ef they was 'way up by James Bay most winter times, and there the cold aer wuss perhaps. They've enlarged our shelter already, and likely as not they've built a fire right inside. As soon as they've had a meal they'll turn right in, and the dogs along with 'em. That'll send up the warmth and keep an Arctic cold out. But it's ten chances to one as they'll try to rush us before the morning. Now ef them steaks is done we'll tackle them, and then get to at building."

There was a delightful odour of cooking about the little island, the overhanging branches of the evergreen pines seeming to hem it in. Joe's mouth was watering before he declared that the meal was ready, and then, having handed a slice to each of his friends, together with a species of damper cake made from flour and water toasted on the embers, he fell upon the food himself with a gusto that told how fear had no place with him. A pipe completed Hank's contentment, then, the moon being now full up, and the enemy out of sight, the trio set to work to erect the walls of their fortification. With their long-bladed knives they cut oblong chunks of frozen snow with the same ease as one would cut butter, and

174

then, leaving Joe alone to do the building, sent block after block of the material sliding to the position he had taken.

"We'll get along quicker like that," said Hank. "It don't take more'n a couple of seconds to lift a block into place, while it takes five perhaps to cut one. So ef one builds, t'others'll be able to keep him supplied."

It was really remarkable how rapidly the wall rose. In an hour there was a complete circle all round the rim of the island, which, being naturally raised, gave greater height to the artificial wall. The second row of blocks was soon added, Joe leaving spaces here and there through which a rifle could be fired. The third and fourth and others swiftly followed, and when four hours had gone the task was completed. Then Hank attacked the ice with an axe which he always carried, and, having cut through a foot and more, came upon water. A tin pot constantly replenished supplied a means whereby the outer face of the wall was drenched, and so fierce was the cold that the liquid congealed almost as soon as it had fallen on the surface at which it was projected.

"We kin make our dummies any time now," said Hank. "Two of 'em'll be enough, and the one who's going to take the first watch'll find they will help to pass the time in making. It's nigh midnight now; I'll take a spell. Joe'll relieve when three hours have gone, and Beaver Jack later. Let's get to and make the most of the time before us."

In a short time silence fell upon this little isolated camp. Down in the depths of the lowest hollow, huddled in their blankets, and as warm as toast, lay Joe and the Redskin, packed close together; for an Arctic winter needs to be treated with consideration. No warmth that can be retained can be allowed to escape, and as two bodies huddled close together generate a temperature which is greater than that generated by one, it follows that campers sleep pressed close together. We have seen the plan put into operation elsewhere. On the high veldt in South Africa, when nightly frosts are keen, and when tents and proper covering are not obtainable, your campaigners soon lose all feelings of foolish pride. Officers divide into couples and bed down beneath the combined allowance of blankets, while we have seen as many as four of the rank and file snug beneath their covering, snoring blissfully, grateful for the warmth of their comrades.

Perched above this tranquil camp, his keen eyes surveying the surroundings with as much ease as a watchman can keep guard from a tower built for that special purpose, Hank looked out across the surface of the lake to the shore where the enemy was lying. His pipe was clenched between his teeth, his hands sunk deep into his pockets, while he himself was immovable. But every now and again the glow in the bowl of his pipe brightened, showing that he was drawing on the weed, while a puff of smoke issued from his lips.

"The critters!" was a favourite exclamation with him; "Them skunks!" another; "Ef I only knew what they was after," an oft-repeated sentence.

"Yer see," Hank was saying to himself, "there don't seem to be any reason in all this business; but there's something behind it all that we can't even guess at. Somehow I can't help thinkin' that this here Joe ha' an importance in the matter."

What would the little hunter have given to be able to peer into the camp of the enemy at that particular moment? He could see the glare of a huge fire, and could imagine men and dogs sleeping together under a shelter. But Hank was an exceedingly practical fellow, not one gifted with an unusual stock of imagination. He could not, therefore, guess that the number of the enemy was divided, that there was one who was a leader. And yet that was the case. Half-breeds formed the backbone of the party—half-breeds of the lowest character, idle vagabonds to be found round and about the forts in the north of Canada. Not, let us say at once, that all half-breeds are idle and worthless; by no means is that the case. There are, of course, black sheep in every flock, and here a number were gathered together, and at that moment huddled fast asleep in the shelter of the lean-to which Joe and his friends had erected. Some ten paces away a second shelter had been constructed, of rather ample proportions, while a fire blazed at the entrance, warming the interior. One side of this structure was filled by a sleigh, which had been put there for a special purpose, the blankets lying upon it showing that it was meant to serve as a couch. On this same sleigh sat a man, a bulky fellow, muffled in furs, bearded, and almost unrecognizable because of the skin cap drawn down over his ears. He leaned over a wooden box which did duty for a table, and at the precise moment when Hank was pulling at his pipe and wondering who these enemies might be, the leader of the band of rascals had his thoughts attracted to one at least of Hank's little party. A long envelope lay beside him, while a document was spread out on the improvised table. As for illumination, some was supplied by the fire, some by the clear moon overhead, and most by a torch of birch bark, the resinous material in which caused it to splutter and burn brilliantly.

Let us take a look at this individual and, lifting his cap, endeavour to recognize him. But time brings changes in all directions, and puts its stamp on the majority of faces. Anxiety may hasten this inevitable change, while ill health, worry, an ill-conditioned mind, grasping and avarice are all capable of imprinting their own particular marks on the features. In the case of the individual in question, a brutal mind was displayed by a face that had never been handsome, and was now heavily seamed and lined, boasting overhung brows, and a mouth which was set in something approaching a permanent snarl. It was a face which had changed vastly in the past few months. For this was Hurley, this was the criminal who had so nearly killed our hero after committing murder, and who had made his escape into the forest, bearing Joe's riches and that all-important envelope with him. We have learned how the man was captured, and how he made good his escape again. We recollect that Joe had recovered his dollars, but that the envelope was still missing. Missing? No. It was there on that improvised table. Right away in the wilds of Canada, in the depths of an Arctic winter, it had come to view again, though now the seal was broken.

"To my son, Joe Bradley," the ruffian leaning over the box read aloud, as if he had an audience, picking up the envelope and holding it closer. "The contents of this letter will explain to you many things which I have never cared to refer to; but I beg of you never to open it till you are in direst need or have earned the right to do so. Make your way in the world, gather riches—then you can open and read."

Hurley sneered at the words. He threw the envelope down with a gesture of impatience. "Of course the fool obeyed," he growled; "waited till he'd come out to Canada—in fact, till it was too late. And think what he was losing. It makes me fair chuckle. There was a home ready-made for him in England; there was gold to fill his pockets and keep 'em filled; and there was servants all round about, so that he needn't have done a hand's turn. Instead the young fool comes out to Canada and slaves on a farm. Well, some people are born idiots!"

Evidently with the reassuring reflection that he, Hurley, was no fool, the rascal turned to the contemplation of the document. He spread it out smoothly, leaned his elbows on either side, and perhaps for the hundredth time read the story enclosed, a tale, let it be remembered, meant only for the eyes of our hero; for therein set down, by the hand of a man now dead, was a history of importance. Hurley gloated over the contents of this document, weighing every word within it; then he sat back on the sleigh and gave himself up to dreaming. His savage, careworn face took on something approaching a pleasant expression, for Hurley's were pleasant dreams. In them he imagined himself entirely successful. He built castles for himself in the frosty air of the lean-to, forgetful that the best of schemes here and there come to a sudden and disappointing ending.

"It can be done," he said aloud; "there is nothing to prevent me, for I have considered the plan from every side. I kill the boy; that is the first move. I take copies of the certificate of death when I leave the country, and when I reach Great Britain I am Bradley—Mr. Bradley, senior. Ha!"

A grin of triumph overspread his features, while he pushed his cap back as if the very thought of success made him hot. Looking at Hurley at that moment, one realized that he was one of Canada's bad bargains and an unscrupulous ruffian. As for the tale which he had gathered from the document which had been stolen from our hero, we will not set it down in full, as had been done by Joe's father. Suffice it to say that the narrative was somewhat unusual. It carried the history of two lives back some fifty years, and told of the birth of Joe's father. Son of a man of wealth, his mother had died soon after his appearance. Then a stepmother had appeared upon the scene, while in due time he was presented with a stepbrother. At that point the tale took on some particular interest, for by the machinations of his stepmother, Joe's father had at an early age found himself almost penniless. To be precise, when six years of age he was banished from the establishment and sent to live with a schoolmaster at the other end of the country. Never once did he return home. Sums for his maintenance were forthcoming, while he drifted unhappily from school to school. He then found himself placed in an office, and hardly was he self-supporting when all allowances ceased. In place he gathered the fact that his stepbrother was now of age and had succeeded to his father's property.

"Succeeded to every penny of it," declared Hurley aloud, "and this here natural son done out of it. But he got to learn that he was the next in succession. He's too hurt with all this kind of treatment, and too proud to go back to the home. He loses himself in some provincial town, and don't say anything. But the chap who gets all the goods don't marry. This Bradley knows that well. Then what does he do? Writes this here, and sends every proof he's got of his own birth and suchlike to solicitors in London. He don't see 'em hisself. Not a bit. He sends the documents, and encloses the receipt which was sent for them in this letter. This here matter can be worked as easy as eating."

The reasoning of this rascal could be followed now with some ease, while it is merely necessary to mention one more item in Mr. Bradley's letter to our hero. He related that his stepbrother, realizing the injustice done to the elder son, had, as the years passed, made efforts to discover him. He had advertised, and put the matter in the hands of searchers.

"In fact, he aer anxious for this here Bradley to turn up, and it aer clear from the letter that when he does, or his son, there's money and a comfortable living. An heir's wanted, that's truth, and seein' as I'm too old to act the son, and am only a trifle younger than this here Mr. Bradley would ha' been, why, here's the heir. Hurley'll fill the bill as well as any other."

There was the diabolical plot in its entirety. That document just went to show that Joe's father was a man possessed of a proud spirit and of good ideas, for he laid it down on the outside of the envelope that he wished his son to earn his place in the world before he opened and read the contents. He would rather see Joe fighting his own battles than coddling in luxury and spending the money of an uncle. He preached independence and energy, and our hero had shown it. It was the fortune of war, perhaps, that the document had come into the hands of such a scoundrel, and, reviewing it and all the circumstances together, one now saw the reason for this extraordinary and unprovoked assault upon the little party. Hurley had gathered means by some dishonest method; he had traced Joe's movements; and now he had rounded him up, and with the rascals he had hired had him almost within the net.

"To-morrow or next day, don't matter which," he told himself; "but kill him I will, then away for England."

For Hurley it was a fascinating conspiracy; for Joe, had he known the ins and outs of the story, it was likely to prove more than disconcerting. But forewarned is forearmed, and there is this to be said for our hero. The first shots had missed him. He was now behind cover, while two of the stanchest friends were there to protect him.

"P'raps them critters will have had enough already and will sheer off," said Hank, still sitting motionless on the top of the snow wall when the watch he had been keeping came to its end. "Ef not, then it proves as there's something deep behind all this here business. Hi, Joe! It aer your turn now, and jest you keep movin'. It's all right fer me as is an old hand at the game to sit tight and look about me. Young chaps feels the cold wuss and soon gets sleepy. Move all the time, and take a fill of 'bacca."

It was a habit into which Joe had fallen, and with very good reason, too, seeing the open-air life he was leading and the companions he associated with; for your Canadian backwoodsman loves his smoke. A short clay dangles from his teeth on most occasions. Joe therefore roused himself swiftly from his blanket; and here again was something more which camping had taught him, namely, to be a light sleeper. Hank might be said to sleep always with one eye open, for he heard the slightest movement. Beaver Jack might often enough appear to be sunk in the deepest slumber, and yet, if one happened to peer into his face, one discovered that both of those deep-sunk brilliant orbs were actually twinkling. Our hero, too, would sit up with a jerk on the smallest occasion, so that Hank's call had brought him to his feet promptly. And now he watched the little man shake himself like a dog and toss a blanket about him. Then Joe crammed weed into his pipe thoughtfully, lifted a glowing ash from the fire, and puffed long flames into the bowl. With a trail of smoke about his head, he began to march the round of this strange fortification.

"Hard as a brick," he told himself, running his hand along the outside of the snowy wall. "Wouldn't turn a bullet, perhaps, but almost, I reckon. Ah! there's the fire the enemy are burning. Jolly cheek they've got to make use of our old camp! Wonder what they're up to? Planning an attack for the early hours of the morning, if I ain't mistaken."

Joe tramped round and round, halting every few minutes to stare about him, a comprehensive look, in fact, which took in his entire surroundings. From his perch on the wall he could appreciate the commanding situation. The countryside seemed to be cut off by that wide-spreading smooth surface, with its soft covering of white snow, unbroken in all directions save for the track which he and his friends had made in gaining the island. The edge of the lake, where the bank rose from the frozen water, was now so merged with the vast sheet of ice itself, that even from the island, the best point of vantage for observation, one could not say where ice ended and solid earth began. Over all the wintry moon threw its own particular magnificence, bathing the scene in brilliant rays which accentuated the pure whiteness of everything.

"Ripping!" Joe exclaimed. "Just fancy if we had such scenes in England! And people grumble at a Canadian winter. I dare say there are lots of reasons for wishing the weather were milder, for a winter such as this is stops a heap of work. You can't sow or plough or harrow. You can't build even a simple shack such as is wanted on the farms. You can't ride a horse, as a general rule, while there isn't feed for cattle. But it's glorious for all that. Give me a bright, sunny winter's day in the Dominion."

"You aer sure as there ain't no movement?" asked Hank, suddenly sitting up. "Seemed to me as ef I heard a sound."

"A dog yelped yonder," answered Joe, who was alert and taking notice of everything.

"A dog?"

"Yes; there's the sound again. I think, too, that it was a different animal."

"Then it aer a case of all hands on deck," whispered the little trapper, become suddenly cautious. "Ef dogs is barking, it stands to reason that they has been disturbed. As a general rule, they'll sleep a night like this through without moving; so, young feller, you kin look to see them critters afore very long. I'll rouse Beaver Jack and then get a kettle o' tea boiling. What's the hour, lad?"

"Five o'clock or thereabouts. Ah! there's another dog, and——"

"You kin see them skunks?" asked the little hunter.

"No—yes! Two sleighs have just shot out from behind the trees where we were camping last night, but I can't make out how many men are aboard them.'

"Wall? Aer they heading straight along here?" came the request in a few moments, while Hank stirred the fire, and, thrusting handfuls of snow into the wide-mouthed kettle, put the latter upon its hook above the flames.

"No; they've run on to the lake surface, and are making a tour round. It appears to me as if they were hunting for an opening."

There came a gurgle of amusement from the little hunter. He presented a grinning face to our hero, and then climbed up beside him.

"That 'ere wall fair bothers 'em," he laughed. "Guess when you look at this island from 'way outside, there's jest a smooth white surface without so much as a break. Now, where aer them critters? Ah! over there, going along easy. I make it that there's two men aboard each sleigh, and that this here's merely a kind of scouting. Keep well down, me lad. We ain't goin' to help them by even a little."

In ghostly silence the two sleighs circled round the island. They kept at a respectful distance, then dividing, ran in opposite directions. After some ten minutes had passed they met again, and, swerving so as to take the same path, went off in the direction of the camp which the enemy were occupying. It was perhaps half an hour later, when the little garrison had fortified themselves with a steaming cup of tea, and pipes were comfortably going, that Joe again gave a warning.

"Coming in full force," he said. "There's four men at least on each of the sleighs. They're making directly for the island."

It was a true report, for when Hank and Beaver Jack joined Joe, there were the two sleighs, their teams spread out in front, tearing along towards the island, while each one of the rascals on the sleighs bent down, hoping thereby to decrease the wind resistance.

"I could plump a shot clear into 'em now," observed Hank, nursing his rifle. "But guess it's better to give 'em what they've been axing for from the beginning. Ef we're goin' to get out of this bother with our scalps, as you might say, we aer got to read them critters a bad lesson. Shootin' at them from a distance won't do it. We've got to run the chance of 'em getting at us, and wait till they're at close quarters."

So they watched the two crews advance, till a sudden shout caused the drivers to draw rein. Then eight figures leaped from the sleighs and, dividing at once, came racing forward.

Joe and his friends watched them quietly and with determination. Ignorant of the cause of the attack, they were naturally incensed, while such a thing as surrender had not occurred to them. But a looker-on must have had serious doubts as to their success; indeed, it may be said that their danger was great and pressing. As for the scheme which the ruffian Hurley had originated, his chances of ridding himself of a rival may truthfully be described as rosy. With Joe Bradley slain in this outlandish situation, there seemed little difficulty in carrying out the remainder of a disgraceful and cowardly conspiracy. Hurley would present himself in England. He would demand those documents and proof of origin. A fine fortune and position seemed to be awaiting him.

CHAPTER XVIII

On the Defensive

A strange silence had fallen upon attackers and attacked, once the former had leaped from their sleighs and had begun to race across the snow-covered surface of the lake. Not a sound broke from them, though now and then there was a whimper from one of the dogs in the teams attached to the sleighs; and neither Hank nor Joe or Beaver Jack so much as uttered a syllable. Perhaps if they had leaped to the summit of the wall they had built, and had shouted and thrown threats at the enemy, it would have had the effect of spurring the latter on; for opposition in any shape or form is apt to stimulate men to courage and exertion, but silence depresses. The attackers seemed to lose heart rapidly; then, as one stopped doubtfully, his comrades slowly copied his example. Thereupon a burly figure turned upon them angrily.

"Forward!" he shouted almost incoherently. "Why stop here? The fools can kill you now as easily as they could if you were closer. Forward!"

"Give 'em a sight of the dummies we've rigged up," whispered Hank at once. "Jest show the tops o' their heads over the wall; I'll lie here and give 'em a shot ef they want to come closer."

He spread himself face downward on the snow and pushed his rifle through one of the apertures which Joe had left. Meanwhile our hero and the Redskin each took one of the dummies which the cunning little trapper had manufactured during his hours of watching, and slowly raised that part which was supposed to be the head over the summit of the wall. Crouching as low as possible themselves, they moved the dummies slowly to and fro; for they were some three yards from one another. At once there came a loud shout from the open, and, staring out through the aperture, Hank saw the same burly figure which he had observed before dashing to and fro haranguing his following; but move them he could not.

A DEFENCE AGAINST ODDS

Page 312

A DEFENCE AGAINST ODDS

"What? You won't come on?" the three defenders heard him bellow. "Never did I meet such cowards! Look at the men we've come for. Fire!"

They could do that even if they would not advance, and in a twinkling the seven half-breeds had thrown themselves into all sorts of attitudes, and were busy with their weapons. There came an irregular volley, while the narrow, elongated bullet of the modern weapon, the larger, squat missile of the rifle somewhat out of date, and even the huge round leaden ball discharged by a smoothbore came hurtling about the fort. Joe heard again the zip-zip of rapidly-travelling bodies cutting their way through a maze of branches, he felt the hail of debris as it fell, while within a foot or more of his head he listened to the dull thud of a bullet striking the hard-frozen wall, and heard the queer ripping sound it made as it forced a way through and sped on across the fort to the far wall. Then there was a pause, during which there was deathly silence.

"I ain't in no hurry to fire," said Hank, in low tones, grinning up at his companions, "and I'll tell you for why. Shouts and firing and sichlike would make them critters come on; silence gives 'em the hump. In any case, they ain't bustin' with pluck, and never did I see men show less dash when attackin'. Say, Joe, ain't I heard that voice before? Seems as ef I ought to know it."

Before he could receive an answer, the burly man was again addressing his men, strutting up and down before them; for though his orders had been that they should divide and approach the island from every point of the compass, the half-breeds lacking courage had held together, as if the companionship of their fellows helped to hearten them.

"Forward!" Joe heard the command given. "You can see where they are now. They've rigged up a wall, and any one of us can hop over it in a twinkling. Now, all together!"

But his orders went unheeded. Instead, a second volley spluttered down the irregular line, while once again a variety of shots swept against the fort. Joe could see Beaver Jack's penetrating eyes twinkling. He even fancied there was a smile on those lips which were always so impassive. In any case, the Redskin pointed overhead to the dummy he held and nodded.

"Fine shooting," he murmured. "Send bullet right through the head; glad Beaver Jack not up there."

Then Hank repeated his question.

"Queer, ain't it, Joe? I'd swear I'd met that chap before. But——"

"I believe——" began our hero doubtfully, "but it can't be."

"Can't be? There's nothing that can't be 'way out here after what's happened. I tell you, man and boy I've tracked the backwoods, and never once have I been set on like this. I've heard o' ructions, in course, but always near the forts and stations, or in the settlements. But right out in the wilds like this—never! I'll eat my boots ef these here critters ain't been set on us. Seems to me that ef we could get a hold on that big chap as seems to lead 'em, and could make him talk, there's a heap he could tell us. Who is he, anyway?"

"Hurley!" exclaimed Joe.

"Eh? What? Hurley? That durned murderer! Shucks, lad, that's too tall for anything!"

"I'm dead sure. Hurley's tall; Hurley's a big man; Hurley's voice is the same as that."

"But—" interrupted Hank hoarsely, keeping his eyes all the while on the enemy, "but, grant you the voice is the same—now that you've said it, I 'low that that aer Hurley's voice—he'd be mad to follow like this. There's a string always round his neck, and he ain't likely to come close to the men who know it. It ain't reasonable. Why, we could hang the scoundrel any day we set hands on him!"

"True enough," agreed Joe, "but—wait, they're moving. That rascal is getting them to their feet; we'd better be ready for trouble."

Joe had managed to squat down close to one of the openings, and as he conversed with Hank had wriggled himself into a position which enabled him to look out. Everything outside on the moonlit snow was visible. Indeed, the white background showed up every detail, though, as it happened that the enemy had their backs to the moon, their features were indistinguishable. But features are of no account when bullets are flying, or when an attack is about to be launched. The enemy had gathered into a bunch, in spite of the shouts of their leader, and now, fortified by even closer companionship, and goaded by the burly brute who stood at their head, they poured in another volley, then, trailing their weapons, dashed toward the fort. Joe jerked his dummy on to the top of the wall and left it there; then his hand sought for his rifle, and in a trice he had the muzzle grinning at the enemy. He jerked back the bolt—for he always kept the weapon at safety—took a rapid aim at one of the charging figures, and pulled the trigger. To his amazement, the man at whom he aimed doubled up into a neat round ball and, tumbling on the snow, rolled rapidly forward. But it was not for long. He straightened himself suddenly, stood erect, and then threw his arms overhead. A penetrating shriek came from him, and a moment later he bounded into the air and fell face downward. Hank's rifle spat forth a bullet in the interval and sent a second man rocking from side to side. Long before Beaver Jack could get to one of the apertures, or Hank push in a fresh cartridge, the enemy were in wild retreat, separating widely and racing away as fast as their snowshoes would take them. As for Joe, numbed fingers do not readily operate the bolt of even a modern weapon, while, for the same reason, cartridges are hard to grip; so that he had not even reloaded. But numbed fingers were not the only reason for such delay; he was watching the man at whom he had fired. A feeling of elation possessed him for one brief second as the rascal doubled up and rolled forward, and then one of terror, of keen remorse.

"I—I killed him," he cried, a waver in his voice.

Hank looked up quickly, his lips moving.

"Eh?" he asked shortly.

"I killed him," declared Joe again, almost plaintively.

"Ah, so you did, young 'un, and a mighty fine shot it war. But you ain't going to tell me that you're sorry? In course in a way one is sorry when one wipes a critter out, but——"

"It's awful!" groaned Joe, huge depression upon him.

Hank scrambled to his feet, dragged our hero to his, and took him away from the wall where the moon's rays fell brightly upon both of them.

"See here," he cried angrily, though those who knew the little man best would have declared that his anger was artificial, "see here, young feller; am I less valuable to you than that 'ere cuss? Eh? You ain't got an answer. You don't seem to reckon that ef you wasn't to shoot, the critter would come right in and kill me or you. Ef it's like that, and you value him higher, why, I'm for moving."

Very slowly he began to clamber on to the top of the wall. He dropped his legs over to the far side, and seemed to be in the act of departing from the fort. Then Joe came to his senses; he caught the little trapper by the fringed sleeve and dragged him back. Indeed, using his strength and height, he gripped the little man and lifted him bodily. He was smiling when Hank at length broke free.

"It's over," he said; "I'm sorry."

"No harm done, lad," came the hearty answer. "No one was ever the wuss for havin' a soft heart. But this here aer war, war to the knife, and, what's more, that aer Hurley. Would a skunk same as him leave us alive ef the call was with him? Huh!"

That was the most expressive sound he could make. It betokened the utmost scorn; it showed Hank when most emphatic.

"It aer Hurley, fer sure," he declared. "But why? Aer he mad?"

"Not mad, but hoping to make something out of us or out of me," said Joe. "At least that is the idea I have, though it seems to be stupid, and there is no apparent reason for my saying so. But what does it matter what the cause of the attack may be? It's Hurley."

"Dead sartin—the skunk!" growled Hank.

"And he means business."

"He aer goin' to wipe the hull lot of us out ef he's able. But he aer come up agin a crowd that's got its dander up, so I tells him. He aer yet to larn what backwoods chaps and others kin do. Next time I makes a particular point o' puttin' my sights on him, and ef I get the chance, I'll roll him over. Let's see what they're doing."

For the next ten minutes the trio sat on the summit of the wall in the full glare of the moonlight, for there was now no object in concealment, and watched the enemy. They had retired as far as their sleighs, and it looked for a little while as if they were about to mount and drive away. But the burly figure of the rascal who led them—now admittedly Hurley, the murderer, the escaped criminal—tramped up and down near them, and though only a faint whisper of his voice could be heard every now and again, when the wind bore it in the direction of the island, it was perfectly evident that he was again using all his persuasive eloquence to induce his followers to repeat the attack. They saw him swing round more than once and point towards the fort. They watched as the enemy actually advanced again; but a shot from Hank surging between them seemed to put their courage to flight, for they went again to the sledges. Then there was a different scene.

"Threatening them," remarked Joe. "Hurley is shaking his fist at us, and pointing his gun at his own people. I begin to believe that we shall win out all right. Say, Hank, how many men can go on a sleigh as a rule?"

"Depends on the teams, lad. Some'll have only a small team, and then one man are a load; some'll take four, same as those, and move sharpish over the snow. Then agin, it depends a heap on the ground. Ef it's smooth and level, the work aer easy; ef there's a hill, folks has to dismount; and ef there's a thaw—shucks! you can't get along nohow."

"But just now, after the 'silver thaw' we've had, the snow is beautifully hard, and if those beggars went the opposite way, the way we'd go if we were making back towards the Fennicks, they'd move."

"Fly," came crisply from the hunter. "It aer a trifle downhill, and since this keen frost set in, the snow aer hard and smooth. Yes, they'd fly. But don't you reckon on that; Hurley'll work them half-breeds up to attack again. They'll wait perhaps till morning, or till it's darker. It'll be that any time now, and I ain't so certain that we ain't in for a little snow. It won't be much, anyway, for there's only a few clouds about; but the wind's got up a little, and clouds have come into sight that wasn't there when we came to the island."

"Ah!" Joe gave vent to the short expression in such a tone of voice that Hank stared at him. It was just as if he had said "Thanks awfully; you've just given me the information I wanted."

"What's that?" demanded the hunter.

"Nothing," answered Joe briskly.

"You ain't goin' to flummox me! You was thinkin' something jest then; you're up to some game and ain't let on yet."

The little fellow was gifted with wonderful intelligence, and picked up Joe's unspoken thoughts with the same intuition with which he would have ferreted out the tracks of an enemy, or guessed at their possible movements. He shook Joe angrily, staring into his face.

"What aer it?" he demanded. "This ain't the time for playing games. But I guess you've something at the back of that head of yours. Now, I've caught you out—-what's the move?"

Joe told him in a very few words; for he had of a sudden come to the determination to move against the enemy.

"I'm going to do a little bit of scouting, Hank," he said. "I'm going across to their camp to see what's happening. What I want to know is this: will those dogs they have set up a racket and fly at me?"

"You bet! In course they will. Only there's snow everywhere now, and ef you're careful—and I've larned ye to be—then you'd be able to manage without rousing the critters."

"And if I took a hunk of meat with me I might manage to quiet them in any case, eh?" asked our hero.

"Might, mightn't; can't say. Jest a toss up—what then?"

"That's telling," smiled Joe. "But you and Beaver Jack be ready. If you see a sleigh coming along quick, with one man aboard it, put it down that it's me. I'm going to make a move to get possession of one of them, and once I have got it, why, we'll make tracks for the Fennicks."

The little hunter regarded his pupil in open-mouthed amazement. He stepped a pace away, held Joe at arm's length, then brought one hand with a bang down on to his shoulder; only, as this young friend of his had grown so prodigiously of late, Hank had to stand on tiptoe.

"Of all the mad ideas that ever was, this is it!" he cried. "But it aer fine, and I'll say more, it aer the only way to pull us out of this business, mad though it does appear. Ef you hadn't wanted to go, I'd have gone. But you suggested, and so you shall make the attempt. And ef they spot you, jest run for your life out on to the lake. Beaver Jack and me'll follow you across and build up a bit of a breastwork close by the shore. That'll give us a sorter place to hold 'em from, and there you could join us. If you succeed, why, off we goes, in course; and, now that I thinks of it more, ef you ain't too proud, I'd like to come with you. Why? I'll tell you. The dogs are bound to be a bother. You ain't never handled the critters, while I have, many a time, and dogs, like hosses, soon gets to know when they're dealing with a green 'un. How's that?"

"Agreed!" cried Joe, delighted to have a companion. "Ask Jack what he thinks of the affair."

Half an hour later there was quite a stir amongst the garrison of the island, for the enemy had disappeared, having returned downhearted to their own encampment. Beaver Jack and Joe were bearing along between them the light sleigh upon which the Redskin's pelts were stacked, and on which their own traps would find a place. They lifted it to the top of the wall they had built and, leaping to the outside, lowered it carefully. Hank then handed down rifles and ammunition, the former of which they slung over their shoulders.

"If the wust comes to the wust, we makes back here agin," he said. "It aer been a proper tight little island; now we kin move. Them clouds has smothered the moon nicely, and it aer snowing enough to hide a man at fifty yards. Guess we'll cross, throw up a wall of snow, making a sorter nest in case we want it, and then get away on to the camp them half-breeds is occupying."

He took the end of the tow-rope, while Beaver Jack went immediately behind him. Joe fell in in rear, and in that order they strode on across the snow towards the shore which harboured the enemy. They halted once to listen, for a dog had yelped. But as the sound was not repeated, they pressed on again, and were soon at the point where ice and solid earth met beneath the all-pervading mantle of snow.

"This'll do," said Hank shortly. "Slip off yer snowshoes and rake the snow up from a central point; that'll leave a deep little hole to shelter us. See here, Beaver Jack, you keep a bright eye open for us. Ef we comes bowling along on a sleigh, get a hold of that sleigh rope of yours, leap aboard us, and make fast. Ef we comes runnin' out, jest see that you shoot at them critters who'll be follerin' and not at us."

That was his farewell to the Redskin. He and Joe helped to erect the wall of snow, and then, leaving Beaver Jack to complete the task, strode on again towards the camp which they had vacated for the benefit of the enemy. Under one arm the little hunter carried a ball of snow, which seemed somewhat curious and unnecessary, especially considering the fact that the ground was thickly covered with the same material. But within the snow there was something of greater value.

"It's that chunk o' meat," Hank had explained, when he first produced his burden. "I set it over the fire till it was wellnigh cooked and the frost driven out of it altogether. Then I cut it into pieces, packed them close in a piece of skin from one o' the beasts we shot, and wrapped the whole again in snow, which'll help to keep the heat in and the cold out. Sounds rummy, don't it? But it'll work handsome."

"Now, young chap," he whispered, when he and our hero had parted from the Redskin and were within three hundred yards of the enemy, "we've got to decide how we'll work this business. How's it to be?"

"You take the dogs," said Joe at once. "I'll tackle Hurley."

"But—but you ain't going to kick up a rumpus with him, surely!" exclaimed Hank, sinking his voice till it was almost inaudible, and almost hissing the words. "It aer the sleigh we want, two of 'em ef we could manage it, though that ain't possible. Ef we get away with one, only four of the critters can follow, and what's four after so many? You ain't after Hurley?"

He was answered by a vigorous shake of the head. "No, I don't want any struggle; I wouldn't shoot the fellow if I had the opportunity."

"Wouldn't ye? Then I would, me lad. It aer human nature to look to number one fust. When a man murders, and aer wanted by the hangman, when he begins trying his best to murder others, then's the time fer him to go under. Hurley has my bullet fust time I kin look straight along the barrel. But what aer you after?"

"I don't know. I want to see what he's doing. I want to find out if he has that envelope he stole from me so many months ago now."

Hank's head shot up quickly. He was a man with such a vast experience of life, and had encountered so many strange happenings, that he was not inclined to think a thing impossible till he had proved it to be so. There was that envelope, to be sure. Joe had often spoken about it. He had told Hank the whole story, how there was something within the envelope which he could have read had he chosen, though against his dead father's wishes. The contents, in fact, were for perusal only when he had made good, when he had fought his own battles. And Hank had been impressed by the recital.

"It aer a queer story," he had said in his quiet little way, "and I 'low as the temptation to open that envelope must have been great. But your dad war right. Supposing the letter told you of dollars to be had for the axing, what would have happened? You'd have stayed back there in England. You'd have lived on the best of the land and become fat and lousy. You wouldn't have had half the fun out of life, for the struggle to make good aer fun to everyone who's got spirit and pride. 'Sides, there's something wuss. This here Hank wouldn't have made your acquaintance.

191

"Supposing that letter had had something to do with monetary affairs?" The little hunter came to a halt promptly and stared before him. He would have whistled but for the proximity of the enemy. Instead, he turned on Joe, and with the snowflakes falling about them gripped him firmly by the sleeve. "By Jingo," he whispered, "I believe you've got it! That there Hurley stole the letter. When he was captured he hid it up, for he'd had time to take a look at it. Perhaps he forgot to hide the dollar notes. But in any case, he put the letter away in some safe place, perhaps in the shack close to that lake where he went into hiding. He'd larned that there was gain to be made by it, ef only he could get clear of the law. Wall, he slipped off. Those police let him out of their fingers. He went back for the letter, and then, because you've something to do with it, as of course is sartin, he sets out to find and wipe you out. Huh! It's all in a nutshell. You ain't wanted, young chap. Soon as you're wiped out, Hurley comes in for something that's waiting."

Perhaps it was native sagacity again, a strange mixture of intuition and intelligence, which helped the little hunter. Perhaps also, taking every point into consideration, it was the most reasonable solution to come to. Be that as it may, Hank at one effort had fathomed the mystery of this unprovoked attack, and at the same time had discovered that Joe was most probably rather an important person.

"But you ain't got the dollars yet, not by a long way," he cautioned. "We ain't got out of this muss, and Hurley'll do his best to hold us. Now, lad, you aer after that envelope. Wall, see here. Ef it's to be had easy, take it; ef not, leave the thing till another time. For ef we clear out of this with our scalps we'll ride for the nearest fort garrisoned by the North-west Police, or some station where there's Ontario Police quartered. We'll inform about Hurley, and we'll lead a party along till the rascal's taken. Life, I guess, aer more valuable than a letter; so bear that in mind, and hold off ef there's danger."

With their plans thus arranged, the two crept forward, and were soon within some fifty yards of the camp. Through the falling snowflakes they could see the large lean-to in which the half-breeds were sleeping, for the band of desperadoes had thrown themselves down immediately on returning. The fire at the entrance burned low, and the light it gave out was feeble. But more issued from a second, blazing some yards to the left, and illuminating the interior of the other lean-to.

"The men!" whispered Hank, pointing to the first. "That 'ere critter yonder! It aer up to us now to locate the dogs. H-hish! Here's one o' them coming."

Joe saw him tear his bundle asunder and extract a piece of flesh. At the same moment he became aware of the fact that a huge beast was slowly crawling toward them.

"Was it actually a dog? No. Yes; that was certain. Then would it suddenly give tongue and fling itself upon them?"

"H-h-hish!" said Hank, making a curious little clicking sound with his tongue. "He's smelt the meat; ef only he'll be quiet, we'll soon have the others."

A low, almost inaudible growl came from the brute advancing on them. Even in that light Joe could see that its coat was bristling. It was slinking toward them now on half-bent legs, looking as if it would make a sudden spring when within easy reach of them. The position of the two might be described, in fact, as more than a trifle embarrassing.

CHAPTER XIX

Across the Snows for Safety

"Hist! Hist! Here, good dog!" Hank called gently to the huge brute slinking towards himself and Joe, as they lay outside the winter bivouacs of Hurley and his men, and held forward a tempting morsel of flesh. Even our hero could scent the pleasing aroma from the morsel; for the little hunter had so contrived with his covering of snow that there was considerable warmth in it yet, while the frosty air seemed to accentuate the aroma. But it was a toss up as to whether the beast would suddenly give tongue or would slink still nearer and accept the proffered dainty.

"Good dog!" called Hank again. "Here's summat for yer."

Perhaps his soothing voice had something to do with the matter. It may have been even that the brute realized, as dumb brutes do, that he was face to face with one well acquainted with his brethren. Suffice it to say that his bristles subsided and he sidled up, wagging his tail, his nose snuffing at the morsel. Hank patted him at once.

"Here's more o' that," he said. "Lie down! Now, where aer the others? It aer more'n likely that they've gone in with the men, and ef that's the case it'll be a job to get 'em out, to say nothing of puttin' the harness on 'em. See here, lad; I'll stay with this brute, so's to quiet the others ef they come out. You creep in a bit closer and scout around; I ain't yet quite sure how things aer. Take a piece of the meat with you, and ef a dog runs out, jest pitch it towards him."

It may be imagined that Joe needed no further orders. He was on hands and knees at once, and began to creep towards the lean-to. In a little while he was within a dozen feet, and, wriggling his way into a position of advantage, he was soon able to look right in, the firelight helping him greatly. A jumbled heap of bodies, legs, and arms met his eyes, with the sleeping forms of dogs inextricably mixed up with them. He saw, in fact, a typical residence of the half-breed. These men, of a degenerate class themselves, and careless of everything so long as their own comfort was assured, had turned into their lean-to without removing so much as a garment, which is not to be wondered at, considering the cold, and, throwing themselves down higgledy-piggledy, had called to the dogs, who had promptly accepted the invitation, and, thrusting their way into any odd corner and the most comfortable nooks, had settled

194

themselves down to sleep till the call of a new day aroused them. But there was something more which attracted Joe's attention. There seemed to be so few dogs, perhaps half a dozen in all, while each of the sleigh teams mustered nine or ten.

"Couldn't swear to the number," he told himself, "but there are not two teams here, of that I am certain. Where, then, are the others?"

Looking to right and to left gave him no help. It was clear that he must search for them elsewhere, so promptly he crept away in the direction of the second lean-to. It happened, too, that his path took him to the end of this farthest removed from the spot where the fire was blazing. Indeed, it was only native caution which caused him to make for that end; for had he crawled towards the fire, its bright flames would have betrayed his presence instantly to anyone happening to look out. Hurley, he knew, was a suspicious, restless individual, so that the merest whimper from one of the dogs, even a rustling of the snow, might bring him into the open.

"I'll give him no chance to spoil our plans," said Joe, kneeling up to take a good look about him. "First thing is to take a squint into the lean-to. There's a light somewhere inside, I fancy, so perhaps Hurley is sitting up and making plans for the next attack. Hope he ain't, though; I'd rather he were asleep, worn out by all that's happened."

Crawling along on hands and knees, it was a little time before he came to the lean-to. A glance over his shoulder now told him that Hank had come a trifle closer, and still had the dog beside him. Knowing, therefore, that he had someone to give him a warning should the half-breeds suddenly emerge, Joe very gently separated two strips of birch bark which closed in a portion of this Canadian dwelling. Then he applied his eye to the aperture, only to find that he was staring right across to the far side of the lean-to, and that neither Hurley nor anyone else was within his vision. There was a roll of flaming bark within two feet, however, spluttering and smoking gently.

"No good here," he thought. "Must try the other side, and a trifle lower down. Hallo—dogs! George—they're lying just outside this shanty!"

Joe had risen to his feet now, though still stooping, and as he peered over the far end of the flimsy erection he caught sight of quite a number of dogs stretched within easy distance of the fire, huddled into one close body, and all fast asleep. After all, there was nothing remarkable in that, or of sufficient importance to cause his exclamations, save, of course, their proximity to himself. For these dogs, bred in the Arctic zone almost, and in any case upon its fringe, can stand a degree of cold which would rapidly kill a human being. Warmth they like, just as do most animals, but they can resist a Canadian winter in remarkable manner, and are capable of sleeping in the open. In any case, there they were, bundled together, sleeping deeply, no doubt tired after a hard day with the sleigh.

"But they'll rouse any time," Joe told himself. "If there weren't snow about to deaden my steps, they'd have kicked up a row already, unless, of course, they take me for one of their masters."

Perhaps that was the reason of their tranquillity. Satisfied that they had not detected him yet, Joe crept round to the far side of the lean-to and, boring another aperture, peered in. And on this occasion his efforts won a greater reward; for Hurley lay before him. His bulky form was stretched full length on one of the sleighs, his face turned away from the light; a rifle was propped beside him, while close against the sleigh was that same wooden box which we have already described. For the rest, there was nothing more to comment on. Travellers during a Canadian winter are few and far between—we speak here of the backwoods—and such as there are carry merely necessaries, so that a humble lean-to contains little else but the traveller. There was Hurley, in fact, alone, and with a weapon beside him. The box was of no consequence, though, if only Joe could have guessed that only a few hours ago that precious document was spread out on it, it is likely enough that he would have shown more excitement. But there was no sign of the envelope. Doubtless the sleeping Hurley had it in an inner pocket. Joe bore in mind Hank's warning, and promptly used all his wits to bring about an escape from the ruffian.

"Can't bother about the document or letter," he told himself. "We'll tackle the man; but how, is the question? It's clear that he has hauled the sleigh in to make a bed, leaving the dogs still attached to it. That would be fine for us, if it weren't for the fact that Hurley has fallen asleep on it. Then there's the gun; fancy I can reach that, anyway."

He stretched the opening a little wider, stood well above it, and reached in.

"Can't!" he told himself, with an exclamation of vexation. "Try again."

This time the roof of the lean-to bent inward as he pressed upon it, then his fingers hit upon the muzzle of the weapon. Joe gripped it firmly, drew gently on it, and slowly extracted the gun through the opening.

"Makes things easier a whole heap. When he wakes he'll have to look about for another weapon, unless he's got——" He pulled at the opening and again stared in at the sleeper. "No sign of a shooter. Hooray! Things begin to look a little better. I'll get hold of Hank and have a chat with him."

Within three minutes the two had retired a little and were discussing matters in voices raised hardly above a whisper. Hank kneeled on the snow, one arm about the dog he had coaxed into friendship, and who seemed to have taken a

196

huge fancy to him. The little man listened carefully to our hero's description, and made no comment for a few moments; then, of a sudden, a gurgling laugh came from some point deep down in his throat.

"Ef we don't win out I ain't Hank," he smiled. "Now, jest listen. This aer the movement; Jimmy here—that's this dog, and I christened him Jimmy 'cos that's the name of a beast I had once when huntin' in the backwoods—Jimmy goes along up to his friends sleeping outside the lean-to and wakes 'em. He lets 'em understand that things are right, and that there's a new friend come to the camp. You needn't look as ef you didn't believe it could be, young chap. You've got to remember that there's a moon. Ef it were pitch dark it would be different, for then the dogs couldn't see us. A beast barks at any sound on a dark night, while with a moon, ef he kin see right off what's caused the ruction, he don't always give tongue. Anyway, we try the plan. Ef it fails, we'll have to make a rush at the brutes, put 'em into line, and drive 'em. But here's the rest of the scheme. This is your part."

"Ah! What? I'm ready."

"In course you aer; couldn't I tell that from what you've done this last five minutes?"

"Well," said Joe impatiently, "you look to the dogs. That's right, for you know a heap about them. What do I do?"

"Settle Hurley."

"Eh? Kill him? I——"

"You don't need to be thin-skinned, young chap. This ain't a time fer killing; I'll do that fast enough ef it comes to a tussle between us. What you've got to do is to rouse him off the sleigh, and then smother him so's he can't get clear of the lean-to till we've got aboard and has set the dogs going. Jest sling that 'ere rifle into the bushes here. Gently with it. Now you ain't bothered with extry weight. You comes with me to the place agin and watches while I get in amongst the dogs. Ef there's a noise, and Hurley rouses, bash the lean-to down on top of his head, jump on it, send the sticks and the snow about him, then leap on the sleigh and look out fer fireworks."

Joe grinned; he couldn't help doing so, in spite of the danger of the situation. "If there's not a row?" he asked.

"Ef there's not a ruction with them dogs and the other men, and things go nice and smooth and easy, I'll lift my hand when I'm ready. Then you get a grip of that thar Hurley, bash him over the head ef you like with your open hand, and, as he rises, bring the whole shanty down on him—eh? You're there, ain't you? It aer a clear and straightforward plan."

"Got it," answered Joe promptly, moistening his lips, and tingling with excitement and anticipation. "Do we start now?"

"This very instant. But supposin' Hurley suddenly rouses as soon as we get close, and afore you kin bring the shack down on him———"

"Leave that to me," answered Joe tersely. "I've had one innings with the ruffian already."

There never were two who understood each other so well and so easily as did Hank and our hero. Their discussion had taken them but a few bare seconds, and now they were creeping back. Joe halted when close beside the lean-to, while the little hunter sat down on his knees and whispered to the dog Jimmy. The hound seemed to have gathered his meaning too as rapidly as had Joe, for he went slinking forward and lay down beside his comrades. As might have been expected, his coming caused many of the beasts to open their eyes, though they did not offer to move. But Hank was watching eagerly, and a second later a morsel of flesh flew across, landing close to Jimmy. Others followed, and in an incredibly short space of time the dogs were all aroused and standing.

"Jest watch fer the signal," whispered the hunter. "I'm agoin' to put 'em into their harness."

It was just at that moment that Joe heard a movement within the lean-to, and promptly applied his eye to the opening he had made. Hurley had turned over, and was now blinking at the spluttering torch, while one arm was spread out over the box. Something seemed to have alarmed him, for he sat up, giving the box a kick, which Hank heard; then he got to his feet swiftly and, bending low, stepped toward the opening, just outside which blazed the fire, and just beyond which Hank was mustering the team of dogs. Hurley saw him; for the instant he took him to be one of his own following, then he became suspicious.

"Who's that?" he called. "Hi! Someone is tampering with the dogs."

Joe did not venture to wait longer. He leaped on to the top of the lean-to, the flimsy thing breaking down beneath his weight at once; he trod upon the wretch beneath, sending him tumbling to the ground; then he stood ready for the next movement. It came with startling suddenness. Hank had found a whip close to the dogs, and sent it cracking over the team. The brutes sprang forward the next instant, and in spite of the fact that Hurley had tumbled across the sleigh, they brought it out from beneath the smashed lean-to with a jerk which tossed snow and sticks aside, and sent the rascally leader of this band of cut-throats rolling backward from the end. Hank seemed to fly to his position at the fore end. Joe fell across the sleigh as it flashed past him, scrambled aboard, and found himself gripping the sides closely; for a sleigh is no easy thing to ride when a strong team pulls it at fast pace across ground which is broken. It jolts and sways abominably, while often enough it will glissade, just like a petrol car rounding a sharp and greasy corner.

"Hold tight," shouted Hank, "and get yer shootin' iron ready for 'em! When we comes up to Beaver Jack, I'll hand the reins over to him. You'll take the centre place, while I'll nip in at the back, so as to be ready to shoot that 'ere Hurley."

Not a word passed between the two from that moment until they reached the spot where Beaver Jack was waiting for them. Swinging along at a glorious pace, and swerving and rolling, sometimes dangerously, they finally dashed up to the heap of snow behind which the Redskin had taken shelter.

"Now, Jack, you take them dogs," said Hank quickly. "Give me a hold of the rope tied on to your sleigh. There! It's fast to this; you kin move off when you're ready."

"But——"

"What?" asked the hunter somewhat curtly, interrupting Joe.

"Why let the dogs haul two sleighs? Cut Beaver Jack's pelts adrift and tie 'em here. We can do it as we go. Our traps can be served in the same way. It isn't the weight that'll tell so much as the amount of ground our runners cover. A sleigh towing behind will hold the dogs more than the load on it will do when added to this sleigh."

"Shucks! You aer got the best head of the three of us," cried Hank. "You git in at them dogs, Beaver Jack. Me and Joe'll fix the kit while we're moving."

Away went the lash of the whip cracking over the leaders. Beaver Jack handled the team as a man does who has had great practice. Anyone could have said that from merely observing his manner of wielding the whip, for the short-handled, long-lashed dog whip employed in the north of Canada is apt to be more dangerous to the amateur wielder than to the dogs. It requires an amount of practice to control it; and as it twirled and cracked, and leaped backwards and forwards, now over the dogs, and then above the heads of Hank and Joe, there was proof positive of Beaver Jack's previous acquaintance with it. Meanwhile, Hank had drawn up the smaller sleigh alongside, and he and Joe rapidly transferred its load to the large one on which they themselves sat, lashing every article into position.

At the enemy's camp there was now huge commotion. At first the confusion had been so great that no one could guess what had happened. Even Hurley himself had little more than an inkling, and it took him a few seconds to pick himself up and free himself of the snow and debris of the lean-to with which he had been covered. Then shouts of rage and fierce orders burst from his lips; in his anger he dashed hither and thither, shouting at his men, and even striking those who seemed to be dawdling.

"Put the other team into the sleigh, quick!" he commanded. "One of you help here to find my rifle. Those men have made a sneaking night attack, and will get clear off if we don't move quick. Here, look for my rifle, I say. How in thunder did it get outside the lean-to?"

There were quite a number of little matters which he was likely to find difficult of explanation. But the gun was found eventually where Joe had placed it, while the second team of dogs were got into their harness. Then Hurley pressed two of the boldest of his followers into this special service, and putting them aboard the remaining sleigh, leaped there himself, and ordered the driver to set off in pursuit of our hero and his friends.

Beaver Jack never hesitated as to the course he ought to pursue once his fingers closed on the reins Hank tossed him.

"Clear back for the settlements," the little hunter had said, and the Redskin obeyed him to the letter. He steered his team over a portion of the lake, set them at the bank where it shelved very gradually to the ice, and, gaining a hollow, aimed directly for a huge patch of forest distinguishable with the aid of the moon's rays in the far distance.

"He war born cute, he war," grunted Hank, some minutes later, when all the loads were secured, and he and Joe had time and opportunity to look about them. "Beaver Jack never stirs a foot, but he watches everything about him, and I reckon that he knows nigh every foot of the country; knows it, too, whether it's fine weather or ef there's snow about and landmarks is wiped out altogether. He aer steering downhill, knowing as the big lake back behind drains along the valley to another, and that again to a third. It means quick travelling all the way, and ef we're to shake off them critters it'll be before we reaches the third lake. Ah! Guess that's Hurley. It's a pity it's stopped snowing."

It was necessary to cling to the sleigh tightly, for the going was fast and furious. There was no time to watch for obstacles ahead, while the snow covered the land so completely that deep brooks crossing their line of flight were not seen till they were on to them, and then there was a mighty shaking. The dogs, spurred on by the cracking whip, leaped across the hollow. The sleigh bumped across with a great jolting which tossed those aboard it to either side; but still they clung tight, while the little hunter, seeing that a sleigh was following, nimbly turned about, spread himself face downward on the top of the sleigh, and placed his rifle before him.

"You jest take and sit on my legs, Joe," he called; "then ef there's a bad jolt I'll still be here. It won't make no difference to my shootin', and it's likely to save delay. Ef I was to roll over you'd have to stop, and that'd be serious."

Joe promptly did as he was asked, tucking the legs of the little hunter beneath him, and placing a blanket across them before he sat down. He could then afford to turn his own head and watch the enemy. Away behind them, tearing along at reckless speed, and at such a rate that a cloud of white was thrown up in front of each runner for all the world as if the sleigh were a ship at sea, Hurley and his comrades came chasing after the trio they had fondly hoped to kill. A figure crouched just behind the dogs, and the frosty air brought the sound of his shouts and the crack of the dog whip he wielded. A second figure was bundled up behind him, the face of the man on the shoulder of the driver, while a pair of staring eyes peered at the sleigh ahead. Hurley sat right aft, his bulky form overlapping the sides of the sleigh, his head and shoulders well above his comrades. The moon, playing upon the scene, showed a rod projecting upward from a point just in front of the murderer, and at once Joe knew it was a rifle. He saw the ruffian lean forward and shout at his men, and then watched as he rose still higher—evidently he was half-kneeling and half-sitting—his weapon was lifted into a horizontal position and went to his shoulder. It was clear, in fact, that Hurley was about to fire.

"Best get down flat, every one of us," cried Hank, in warning tones. "Beaver Jack, you lie flat same as me, facing forward. You'll still be able to steer, and kin use the whip ef it's wanted. Then Joe kin stretch hisself out on top of the two of us. It'll be a cramping business, but it aer better'n bein' shot."

Such gymnastic efforts upon a sleigh rocking from side to side was no easy matter. But when there is a man within reasonable distance whose rifle is presented, and any moment may bring a bullet, the most difficult of evolutions are carried out with wonderful rapidity. In this case, Beaver Jack swivelled himself round with a dexterity there was no denying. Then Joe turned entirely, for he wished to have his eyes behind him all the while and watch Hurley. A second or so later he was also lying flat, his weight helping to hold the Redskin to the sleigh, while he gripped Hank now by the ankles. But he was hardly in position when a puff of smoke burst from the rifle held by the burly figure at the back of the pursuing sleigh, there was a dull flash, then a bullet screamed past the heads of Hank and his friends. The reply to this was sent without delay by the little hunter.

"Missed!" he grunted. "Shootin' at a moving object ain't never too easy with a rifle, but when the consarn you're fixed on is movin' itself as well, why, a hit aer often a chance. Guess Hurley ha' got his eye in."

It was a cold-blooded observation, hardly likely to encourage either. But the grin on Hank's face showed that he himself was not greatly concerned by the close approach of a second bullet which Hurley had fired. For Joe, one can only say that he watched the duel fascinated, fear for his own person lost in his interest. Once again he saw Hurley's rifle lifted, saw the smoke belch from the muzzle, and then heard—almost felt, one might say, without exaggeration—the passage of the bullet.

Hank chuckled. "This here lyin'-down position bothers him fine," he cried. "He aer got to drop his muzzle a whole heap before he hits us. But I'm not the one to give chances; I'm going to pick off that Hurley."

Up went his own rifle, for Hank leaned on one elbow. He took a long and careful aim and then pulled his trigger; but the result was not what he had anticipated. As he himself had said, shooting was extremely difficult under such circumstances, for the sleigh swayed and jolted horribly. But the bullet missed the ruffian at whom it was aimed only because there was another man in front of him. Of a sudden the driver of the pursuing sleigh dropped his whip and doubled up, his chin on his chest. Then he swayed a little, and, as if with a mighty effort, gathered all his strength and threw himself backward, pulling on the reins and bringing his team to a standstill. But it was his last action. He toppled over to the left and fell into the snow.

"Wrong man; sorry," Hank jerked out grimly. "Hurley'll have it next time. I'll wait a bit to get him closer."

The chase after that settled down a little, Hank holding his fire, while Hurley himself copied the example of the little hunter and spread himself out flat on his sleigh, his new driver also. But this was apparent, with a lighter load the enemy were getting nearer.

"Ef that's the case, we'll make a stop precious soon," said Hank. "What say, Joe?"

"I'm with you. We're three now to their two, and if we could face eight of them some little while ago, surely we could——"

His argument came to an abrupt ending at that moment, for a wide ditch with vertical banks carved out by nature crossed their path, and the snow hid it from view. It was more than likely that the snow had formed a species of bridge over this deep hollow; but, in any case, it broke down as the last of the team of dogs crossed, causing the front end of the sleigh to dip suddenly. The runners cannoned against the iron-hard banks, and in a twinkling sleigh and men went flying.

"Surely we could face those two," gasped Joe, as if continuing the sentence where circumstances had caused it to be so abruptly broken, and at the same time picking himself up from the bank of snow into which he had been thrown. "Here's fine cover. This ditch will hide us completely."

He threw himself down into the deep hollow at once, and found that he had quite a high bank before him, over which he had to lift his head to see the enemy. Hurley marked the occasion by firing at him, and his bullet swished past within an inch, causing Joe to duck suddenly. As for Hank, the sudden upset seemed to have caused him vast amusement, and certainly he wasn't in the smallest degree hurt, though, being at the rear of the sleigh, he had been thrown over the heads of his comrades and had come down sprawling amongst the dogs. He picked up himself and his weapon instantly and crept to Joe's side, still grinning widely, while Beaver Jack, undisturbed by the upset, his gravity of demeanour and his native dignity not in the least degree ruffled, coolly turned the sleigh the right way up, dragged it backward, and called hoarsely to the dogs to lie down.

"We war jest meant to stop and have it out with them critters," said Hank, when he had shaken the snow out of his eyes and mouth. "Gee! that war a tumble. Lucky fer us there's soft snow. Ef it had been on bare ice, there's some of us would have had cracked heads. Ha! Hurley ha' thought better of coming along towards us. Guess this business is gettin' a little more serious than he wanted. Yer see, he had jest three at fust, three as didn't know he was following. Now he's got the same three, and only one to help him agin them. You sit low, lad; bullets has a way of striking jest when they ain't expected."

His own head went down of a sudden, while a bullet buzzed above them. Evidently it must have gone extremely near to the Redskin, who was then crawling towards them, for Beaver Jack's impassive face broke into a smile. His sensitive lips actually curled, those deep-set, penetrating eyes twinkled, while his curious chin went up and seemed almost to embrace the tip of the hooked nose.

"None the wuss if you ain't hit, mate," laughed Hank. "Joe, how do yer like bullets flyin' close beside you?"

To look at our hero it was an experience which he enjoyed, for he was smiling. But it was not because of the bullets. He was smiling at the sudden change in their fortunes, at the complete success of the special efforts which he and Hank had made, and at the thought that, instead of being chased by Hurley now, they might well turn the tables on him.

"We've a duty to do," he said so sharply, that the little hunter swung round upon him.

"Eh? Duty?" he asked.

"Yes; there's a murderer, a criminal wanted by the law. Our duty is to take him, so that he can do no more mischief."

"In course," came the ready answer, "that's what we're going to do. See here, Joe, I don't return to the settlements till we've got our man or rubbed him out entirely. It's the same thing to me whichever happens; only stop his game we will."

"Right! I'm with you," cried Joe.

"Then jest look spry and don't get standin' in the way of his rifle," grunted Hank, as he peered cautiously at the enemy.

CHAPTER XX

Back to the Farm

The minutes which passed as Joe and his friends lay in the hollow into which the upset of their sleigh had thrown them proved, as they rapidly increased in number, that plans, however carefully made, do not always become accomplished. It had been agreed between the little hunter and our hero that it was their plain duty to capture Hurley; for was he not an escaped criminal, a murderer, a brute who sought to slay them? But try as they might to circumvent the rascal, he outwitted them.

"It aer one of them tarnation difficulties that one don't realize till one comes up agin them," said Hank after a while, for immediately on their upset Hurley had caused his own team of dogs to be pulled up short, and had himself taken advantage of a hollow. Hidden in it, he bobbed up every now and again and sent a shot swishing over the little party, while apparently the bullets fired by Joe and his friend had no better effect. They were, in fact, merely wasting time.

"Doing no harm, and just keeping us here till his men come up to join him," ventured Joe.

"Huh!" grunted the trapper. "But we'll see as they don't get quite up to him, unless, of course, there's a hollow which will give them cover all the way. Lad, this aer likely to get serious."

"Then why not make a bolt for it?" asked Joe. "I don't mean run away altogether," he added, as Hank flashed round upon him, "but make a rush and draw him after us. If Beaver Jack steers so as to take us into broken country, where there are patches of trees and undergrowth, we could select a suitable place, stop suddenly, and then shoot as Hurley came after us."

Hank struck the butt of his rifle violently. "Ef that ain't a wheeze!" he cried exultantly. "Ef he follows us—and it ain't dead sartin—but ef he does, Beaver Jack'll manage the move for us easy. Let's see; yes, there's trees 'way ahead—only to reach 'em we've got to run the gauntlet."

"Well? What matters?" asked Joe. "Better that than have all those rascals close up to us and shooting."

"We'll do it," exclaimed Hank. "Beaver Jack, you aer heard this proposition?"

The Redskin hardly deigned to answer; instead, he swung his dogs round, pulling them by means of the reins, till he had them lying in the hollow itself.

"Not do mount here," he said. "P'raps bullet hit us. But creep away down there till we reach trees. Leave one here to fire now and again; then, when all ready, jump on the sleigh and get away behind cover."

He held out an attenuated hand, the fingers of which were as fine as any lady's, and pointed to a patch of trees springing from the side of the hollow a hundred or more yards away. The gesture and his words were sufficient explanation of his meaning. If the sleigh were taken there without its human load, and the feat could be accomplished without Hurley seeing, then all could mount and start away before the murderer had become aware of their intentions.

"It aer a cute move, and we'll work it," said Hank instantly. "Now, Joe, which of us'll stay; you or me?"

"My place," came the ready answer. "I suggested going, therefore I do the work which will help us to fool Hurley. I'll give him a shot now and again."

Hank at once slid down into the hollow and joined Beaver Jack. Joe watched them as they sprawled on their faces, first placing their weapons on the sleigh; then he saw them slowly move away, the Redskin beside his team, crawling on all-fours, talking to the dogs and keeping them well under cover.

Crack! crack! Zip! zip! Two bullets swished overhead, the crisp sounds they made proving that they had been aimed at Joe and not at his comrades. At once he bobbed up, aimed for the place where he knew Hurley was in hiding, and fired; but he saw nothing of the enemy. This was a duel waged between contestants who kept beneath cover, and hoped only for a lucky chance to hit an enemy. Joe waited again, and once more the exchange of shots was repeated. Then he turned his head, to find that Hank and Beaver Jack had reached the trees and were waiting for him.

"I'll give 'em one more," he told himself, raising his rifle, "and then join the others. Hallo! What's this? One of Beaver Jack's pelts. Suit my purpose admirably."

Two shots rang out again in the distance, and Joe's followed swiftly. Then he placed the dark-coloured skin on the top of the bank, and within sight of the enemy, and at once sprawled on hands and knees and crawled along the hollow. He accomplished the distance to the rat-a-tat-tat of rifle shots, for Hurley and his comrade had found a mark to aim at. Then he took his place on the sleigh, on which Hank and Beaver Jack were already seated, and which they had hauled in behind the cover of the trees.

"Best get into position and comfortably settled afore we set out," said the little hunter. "Gee! What a racket they're making! They ain't spotted this business, I hope?"

"Shooting at one of Beaver Jack's pelts," said Joe dryly. "He left it behind. I thought he'd be able to spare it."

"My, you'll do!" exclaimed Hank, laughing outright. "I've known young chaps as could fight all right, but who were always mighty serious when bullets war flying, and couldn't think of things like that. You'll do, Joe. You aer got a sense of humour. Now, Beaver Jack, you get in at it, and don't drive 'em too fast after the fust bust of speed. We aer got to draw that Hurley cuss close up to us."

Shouts of anger and disappointment greeted the party as they swung out from behind the cover and into the open. Shots were fired in their direction also. But Beaver Jack was a master of stratagem; he kept the patch of cover that had already helped them so much between the sleigh and the enemy, and Hurley, seeing that the men he desired to kill were rapidly increasing their distance, rushed for his own sleigh, leaped aboard, and bellowed to his driver to set the team in motion; and, thanks to the lighter weight the pursuing sleigh bore, and in no small degree to Beaver Jack's skill and cunning, Hurley slowly gained upon the three men flying before him. He leaned upon his elbow, for he had again adopted the position which Hank had first shown him, and, taking a long and careful aim, sent a bullet flying after them.

"Time we stopped!" cried Joe abruptly, gripping his elbow, for the missile had struck him. Not that it was a severe wound—on the contrary, it was little more than a graze—but even that causes pain and rouses a man to exertion. Joe was determined to put up no longer with Hurley's attempts upon his life and upon those of his comrades.

"Let's stop this business right here and now," he cried hotly. "There's a long patch of wood ahead; let's fix to pull in the team there."

"Good fer you, lad!" answered Hank. "Beaver Jack, you aer heard the order? Now, Joe lad, listen to this. I has fust shot; ef I miss, you're welcome to try; only I somehow feel as ef this war my special business. Here we are; now fer it."

Beaver Jack brought the team to a halt in masterly manner, while Joe and the hunter rolled off the sleigh. Then Hank took post close to the edge of the wood and just in the open.

"I ain't the one to fire at a man without giving him a chance," he said. "Ah! he's seen us; he's stopped. That was a near 'un!"

There was a heavy thud as Hurley's bullet struck the tree beside the hunter. Then up went Hank's weapon. He took a rapid sight, and then flung down his rifle almost before the report had come to Joe's ears, while the latter watched for the result of the shot with more than a little anxiety. A little time before he would perhaps have wished Hurley to escape injury, for Joe possessed a soft and forgiving heart. Now, however, he had a different opinion as to his merits. It was, therefore, with no great amount of sorrow that he saw the ruffian suddenly throw up his arms and tumble over.

"Wiped out clean," growled Hank. "Dead as a trapped beaver."

There could be no doubt that that was the end of the murderer. Hank's bullet had, in fact, killed Hurley instantaneously, and had thereby provided a fitting punishment for the detestable crime he had committed. As for Hurley's companion, the half-breed leaped on to the sleigh which, like his master, he had abandoned for the moment, and sending his whip cracking over the dogs, turned them in the opposite direction and raced away for safety.

"Not as he's got anything to fear from me," said Hank; "I aer done what I promised. And now, young chap, guess there are something more for us to look into—there aer that letter."

It was uppermost in his mind as in our hero's, and it is not to be wondered at that they boarded their sleigh and swung their team back towards the dark figure lying prone in the snow behind them. But would Hurley have the document still? Had he destroyed it? In fact, had he ever had it, or was it possible that both Hank and Joe had conjured up a conspiracy which had never existed? Supposing Hurley had merely fallen upon their trace by accident, and then, learning that two of the men who had previously helped to hound him down were of the party, had endeavoured to slay them?

Those were the fears and the questions which raced through their minds as Beaver Jack sent the dogs straining across the snow towards the body of their enemy. They found him lying face downwards, a crimson stain spoiling the beautiful white of Nature's own making.

"Search him," said Joe, turning his head away from such a gruesome sight. "Search him, then let us go."

"Got it! Huh! I said so, didn't I?"

Hank's face was radiant. He held aloft a long envelope, stained with much handling, and then, having run through all of Hurley's pockets, he dragged the document from the envelope and coolly perused it. Joe himself had now no qualms as to reading it also.

"You are on the high road to 'making good'," said Hank. "There ain't no reason now in waiting longer. Read! It aer as clear as daylight that Hurley had made up his mind to wipe you out and then to make for England with the idea of passing himself off as your father."

When they were able to gather all the details, this, indeed, proved to be the crux of the whole conspiracy, and the death of Hurley had alone put an end to it. It is not for us to raise doubts here as to his prospects. Doubtless there was many a slip which he might have made, for criminals are ever careless; but matters were decidedly in his favour. That receipt, still within the envelope, would obtain for him all the proofs of Mr. Bradley's birth and life and parentage. The signature, doubtless, he would learn to copy, while the very fact of Joe's father having kept so much to himself would have made Hurley's non-recognition at the Bradleys' old home of no moment. The weak point, however, arrived when he expected residents in the little provincial town where Joe had spent his early existence to recognize in Hurley the cycle maker who they knew had died quite lately.

"He'd have been had there," said Joe thoughtfully, "unless, of course, he had declared that he never lived in England after he was twenty years of age. Ah! that was his game; he had become a colonist. No doubt he could have imported some scoundrel to swear to the fact that Hurley was not known as Hurley at all, but as Bradley. However, there's an end to the matter. Wonder what this uncle of mine's like? Don't feel over-keen on writing to him."

Circumstances saved Joe that necessity, for no sooner had he sent information to the London solicitors who held the proofs which his father had deposited, than he learned that his uncle was dead. He had, in fact, survived Mr. Bradley but a few months. Thus Joe was the heir to the property.

"Let it go hang for the time being," he said, when he and Hank and the Fennicks were discussing the matter together; for the trio had safely returned to the settlement at the head of the valley in New Ontario. "I've something far more interesting here, I can assure you."

He said that with truth, too, for never was there a more fascinating business than Sam Fennick had created. That spring, in fact, more than twenty families joined him, shacks were run up rapidly by the corporation into which they formed themselves, while machinery was already arriving. Soon the workers were divided into parties, each with their tasks assigned, and by seeding time not only had every family a good roof over its head, but an extraordinary amount of ground had been broken.

There is little to add with regard to our hero. That winter which followed he ran over to England, and then, having placed his affairs in the hands of lawyers, and having let the property to which he had proved his title, he returned to join his comrades. Up at the end of that valley Peter Strike, and Hank, and many another are now located. A railway draws its steel lines through the heart of the settlement, while a school is already building. That is the way with Canada, red tape has scarcely an existence; it is merely a bad memory imported from the old country. Yes, there is a school building, while the telephone is fitted to houses rapidly replacing the rough shacks. But that is not all. Electric light is generated by water power at the foot of the lake, while there is a lumber mill down south, and logs pay handsomely. Motors buzz, too, out on the fields, and acres of soil are ripped open and ploughed in as many hours as days were taken formerly with horse tackle. Joe himself is rather proud of the potatoes he grows on his holding, while he has hopes some day of beating all at the annual fruit show in Toronto. You may ask with reason, perhaps, whether he ever pines for London or a city. No, emphatically no! Joe is an open-air man, a jovial, hard-working, contented fellow, who loves the wilds of the Dominion, and who now and again sneaks off into the backwoods with his old chum Hank. But business is his main consideration. His purchases close to Peter Strike's old settlement have increased enormously in value, while elsewhere he is making money.

"Not as it matters much to a chap same as you," said Hank one night, for he and Joe lived together; "you're rich without these here acres. But guess it's not the dollars you're after; it's makin' good, eh, Joe? Making good 'lows a man to be proud of hisself, and, jingo, it aer worth doing!"

The End